TOM PATTERSON
Colorado Crusader for Change

Sybil Downing
and
Robert E. Smith

UNIVERSITY PRESS OF COLORADO
1995

© 1995 by Sybil Downing and Robert E. Smith
Published by the University Press of Colorado
P.O. Box 849
Niwot, Colorado 80544

The University Press of Colorado is a cooperative publishing enterprise supported, in part, by Adams State College, Colorado State University, Fort Lewis College, Mesa State College, Metropolitan State College of Denver, University of Colorado, University of Northern Colorado, University of Southern Colorado, and Western State College of Colorado.

The paper used in this publication meets the minimum requirements of the American National Standard for Information Sciences—Permanence of Paper for Printed Library Materials. ANSI Z39.48—1984

Library of Congress Cataloging-in-Publication Data

Downing, Sybil, 1930–
    Tom Patterson: Colorado crusader for change / by Sybil Downing and Robert E. Smith
        p.   cm.

    ISBN 0-87081-364-1
    1. Patterson, Thomas McDonald, 1840–1916. 2. Politicians—Colorado—Biography. 3. Legislators—United States—Biography. 4. Colorado—Politics and government—1876–1950. 5. Colorado—History—1876–1950. 6. United States. Congress—Biography. I. Smith, Robert E., 1928–   II. Title.
    F871.P38   1995
    978.8'03'092—dc20
    [B]
                                                                95-2671
                                                                CIP

10   9   8   7   6   5   4   3   2   1

Tom Patterson

*We dedicate this book to
Mancourt Downing and Jean Smith
for their encouragement, insights,
and remarkable patience.*

Contents

Preface

Thomas McDonald Patterson, once described by contemporaries as the most conspicuous figure in Colorado history,[1] achieved a degree of political influence, professional fame, and financial success that makes his relative obscurity a strange phenomenon. Controversial in public life and then a vortex of Denver city politics for more than forty years, Patterson helped to bring about an effective two-party system in Colorado and became the state's most notable political maverick as he struggled on behalf of causes he regarded as essential for the improvement of the fortunes of the common people.

Despite an often tragic personal life, Patterson achieved spectacular success as a criminal and civil lawyer, and amassed a fortune through shrewd real estate investments in Denver. Tenacious and energetic, he became the acknowledged leader of the Colorado Democratic party from 1876 to 1892. As Colorado's last territorial delegate to Congress, he defended sectional interests and helped achieve statehood for Colorado. In 1876 he was elected to a single term as representative to Congress, and from 1876 to 1892 he regularly served as a delegate to Democratic national conventions.

As a member of the Democratic National Committee in 1892, Patterson presented a minority report favoring free silver coinage. He refused to support President Grover Cleveland's stand for gold, and joined the Populists, helping to carry Colorado for the Populist presidential candidate, General James B. Weaver. In 1896 and 1900 Patterson played a key role in committing Colorado Populists to support Democrat William Jennings Bryan for president. Though he effectively reduced the influence of Governor Davis H. Waite within Colorado's Populist party, Patterson still was elected permanent chairman of the 1900 Populist national convention.

Patterson's greatest impact was on Colorado and Denver politics. Often frustrated by election swindles, he steadfastly supported nonpartisan efforts to eliminate corruption in municipal and state government and to reduce the political influence of Denver's private utility companies. Alongside reformers such as Judge Benjamin B. Lindsey and Edward P. Costigan, Patterson helped bring home rule and commission government to Denver as well as municipal ownership of Denver's water supply and a weakening of Mayor Robert W. Speer's Democratic political machine.

During an era of personal journalism, Patterson's *Rocky Mountain News* effectively and often self-righteously supported unpopular causes, such as organized labor. In defense of freedom of the press, Patterson survived serious boycotts by large advertisers and a contempt citation by the Colorado Supreme Court.

Despite his numerous achievements and contributions, today few residents of Denver and the state are even familiar with his name. Unlike other leaders of his era who had their names attached to some public monument, Patterson did not leave behind a permanent record of his name. There is no Patterson County like the Teller County named for Senator Henry Moore Teller; there is no Patterson Boulevard like the Speer Boulevard in Denver named for Mayor Robert W. Speer.

Patterson's efforts to fuse the Democrats and the Populists so weakened traditional voting loyalties that Colorado became a state with an effective two-party system, which led to his election to the United States Senate in 1901. Though he announced his intention to act with the Democratic caucus, he often pursued an independent course. During his single term as a member of a fragmented minority in the Senate, Patterson opposed American imperialism and urged domestic reform. He appeared most enthusiastic when calling for such radical and hopeless proposals as nationalization of the railroads. Refusing to compromise to help progressive legislation pass, he withheld his support from measures he regarded as inadequate.

Patterson's rhetoric and actions raise questions involving his philosophy, motivation, and effectiveness. What events caused him to assume an extreme position as an intractable foe of trusts and an outspoken defender of organized labor? If socialism dominated his economic thinking, how was he able to become a senator from Colorado? Was he the spearhead of a class-based social and political revolution in a frontier mining state? Did he genuinely seek economic and political reforms, or did he seek personal political success based on the votes of unhappy workers? Was he an impractical dreamer, out of touch with political reality, or an effective agent for change and a significant factor in Colorado politics?

Although opponents attacked Tom Patterson as a dangerous radical, the evidence indicates that he rejected socialism and was an upward-striving entrepreneur who opposed combinations of wealth that might handicap ambitious men like himself. To that end he wanted a strong government not only to act as an arbiter but also to be increasingly responsive to popular control. He held deep commitments to the support of "the common man" and to the furtherance of his own fame and fortune. Through the law, political leadership, and the agitation of public opinion, Tom Patterson contributed significantly to Colorado's history, creating a climate in which reform movements finally received fair and serious consideration.

Acknowledgments

A childhood fascination with tales of a feisty great-grandfather and questions raised by a doctoral dissertation converged to produce this effort to clarify Tom Patterson's contributions in the areas of politics, labor, journalism, business, and the law.

The authors cannot adequately express their appreciation for the important contribution and the cooperation of Senator Patterson's grandson, the late Thomas Patterson Campbell. The interest and help of Mrs. Harry Lou Gurtler, grandniece of Senator Patterson, was invaluable. Also essential to the effort was the guidance of the late Professor Lewis E. Atherton of the University of Missouri. Special thanks are due to several colleagues for their suggestions concerning grammar, style, and content, especially professors Louis G. Geiger, Ray O. Werner, Harvey Carter, Arthur Pettit, Robert McJimsey, Christopher Griffiths. Thanks also to Mr. Ralph Conner, Rhonda Crossen, and Scott Smith.

The directors and staffs of the following institutions and repositories have been most considerate in their assistance: the Library of Congress, the Colorado State Historical Society, the Charles Leaming Tutt Library of the Colorado College (particularly Ginny Kiefer in the Colorado Archives), the Western Historical Collection of the University of Colorado at Boulder, the Archives of the State of Colorado, the Western History Department of the Denver Public Library, the El Paso County Bar Association Library, the Southern History Collection at the University of North Carolina, the Library of Duke University, and the Philip Miller Library at Castle Rock, Colorado.

*But for Tom Patterson, folks like you and me could not live
in this city. He is the one man who has put up a continuous fight
for the rights of the common people, and kept it up, year after year.
You can be thankful that he is a fighting man with the
courage of his convictions.*

— Judge James B. Belford

Tom Patterson

1
The Young Man From Indiana

This thin air and alkali water agrees with me amazingly well. I have now been in Denver four days. . . . Everybody . . . with energy and ordinary prudence is growing rich.

—Tom Patterson, to K. M. Patterson
July 10, 1872

Thomas McDonald Patterson was the embodiment of the great American dream. An emigrant from Ireland, a man who had known hard work since childhood, Patterson went West to make his fortune and a name for himself. He did both.

The first son of James Patterson and Margaret Montjoy, he was born on November 4, 1839, in the Irish town of Carlow, County Carlow, with its somber grey stone houses and surrounding fields of brilliant green.[1] His Irish outrage over England's cruel domination of his native land would stay with him until the day he died. In later years, one newspaper associate claimed that Patterson's finest speech was his scathing censure of England for its practice of taking Irishmen to England for trial.[2]

Patterson's grandfather, James, was a landed farmer who learned the watchmaker's trade and lived near Portaferry in Northern Ireland. He had married Catherine, a daughter of the aristocratic MacDonalds, who never forgave her for marrying beneath her station and cut her off without a cent. One of their nine children was Tom's father, James, who also took up the watchmaker's trade. James met and married Margaret Mountjoy in 1834 in Charleville, County Cork.[3]

Margaret's life had been hard and drab, her schooling neglected because her stepmother used her as a mother's helper in rearing the other children. Yet, according to the description handed down through the years, she was "a beautiful girl with flashing dark eyes, a quick tongue and a proud spirit."[4] In

1848 the Pattersons and their three children—Catherine, Tom, and the youngest, James—boarded the sailing vessel *Minnesota* in Liverpool bound for New York City, where they lived for a brief time. Perhaps because of the outbreak of cholera or the violence that plagued the city, the Pattersons soon moved from the city to new quarters on the main street of Astoria, Long Island.[5] Tom attended a public school, and, if family lore is to be believed, he was already at that time expounding to his classmates on politics. Four years later, in 1853, the family packed their belongings and moved again, this time to Crawfordsville, Indiana.

In the 1800s prior to the Civil War, Crawfordsville was no more than a village. Located in the center of broad, shallow valleys and low hills of thin soil—a region known as the till plains—it was the hub of the surrounding farms. Indiana was a growing state, with a population of close to a million, the seventh largest in the Union. At the time of the Patterson family's arrival, a quarter of Indiana's foreign-born population was Irish.[6] The state called itself the Crossroads to the West, and economic opportunities seemed to abound.

At fourteen, drawn by the lure of newspaper work, Tom took a job in the composing room of the *Crawfordsville Review*. He worked there for three years. By his own account, he also became obsessed with the game of poker around that time, at one stretch playing every night until he had lost his entire savings of $1,800. After a night spent in self-evaluation he left Crawfordsville, walking the forty miles to Indianapolis. He paid his way by repairing farmers' watches and clocks, and never forgot the kindness he was shown.[7] Once in Indianapolis, he found work as a printer for the *Indianapolis Journal*.

By February of 1861 the issues of the preservation of the Union and the abolition of slavery had brought the country to the brink of war. Six states had already seceded, and with Kentucky as Indiana's neighbor, strong ties to the South, both family and business, existed in thousands of Indiana homes. Article XIII of the Indiana state constitution of 1851 prohibited the immigration of blacks into the state,[8] and to most Hoosiers, blacks were inferiors.

On April 15, three days after the firing on Fort Sumter by South Carolina forces, President Lincoln called upon the states' governors to gather volunteers for three months' service. That day, ten thousand men across Indiana rushed to enlist.[9] Tom and his brother, James, signed up on April 18 and were assigned to Company I, Eleventh Regiment, Indiana Infantry. Like most other men whose purpose was to preserve the Union, Tom would always refer to the Civil War as the War of the Rebellion.[10]

The Eleventh Indiana Infantry was among those regiments known as Zouaves, whose distinctive uniform included a cropped jacket, baggy trousers to the knee with gaiters snug about the calves, and the flat-topped blue cap of the Union forces.[11] Family stories, handed down through the years, recount forced marches through the night with Tom literally asleep on his feet.[12] During those ninety days, the Eleventh Indiana saw little action. The men were assigned picket duty along the Ohio near Evansville. In June, they marched to Cumberland, Maryland, and Bunker Hill, Virginia, where they came under the command of General Patterson, who was no relation. From there, they marched to Romney, West Virginia, and home to Indiana.[13]

On August 4, their enlistment period was up. James volunteered for another three years. In October of 1864 he was killed at the battle of Winchester, while serving under General Philip Sheridan in Virginia's Shenandoah Valley. In later years Tom recounted the months he spent searching for his brother's body, and how he briefly took his place in the ranks.[14]

In 1861, when his own enlistment was over, Tom was eager to get on with his life. He was twenty-two. Not wanting time to pass him by and determined to get ahead in the world, he decided on a career in law and he moved to Greencastle to enter Asbury College, now DePauw University. In spite of a heavy schedule—attending classes in the morning, working as a printer in the afternoon, and studying at night—he managed to maintain a reasonable if not outstanding record in all but mathematics. A tutor seemed the solution. After asking about, he was referred to Miss Katherine Grafton.[15]

Kate was born on January 1, 1839, in Wellsburg, Virginia (later to be West Virginia), the daughter of Dr. Samuel Grafton and Jane Bryant Grafton and the grandniece of Alexander Campbell, founder of the Wellsburg Christian Church. The family was deeply religious and Kate planned to become a missionary to India. After graduating with highest honors from Bercan College in Jacksonville, Illinois,[16] she went to teach school, as part of her missionary training, in Greencastle, Indiana—and to tutor Tom Patterson in mathematics.

In 1866 Tom switched to Wabash College in Crawfordsville, where he remained until the end of his junior year. He again maintained a full schedule, and again his grades were not exceptional. Involvement in extracurricular activities may have been one of the contributing factors. He was president of the Lyceum debating society in 1866, no doubt honing his oratorical skills in the weekly contests. Probably because of his friendship with some members of Phi Gamma Delta fraternity in Greencastle, Patterson brought a petition for founding a chapter at Wabash. Meeting at his father's bookstore/jewelry shop, he and ten others founded the Wabash chapter, with Patterson serving as its first president.[17]

Tom and Kate had been married in Watertown, New York, in 1864.[18] In September 1866, their first son, James, was born. Faced with the responsibility of providing for a wife and child, Tom knew that his college days were at an end. Still he had no intention of abandoning his goal of the law, so he went to work as a clerk for the law firm of Michael D. White, where he "read the law." Years later White would proudly claim that he "gave Patterson his start."[19]

The War of the Rebellion was over. Lincoln had been assassinated in April at the Ford Theater, leaving his vice president, Andrew Johnson, to wrestle with a radical Republican Congress over the mounting problems of Reconstruction. Political tempers flared as the nation struggled to put itself back together. Tom, influenced by his father, who was an ardent admirer of Andrew Jackson, threw himself into Indiana's Democratic politics. The party that year denounced "greenbacks" and called for the increased use of gold and silver.[20] It was an issue that would later reappear and in no small way shape Patterson's political life. He was committed to President Johnson's program, inaccurately predicting "a glorious victory" for Johnson, the Constitution, and the Union.[21]

Patterson reveled in the political battles, and much to his delight he became increasingly sought after as a public speaker. He proudly wrote Kate that though his "caliber commenced to shine" and he could speak three times a week, he preferred to stick to his studies.[22] His married life was equally fulfilling, marred only by his frequent absences on legal business. From Lebanon, Illinois, he wrote to his dear Kate, "Why, last night I dreamt of you through the whole long night, dreamt you were lying by my side, that we both indulged in all the blissful endearments which it seems the dark canopy of night and the general canopy of bed clothes are best adapted to call forth."[23] Their second child, Mary Grafton, was born in January of 1867.

Tom Patterson was deliberate by nature. Like other ambitious young men of the time, he believed that hard work, frugality, and perseverance were the keys to rising in the world. He knew there was nothing accidental about success. Tom passed the bar examination in 1870 and became the partner of Judge J. R. Cowan.[24]

From all appearances, Patterson's future seemed promising. He had an attractive wife with a good head on her shoulders and two fine children. He made a good appearance, being five feet, seven inches tall with a trim figure and a neat mustache. He spoke easily with a booming tenor voice that carried great distances.[25] Though only a nominal Episcopalian and holding organized churches in somewhat low regard, he was well versed in the Bible and could quote Scripture at length.[26] He had taken part in the community, serving as a school examiner from 1868 to 1871, responsible for certifying applicants for positions in the county schools, and for a brief period he was the county superintendent of public instruction.[27] He felt well prepared for whatever lay ahead. If he played his cards right in law and in politics, he would someday be a U.S. senator.

He was appointed a delegate to the Democratic congressional convention in July of 1868. Unfortunately, a Republican was the governor of Indiana and Republicans controlled the state legislature.[28] Though he had full confidence in himself, as a young Democrat, his political road looked steep. In addition, Kate's family disapproved of his politics,[29] and Indiana's bitterly cold winters and hot, humid summers were not good for her fragile health.

Tom began a search for greener pastures. In a letter to him in July of 1869, when he was looking over Kansas City, Kate said, "I feel more and more anxious to go to some *live* western town every day."[30] Apparently, she was in agreement with his plans. By 1872, perhaps in part because of the climate, he had eliminated Sioux City, Iowa, and Kansas City, Missouri. He turned his attention farther west and wondered about the possibilities in Colorado Territory. Two railroads now connected Denver with both coasts. From all reports, what remained of the Indian problem appeared to be under control. He decided to go see for himself.

On July 10, 1872, he wrote to Kate:

> As for myself, I never felt better. This thin air and alkali water agree with me amazingly. I have now been in Denver four days. I like it the better the longer I remain.
>
> I have conversed with a hundred persons and out of them all I am safe in saying that not one in ten have resided here over a year. . . . The city is as substantial in point of buildings and public improvements as you can find in Indiana. . . .
>
> I have bought four acres of land for which I am to pay $1650 . . . I have paid cash upon it—$450 (2% interest). . . .

A person can't be in Denver and not be infested with a mania for speculation. I confidently expect to double my money within three years. In my opinion, this is the place for an energetic man with some means to make money. Everybody who acts with energy and ordinary prudence is growing rich.

In spite of his initial enthusiasm, Tom had to be assured there were sufficient opportunities for a lawyer with an interest in politics. He called on Territorial Governor Edward McCook, only to find him in Pennsylvania. As he strode along the dusty, busy streets lined with prosperous-looking brick buildings, he kept an eye out for indications of potential competition. Finally, spying an unpretentious shingle hanging from the Tappan Building on Fifteenth Street, he decided to make inquiries. Mounting the stairs to the second floor, he knocked at the door lettered Charles S. Thomas, Attorney-at-Law.

The office was a single room with a pine table for a desk. Charles Thomas introduced himself as a recent graduate of the University of Michigan Law School.[31] He had lived in Denver since December. Patterson liked the determined set to his jaw and the level look of his eyes. Here was a man, though ten years younger than himself, who obviously had known hardship and accepted work as a way of life.

Tom said only that he was interested in a piece of property at the west edge of the city and asked him to examine the deed. They talked of the expanding population and the growing development of gold and silver mines in the mountains to the south. Every sign pointed to ample opportunities for qualified attorneys, Thomas said. Still testing the waters, Tom decided not to reveal that he, too, was a lawyer. Only after he returned to Indiana and began a correspondence with Thomas did he divulge the truth.

In December of 1872 Tom Patterson moved his wife and three children—James, Mary, and Margaret, who had been born in 1870—west to a red frame cottage at West 34th and Tejon Streets and immediately surrounded the dwelling with saplings.[32] In an earlier letter to Kate, he had described the lot as "exactly one mile from the Post Office which is the business center of the city. It is across the Platte River from the business part of the city and as yet is but little built upon. . . . My only worry is that it is far from the center of goings on and away from society."[33]

Tom entered the law office of France and Tofer in June 1873 as a sort of understudy, his purpose being to familiarize himself with the law and procedures of the Territory.[34] When Tom took a particularly thorny case of one of the firm's prominent clients and proceeded to win it, receiving a good deal of attention as a result, Mr. Tofer resented the young Mr. Patterson's success and Tom was out of a job. He looked up Charles Thomas, who agreed to join him as a junior partner, and they opened a one-room office on what was then Holladay Street in the old Crow and Clark Block. But faced with the mounting costs of supporting a wife and three children and with another child expected by early summer, Tom was obliged to return to Indiana to wrap up unfinished cases and to collect his fees. Yet with Kate's history of difficult pregnancies, he couldn't help worrying. On May 6, 1873, he wrote from Crawfordsville:

> How are you getting along is the question I ask myself a thousand times a day since I left you? Are you yet safely through the suffering consequent to giving birth to another soul? I am nervous and anxious and will be until I hear of your safe delivery.

A week later:

> I almost curse the fate which drives me from you at this juncture and at times I am almost tempted to let all business go and hasten back to Denver. But unless necessity forces it, it would never do as money must be had for future needs that can only be obtained by work and hard too for the next four weeks. Since I reached here I have been constantly employed in Court from 8 a.m. till 6 p.m. and twice this week I did not get to bed until one o'clock in the morning.[35]

Fortunately, his final appearance in Indiana courts was financially rewarding. He observed to Kate that people there generally acknowledged his marked improvement as a lawyer. And Charles Thomas had assured him in a number of letters that their new firm was doing exceedingly well in his absence.[36]

Home again, Patterson immediately threw himself into Democratic politics and was elected city attorney in the spring of 1874.[37] His aggressive nature led him to prosecute vigorously, and defendants and opposition lawyers resented his manner. One defense counsel accused Patterson of seeking convictions in a spirit of vindictiveness;[38] and a defendant, though acquitted of charges, claimed that following the decision Patterson had spread derogatory rumors about him.[39]

Denver's mayor, Joseph E. Bates, also had reason to be unhappy with Patterson. As the local Republican party boss, Bates had easily secured his own renomination by the Republican city convention and then set out to

Thomas McDonald Patterson, thirty three years old, at the time of his arrival in Denver, Colorado. (Courtesy Archives, University of Colorado at Boulder Libraries, Patterson collection, Bx 8, Fd 1.)

ensure his election by acquiring the endorsement of a separate Independent citizens' convention. Patterson was furious. Determined to thwart Bates's election, he gave a stirring denunciation of political bosses in general and Bates in particular.

A few days later, Bates and another man approached Patterson on the street and attacked him. The brawl was indecisive, but it drew front-page coverage in the *Rocky Mountain News,*[40] gaining publicity for Patterson that, according to his law partner, resulted in a sharp increase in the firm's business. The widespread version of the fight pictured Patterson running his attackers up an alley after a vicious ten-minute battle. But a newspaper account immediately following the occurrence, and based primarily on Patterson's account, indicated that he was in serious difficulty until bystanders, upset over the odds, intervened.[41] At the very least the fray was a foretaste of future battles against intimidation and "bossism."

In the little less than two years since his arrival in Denver, Tom had become a man to reckon with. Some claimed he was cocky.[42] He had more business than he and Thomas could handle, and he was frequently forced to travel to make court appearances and see clients as far away as Cheyenne, Wyoming.

Kate had a hired girl who helped her with the children, but after the baby's birth Kate's strength was slow in returning. She had little opportunity to socialize and was shy by nature. Her letters began to express her increasing frustration, almost her desperation, over Tom's absences and late hours. Though no substantiating records exist, her written pleas for Tom to come home and his apologies for his absence might indicate that it was sometime in the spring of 1874 when their infant daughter died. As he would do three more times in his life, he put his personal sorrow behind him and went on with his life. Though statehood had been talked about for a decade, Colorado remained a territory and as such sent a single nonvoting delegate to Congress. The election would take place in November, and Tom saw an opportunity at hand.

On the national scene, a growing disgust with the excesses of the Republican-led Reconstruction was emerging. The country was gripped in an economic depression. To the Democrats, it was an issue that might—and did—send enough party members to Congress to at least regain a majority in the House.[43]

Colorado Territory was another matter. Jerome B. Chaffee, who had come to Colorado in 1860, had been the territorial delegate for the last two terms. Well-to-do and influential in Republican party and business circles, he was a

Jerome B. Chaffee, founder of Denver's First National Bank, defeated for
re-election as territorial delegate by Patterson in 1874, later U.S. senator.
(Courtesy Colorado Historical Society.)

close friend of President Grant's. As a result, Chaffee had managed to secure dozens of federal appointments for his supporters.[44]

But early in 1874, according to local rumor, Chaffee quarreled with Grant over a poker game.[45] Without warning, the president began to remove the territorial officers who were Chaffee's friends and appointed others in their position.[46] Among the casualties was Samuel M. Elbert, removed from the position of territorial governor and replaced by Edward McCook, in spite of evidence that McCook had earlier robbed the government of nearly $30,000. In the process, McCook had alienated much of the political community, particularly when he allowed his brother-in-law, James B. Thompson, to line his pockets while serving as a special agent to the Ute Indians.[47]

In Washington, Chaffee led the fight to prevent confirmation of McCook and, failing that, set out to arouse public indignation in Colorado against misgovernment by federal appointees.[48] He called for statehood for Colorado to eliminate the influence of the president on territorial affairs. Another leading Republican, Henry Moore Teller, blamed all the trouble on Chaffee and defended Grant.[49] The Republicans were at each other's throats. Tom saw his chance, and threw his hat into the ring.

2
Hurrah for Colorado!

Coloradoans are roving hordes of semi-barbarous adventurers, with vagrant habits.

—New England Press

In its fifteen years as a territory, Colorado had never elected a Democrat or someone not native born as a delegate to Congress.[1] To Tom Patterson, neither fact was insurmountable. He had cut his political teeth as a member of another minority party in Indiana.

A territory was like a poor relative. With no direct voice in Congress (territorial delegates had no vote and could serve only on the Territorial Committee of the House), Colorado was dependent on patronage and friends in high political places to secure aid for its railroads or helpful mining laws. Since the Republican party had dominated Washington from 1861 to 1876, the majority of Colorado citizens had long seen the wisdom of being Republicans.

But the Republican party was not of one mind. Members from the southern part of the territory demanded their fair share of political and economic spoils. Bad feelings remained from the fight between "the old Denver group" and the "Golden crowd" over the location of the capitol.[2] When the Republicans met on August 5, 1874, their ranks were severely divided between the McCook and the Chaffee factions. A lengthy nomination fight ensued until finally a man who was supposed to be a compromise candidate, H.P.H. Bromwell, was chosen.[3]

Meanwhile, delighted over the disarray in the Republican ranks, the Democrats met in Colorado Springs to nominate their candidates. For months Thomas Patterson had worked to increase his influence in the Democratic party. On March 3, 1874, he helped draw up a resolution calling for a revitalized party that could become a real political force in the state.[4] During the Denver City Democratic convention, he held a position on the Credentials and Organization Committee and presented the committee report to the convention.[5] On April 15 he drew praise from a Denver newspaper as the new city attorney and a lawyer of "marked ability" who could not fail to make an efficient officer.[6]

Encouraged by this growing attention, Patterson announced his candidacy for the office of territorial delegate. He was joined by a stampede of nine relatively obscure candidates, each man eager to capitalize on the Republican split. At the convention, the tedious process of taking twenty-two ballots ensued until finally—probably because of the hard work and support of his law partner, Charles Thomas—Patterson garnered the two-thirds total necessary to win.[7]

Some Democrats were displeased, especially those who resented the success of Tom Patterson, a relative newcomer to Colorado. Others disliked the support he had gained from many young people in the party. An intraparty fight loomed. In addition, a group of disgruntled Democrats persuaded Daniel Boone's grandson, Albert Gallatin Boone, to run as an independent candidate, a move that threatened to further split the Democratic vote. Fortunately, Boone soon withdrew from the race, and the Democrats achieved a shaky solidarity.[8]

With the campaign under way the *Rocky Mountain News* reneged on its earlier kind words for Patterson, declaring that the Democrats had weakened their hopes for victory by nominating him. In its new evaluation of Patterson, the *News* said:

> He is a comparatively young man; has been a resident of Colorado about two years; is possessed of considerable energy, cunning, and ability; is a fair lawyer, and an interminable talker. His personal character is beyond reproach. He has not the caliber, character, brains or experience to properly represent Colorado at the national capitol.[9]

As the weeks unfolded, the campaign between Patterson and Bromwell remained free from personal invective but also struck observers as exceedingly dull. In a letter to the *News,* one Democrat said his party's platform was "as dead as the clammy vapor of a toad's dungeon," and he did not like Patterson as a candidate any better than the platform.[10] The *Pueblo Chieftain* suggested that Patterson and Bromwell should stop complimenting each other so much, drop their campaign clichés, and give the people sound information on how to remedy existing evils.[11]

Both candidates droned on with excessive oratory. Bromwell was pictured as an "artful dodger" and Patterson as a "declaiming schoolboy" prone to demagoguery. The *News* sarcastically declared it had engaged a corps of shorthand reporters to spell each other during the speeches and suggested the crowds fortify themselves with crackers and cheese or "take an armchair for an occasional snooze whenever either of the speakers get back into antediluvian periods of our political history."[12]

The *News* asserted that the only two qualities displayed by Patterson during the campaign were "cheek and talk," and itemized major "blunders" committed by the fledgling politician: He had resorted to the use of vulgar jokes while speaking in Boulder; he had denounced corporations while speaking in Colorado Springs, a city made by corporations; he had attacked capitalists, high tariffs, and national banks in front of audiences unsympathetic to his point of view; he had eulogized the "horny-handed men of toil" when he had very little in common with them; and he had raised opposition within his own party while failing to exploit the dissension within the Republican party.[13]

But Patterson rapidly grew more politically astute as the campaign wore on. He maneuvered deftly when the Republican Central Committee challenged him to debate with Colonel W. H. Parker, a recent arrival from Mississippi. The geographic area to be covered during the debates, said the Republicans, should start at Del Norte and range throughout southern Colorado. Patterson rejected the suggestion in one of his rare attacks on "carpetbagging":

> In response to your request I must say that I am not personally acquainted with Colonel Parker, but upon inquiry find him to be a resident of Mississippi, temporarily absent from his home, filling a federal appointment in Colorado. Such being the case, he has no authority to bind any person or party in this territory by his declarations, and I emphatically decline to divide my time with a gentleman of his political irresponsibility. . . . This contest is between Judge Bromwell and myself, and to him, as I have in the past, I extend a cordial invitation to discuss with me at any of my appointments, the political issues of the day.[14]

Suggestions of further joint debates came to an end. By early September, even the *News* conceded that Tom Patterson had learned his lessons well and appeared to be a more attractive candidate than he had been early in the campaign.[15]

At home, Tom's relationship with Kate was badly strained. Three months earlier, in June, when Tom had been out of town on business, Kate had written him a wrenching letter, begging him for his love. In a tortured scrawl on a small piece of pink notepaper, folded in half, she pleaded:

> Oh, Tom, before God, I could not help the bitterness and anguish that came with what to me was evidence of your indifference and undeniable estrangement.
>
> I ask you to love me again with the tender and exclusive love that you once gave me. . . . I cannot live and be sane without our love. . . . I am so ambitious as to long to rank above them all in your esteem and spontaneous confidence.[16]

Whether Kate was distraught over the death of their infant daughter or resented all the attention Tom received is unknown. On August 8 Tom wrote to her from Fairplay, where he was giving a speech in the mining camp: "I am torn between the love of my wife and the people whom I must convert to my same frame of mind."[17]

In late September, in the midst of the campaign, Kate left Denver and her children to visit her sister in Kansas City. In one of his letters to her, Tom wrote:

> You would be very unhappy of my late hours and perhaps accuse me when I did come home of being indifferent to both you and the family. Now, Kate, of late we have had some severe misunderstandings upon this subject—but I think I can lay my hand on my heart and say 'not guilty' to any of the charges you prefer and infer against me. When I am immersed in business—and weary and almost worn out with law and politics, I confess to not being very companionable—and although at such time I may *seem dreary* and uninterested—yet I know that missing my wife and nanny—even at midnight upon my return home—makes life seem more unbearable. But why talk of these matters—I suppose when we are both grey and wrinkled—the folly of our middle life will be made apparent and we can both regret the unhappy days, suspicions and doubts upon the one side and too much indifference upon the other, have caused us.[18]

In the same letter, Tom talked of plans for Ernest Campbell, Kate's brother-in-law, to join the firm, proposing that Campbell receive a quarter of the income. Upcoming election or not, business had to be attended to.

As the election approached, the citizens of Colorado seemed to feel that a Democratic victory would be a properly stinging rebuke to President Grant and his "carpetbag" federal appointees. Tom took full advantage of the growing groundswell of antiadministration sentiment. He won the election—defeating his opponent by a vote of 9,333 to 7,170—and became the first Democratic territorial delegate to go to Congress from Colorado.[19]

Tom Patterson arrived in Washington in February of 1875. Fired with the enthusiasm of victory, he was determined to do his best for the territory and to wage a serious battle for Colorado statehood. Kate cheered him on from Denver, writing "Hurrah for Colorado! is the first cry I send you across our plains. . . . If there be any hesitating eyes which hold her trembling in the balance, your voice will let them hesitate no longer."[20]

But like many newcomers in Washington that year, he found Washington crowded and was "forced to take a room on the fourth floor" at the National Hotel.[21] Further, his initial dealings with official Washington were disillusioning. "My opinion of the average congressman is lowered. Ditto of senators. They are all with few exceptions very common stock."[22]

Whether he liked certain men or not was immaterial. He was committed to representing the territory to the best of his ability. Of equal if not greater importance, he also was determined to convince his fellow Democrats that admission of Colorado was desirable from a partisan viewpoint. For the first time since 1860, Democrats were in the majority in the House. Yet the presidential election of 1876 loomed as a close race. The proposed new state's electoral votes might thus become crucial, and Colorado had traditionally been Republican.

This would be Colorado's fourth try for statehood. The lack of a regular two-party system in Colorado may have been a contributing factor to previous failures: A potpourri of Spanish-Americans and Southern Democrats in the lower half of the territory and factions clustered in Central City, Golden, and Denver were more cliques than parties. Colorado's population was too amorphous and its resources too underdeveloped to make the two-party system and statehood feasible.[23]

But by 1875 conditions for statehood finally seemed favorable, and the battle took on an interesting flavor. Joining Tom Patterson in the effort was the previous territorial delegate, a Republican, Jerome Chaffee. In spite of Patterson's recent triumph, Chaffee still believed that Colorado would continue to be a Republican territory. Tom, on the other hand, saw his recent political victory as a rise in Democrats' fortunes. Whatever their individual views, the two men formed an alliance, each determined to recruit votes for statehood from his respective party.[24]

Patterson's strategy involved offering himself as living proof that the fortunes of the Colorado Democratic party were on the upswing and that the state would indeed go Democratic, not Republican, in the national election of 1876. Through Senator Boggs of Missouri, Patterson gained admission to the floor of the Senate. Recounting the experience to Kate, he wrote that as a result he had caused several senators and representatives to recognize his views as sound and to promise their support for statehood.[25] Years later he conceded that some Democratic congressmen had regarded him as "something of a nuisance," but he expressed satisfaction that he had persevered until he and Chaffee could count the necessary votes to ensure consideration and passage of the enabling act.[26]

Working diligently, Chaffee successfully held in line some Republican congressmen who feared that Patterson's presence indicated a Democratic shift in Colorado.[27] At one point, Patterson accused the Republicans of using delaying tactics to postpone statehood for Colorado.

> If the state bill should fail, it will be from the treachery of its professed friends in the Republican Party. The danger is, that in their anxiety to saddle the southern states with a military tyranny so that the next election may be secured, our Republican Senators will forget the justice to Colorado.[28]

Though Patterson never doubted that the bill would pass and that Colorado's first electors would be Democrats, the bill faced an increasingly hostile Eastern press, particularly in New England. Editorials and articles decried the bill. One such attack described "Coloradoans as roving hordes of semi-barbarous adventurers, with vagrant habits."[29]

He tried to counter such feelings by making several speaking tours, one of which took him through much of Massachusetts and New Hampshire. After the *Boston Post* carried one of his speeches in March, Tom reassured his family in Colorado that "we have been everywhere received and treated splendidly and I think I have done some good."[30]

17

Patterson took to the political intrigue as if he were born to it. He had a ten-minute chat with President Grant and met several cabinet members. A month after his arrival, Patterson's opinion of the capital was softening. "Washington grows on me daily," he wrote Kate. "With its grand public buildings, wide streets, numerous public gardens filled with statuary, it is a magnificent city."[31]

Much to his frustration, however, Patterson was able to exert little influence in his role as a territorial delegate to the Forty-fourth Congress. He was handicapped by having no vote, and was able to serve on only the Committee on Territories. Yet even that did not stop him, and he forced his way into the action whenever possible, frequently reacting angrily when he spotted cavalier treatment of the problems of the West.

Before his election, Patterson had been outspoken against the appointment of Easterners to prominent territorial positions. In April of 1875 an amendment to the Deficiency Appropriation Bill came before the House, providing that officials in the territories be appointed from among the citizens of the territories. In arguing for the amendment, Patterson said that the people of the territories reacted with rage when men with no thought for the welfare of the territory were sent to control their interests. Such appointees, he said, had only their personal profit in mind.

He particularly objected to the appointment of "judicial incompetents." He complained frequently that the judges sent had neither judicial capacity nor experience in the particular judicial system existing in the territory. As a result, "the whole judicial system is in chaos; cases pending in the courts are predetermined ill-advisedly; they are not and cannot be properly considered."[32] He called for bona fide residents to be assigned to these positions.

Patterson promoted a bill to allow the people of a territory to elect their own officials.[33] The ability to choose whom they wished was important, because the qualifications for the offices were to be determined by the territorial legislatures. He hoped that Eastern objections would be silenced by a provision subjecting all elected officials to possible presidential removal.

He appealed to patriotism and nonpartisan justice in the centennial year, "when the people are returning to the foundation of their liberties for the purpose of drinking anew the water of freedom."[34] When defeated on a point of order, Tom engaged in a sharp and bitter attack on the rules of procedure.

Convinced that Easterners utterly failed to grasp the problem of distance in the West, he saw the real needs for development in the territories routinely blocked. Further, he was impatient with federal attempts to economize by curtailing expenditures in the West. For example, he strongly objected to a move aimed at reducing the salaries of judges in the territories from $3,000 to $2,500 a year.[35] Already unhappy over the downgrading of Colorado's judiciary through carpetbag appointees, Patterson insisted that with the cut in salary it would be nearly impossible to secure qualified men, even among territorial residents. The $2,500 might be common in the East, but in the West judges had to travel greater distances and cover circuits of eight or nine counties, as compared with one or two in the East.

While he was at it, he attacked territorial railroad rates. He argued that although travel in a state like Indiana ran two to three cents a mile, a territorial judge in Colorado or New Mexico should be paid at a rate of 25 cents a mile. He contended that even the $3,000 salary was unrealistic. If the proposed reduction went through, it would lead to a situation in which "lawyers who pettifog about the police courts of Eastern states and cannot make a living at home are sent to the territories and quartered."[36]

He also objected to a suggestion that would deprive members of Congress of mileage allowances. He pointed to the special hardship such a move would cause delegates who in some cases would spend up to one-third of their regular salary on transportation for their families. "Surely," said Patterson, "Congress wanted the wives with their husbands, if only for the sake of morality."[37] When he referred to the multiple needs of some delegates from Utah, laughter rippled through the chamber. At one point during this discussion, Patterson bitterly accused an Eastern colleague of supporting a salary boost because "he got it all," but when it comes to mileage "he is attacked with a sudden spasm of retrenchment and reform."[38]

On the issue of extending the survey of Western lands, Tom Patterson maintained that Easterners did not understand the importance of the service, and he opposed any measure he thought would interrupt the survey process. He insisted that appropriations for surveys be applied to mineral lands and asserted that miners should be aided in getting entry to and patents on public lands. When several efforts to make appropriations for surveys apply also to mineral rights and timberlands failed, an irritated Patterson accused the Easterners on the Committee on Appropriations of favoring their own states in the distribution of money. To add to his other defeats, Patterson also failed to secure public lands for the establishment of an agricultural and mechanical college in Colorado.[39]

In the end, it was the Indian issue that caused Tom some of his greatest frustrations. There the East lined up squarely against much of Western opinion. Though he defended his constituents and their frequently hostile attitude toward members of the various Indian tribes, Patterson also called for justice and fair treatment. To him, the possibility that unhappy Indians could cause serious trouble for territorial settlers was very real. Following that logic, he presented a resolution empowering the Committee on Indian Affairs to investigate the government's integrity in its dealings with the Ute Indians.[40] He questioned whether the United States had been complying with the terms of a treaty under which the government had agreed to pay the Utes $25,000 a year in return for the Utes' giving up their claims in the San Juan mining district of southwestern Colorado. Patterson wanted the government to meet its obligations to preserve frontier peace and prevent retaliation by disgruntled Utes against miners and settlers.[41] He feared, correctly, that the killing of cattle and the burning of farm buildings would be the result when the government neglected to live up to its end of the agreement.

He also suggested that Indian unrest developed because of the methods and personnel of the Indian Bureau. He accused the bureau of unfair treatment of the tribes, of gross inefficiency, and of failure to maintain a peaceful environment. Consequently, he supported legislation providing for the transfer of the Office of Indian Affairs from the Department of the Interior to the Department of War.[42] Further, he introduced a bill for appropriations to construct a military post near the Ute Reservation as a precautionary measure.[43]

One student of Patterson's actions on the Indian issue found that he showed no real moral indignation and made no serious defense of the rights of the Indians—he simply wanted to preserve frontier tranquility.[44] Judging by the letters to his wife during this period, however, such an evaluation seems unfair. Patterson refers in his letters to the "shameful" treatment of the Utes by both the federal government and members of the Indian Bureau. He apparently was convinced that humanitarianism was his motivation.[45] Years later, he publicly attacked the Indian agents as dispensers of moldy flour, shoddy blankets, and gratuitous brutality, arguing that from the Indian point of view it seemed improbable "there were any good living white men."[46]

In spite of his compassion for the Indians, he still disagreed with Eastern idealistic concepts of the "noble red man" and believed that any efforts to civilize the Indian would prove futile. On occasion, he passionately defended such episodes as the much-criticized Chivington Massacre, named after John Chivington, commander of the military district of Colorado, who with his men allegedy slaughtered the sleeping village of Cheyenne at Sand Creek in 1864.[47] He challenged his colleagues to put themselves in the place of the frontiersman, who might "have a band of these marauding savages come upon them in the night time, applying the torch to the cabin, taking out his wife and ravishing her in their sight, then destroying her and her children, leaving the husband and father with all the fond recollections and all the fond hopes blasted forever."[48]

On the subject of finance, Patterson condemned the government's curtailment of the purchase of silver long before it became a popular theme. In 1873, Congress had passed a law that officially discontinued coinage of silver dollars. Few objected at the time, but within a few years the measure began to create controversy. Because of the discovery of huge amounts of silver in Comstock, Nevada, and Leadville, Colorado, silver prices began to fall; it soon became clear that Congress had foreclosed a very real method of expanding the currency in a time of increased industrial productivity. Many Americans concluded that a conspiracy of big bankers had been responsible for the "demonetization" of silver.

Patterson believed that the prosperity of the country depended upon the economic condition of the gold and silver states and he warned that the "stupendous swindles—the Crime of '73—" would come back to haunt the country in the future.[49] His strong support of free coinage of silver was a position that later would link him with the Populists and William Jennings Bryan during the 1890s.

But no matter what else Patterson tackled, the passage of the enabling act for Colorado statehood was uppermost in his mind. He worked almost around the clock, getting little sleep, always believing that action on the bill was only days away. Finally, the Enabling Act was passed on March 3, 1876. A week later, Tom wrote to his wife: "My work in Washington is done, and I start for Indiana tonight. I feel quite happy that Colorado has run the gauntlet safely and that we now live in what will soon be a full fledged state."[50] Historians agree that Tom Patterson had exerted a critical influence in its eventual passage.[51]

Back in Colorado, the electorate prepared to vote on a proposed state constitution. Statehood supporters became worried over a rumor that a determined last-minute opposition might arise because of the anticipated expense of financing and operating a state government. To be on the safe side, on election day—July 1, 1876—a number of statehood supporters voted at more than one polling place. Conceding that "much chicanry had taken place," Charley

Thomas, Patterson's law partner, was relieved that no formal challenge to the election results occurred.[52]

On August 1, 1876, Colorado became a state—the first to be admitted to the Union in thirteen years. A jubilant Tom Patterson telegraphed, "I greet the Centennial state—the latest but the brightest star in the political firmament. I am proud . . . of representing the grandest state, the bravest men and the handsomest women on the continent."[53] Once in the Union, Colorado raced to qualify and participate in the national election of 1876, only a few weeks away. The state constitution provided for direct election of electors by the people only *after* 1876. To save the three electoral votes in 1876, the Colorado General Assembly (the state legislature) was nevertheless allowed to make the selection of the electors *in* 1876. In spite of all of Patterson's earlier assurances that the electors would be Democrats, the fact remained that the Republicans controlled Colorado's legislature. There was no possible way that Patterson could make good on his promise. Because both political parties knew that the presidential race would be close, Colorado's three electoral votes were crucial. They not only triggered the most dramatic contest of any presidential election in the country's history, they also determined its outcome.

The respectable Rutherford B. Hayes, burdened by the moral bankruptcy of the Grant administration, appeared a certain loser when Democrat Samuel J. Tilden piled up a popular plurality of 250,000 votes and led the electoral count by 184 to 165, including 20 votes from four states—South Carolina, Florida, Louisiana, and Oregon—that were in question. Yet even with the votes of these states Tilden had only 184 electoral votes, and 185 were necessary for election.[54] In each of the three Southern states (still under Reconstruction) two governments—one representing the white vote, the other the carpetbag vote—sprang up after the election. Each claimed to be legitimate, and each called upon federal authority to settle the dispute in its favor. Intimidation and fraud were rampant on both sides. Hayes appeared to have carried South Carolina, but in Florida and Louisiana Tilden seemed to have a safe majority. Republican reporting boards threw out about 1,000 Democratic votes in Florida and over 13,000 in Louisiana. The electoral vote of a fourth state—Oregon—was questioned when one Democratic elector was replaced with a Republican by the Republican governor.

With no mechanism in place to handle the dilemma, the leaders of the House and the Senate conferred and came up with the idea of an election commission, the only such group in all of American presidential politics. The commission was to determine to whom the contested votes should be

Downtown Denver, Colorado, in the 1870s. Note Jerome Chaffee's First National Bank on the corner. (Courtesy Colorado Historical Society.)

awarded. There was one proviso: Each house had the right of veto over the commission's decision.

The Election Commission was composed of five members from the House, five from the Senate, and five from the U.S. Supreme Court. The House being Democratic, three of its five commission members were Democrats. Conversely, the Senate, with a Republican majority, appointed three Republicans and two Democrats. Finally, there was the Supreme Court. Only two justices were Democrats, holdovers from pre–Civil War days.

Denver, Colorado, in the 1870s. (Courtesy Colorado Historical Society.)

Two other justices appointed to the commission were Republicans. The fifth man, David Davis from Illinois, was of neither party.

The appointments made, the commission consisted of seven Democrats and seven Republicans. The tie vote was David Davis. Refusing to accept the immense responsibility of determining the next president, Justice Davis resigned from the court and returned to Illinois. Because the only remaining justices on the court were Republicans, his replacement necessarily was a Republican.

Though the majority of the commission members were now Republicans, the Democrats in the House could conceivably exercise their vote to veto a Republican outcome. But inauguration was by now only days away, with no president yet chosen. One night, a contingent of Southern Democrats called on Rutherford Hayes and struck a deal. If he would agree to remove the remaining U.S. troops from the South, they would break the logjam facing the Election Commission. Unenthusiastic about Reconstruction, Hayes agreed. The Commission declared Hayes a 185 to 184 winner.

Throughout the entire stalemate it was obvious that had Colorado not acquired statehood and cast its three votes for the Republican Hayes Samuel Tilden would have won the election—even if all twenty of the disputed votes had gone to Hayes. The Hayes victory particularly incensed Democratic party leader David Bennett Hill of New York, who never forgave Tom Patterson.

Years later, while serving as senator from Colorado, Tom recalled that he had been widely condemned as the man responsible for Tilden's defeat. He did not explain the motivation behind his guarantee to the Democrats nor did he defend his conduct.[55] His speech, however, reflected a note of pride over the fact that it was generally believed that a presidential election had been lost because of a lowly territorial delegate.

Although Tom Patterson eventually succeeded in making the Democratic party a consistently formidable force in Colorado politics, in the beginning years of his political career, well-entrenched vanity and political inexperience led him to unfounded optimism. In 1876 one such miscalculation produced both statehood for Colorado and the election of a Republican president.

3
Meeting the Challenge

I leave the case, gentlemen, with you. . . . In so doing you will teach these Colorado conspirators that they know neither the law, the ballot box, or the people.

—Tom Patterson, *Congressional Record,* 45th Congress

During the steamy, early summer days of Washington in 1876, before the fateful presidential election, Tom Patterson considered his political future. Measuring his accomplishments against the cost to his private life, he occasionally became despondent. Writing to his wife in June, he complained, "Why did I ever allow myself to be torn from my bucolic home to be imprisoned in this metropolitan bastille, under the mistaken assumption that I was having honor conferred above that of my fellows?"[1]

But the letters and newspapers from Colorado were filled with talk of Patterson's political future. When he professed indifference, Kate did not believe him. She even went so far as to suggest that he cast his lot with the majority Republicans to ensure a more successful career.[2] After recoiling in mock horror over the suggestion, he described a frightening daydream he had conjured up while trying to picture himself as a Republican:

> I realized that I was in part responsible for the fearful crimes of that party, and I feel as if I ought to be in jail. I wanted the Credit Mobilizer to come along and bribe me. I found a man who had some of my letters and I threatened to commit suicide if he did not return them. I then got up in the House to make a speech and I commenced to lie and lie and then to swear to their truth. But then the spell was broken, and I am now once again clothed in the full robes of my Democratic virtue, and such advice from you again will be considered a good ground for a divorce.[3]

By mid-July Patterson appeared to be only half joking when he asked Kate whether she had learned of "hordes" of delegates from Colorado begging him to consent to be senator, governor, or any other office provided for in the Constitution.[4] Perhaps his vanity had been piqued after a triumphant speech he gave at Martinsburg, West Virginia, when he was the only one of several speakers to receive calls for an encore and was presented with a wreath and a bouquet.[5]

Patterson took notice of "the political hell being fired up in Colorado." He complained that the *Rocky Mountain News* had started its usual warfare against him, pending the upcoming election.[6] In spite of his earlier protests, he told Kate that he would not resist a draft as a candidate for the House of Representatives. He placed the weight of his decision on his duty and obligation to the people of Colorado.[7]

But on the home front, Tom's problems were not as easy to solve. He was having a house built on Fourteenth and Welton Streets and it would have to be furnished. Kate was in the early stages of her fourth pregnancy and often in bed. He arranged for his mother to stay with her and care for the two girls. Their eleven-year-old son, James, had been with Tom in Washington since January.

Ever since Christmas, the strain of their separation had taken its toll on Kate. Writing after a long day of looking after two young children and bogged down with household chores, Kate saw Tom's life in Washington as carefree. Jealously, she wrote:

> If it is not too much to ask I should prefer that you would not take my pretty young cousin to the theater or recognize any special claim she may assume to have upon your attentions *until I come.* ... You will understand, I know, and be a good boy till I come and I will not be obliged to suffer any more from the bitter consciousness of my last departing you—while I have so little else to compensate for it or to cloak my real feelings in frivolity.[8]

Tom tried to assure her of his lack of interest in any other woman. "I could never love any one but you," he wrote. "If I don't love you, I am incapable of love. If you were to die tomorrow, I would be as dead to love except for children and parents as the marble of the statue. *No* woman ever could awaken love in me again. ... Business, politics and other cares have changed my manner, I suppose, but no matter what the outward show may be my heart is warm for you and its love is only yours."[9] After a brief trip back to Colorado, Tom

The Patterson home, 17th and Welton Streets, Denver, Colorado, in the 1880s. (Courtesy Archives, University of Colorado at Boulder Libraries, Patterson collection, Bx 8, Fd 10.)

continued his reassurance. "I want you to know and feel that you and you alone are my only womanly love upon this earth."[10]

Not only was he beset with a lonely wife, but the handling of his law office and business dealings was creating troubles. He had taken Ernest Campbell, Kate's brother-in-law, into the firm the year before. At the time, Kate was distraught over his seeming indifference, and he had offered to take Campbell into the firm as a kind of olive branch. But from the beginning, Tom had to plead with Campbell for accountings of the firm's position. On June 15, 1876, he wrote to Kate, saying, "I am perplexed at Ernest's silence on this and other matters touching my business affairs since I have been away. He has not condescended to give me one word upon the subject."[11] Not surprisingly, when Kate wrote to discuss the need to finish the house, he responded that "I will make no arrangements about finishing the house until I get back—and I am very certain I will not have it finished on credit."[12]

Still, the question of his candidacy was never out of Tom's mind. As he had in the past, he turned to Kate for advice. "I sent you yesterday a *Record* containing my speech on the silver question. I want you to read it and criticize heartily when you write. I confess to a high regard for your sincere views on any subject involving taste, good sense, and grammar."[13]

Returning to Colorado, Tom planned to attend the Democratic convention, where the party's candidate for representative to Congress would be nominated. If elected, he would serve for the unexpired term of the Forty-fourth Congress and the full term of the Forty-fifth.[14] But, since his election as territorial delegate, Colorado Republicans had closed ranks and fully expected to regain the ground they had lost two years earlier.[15] Meeting in Pueblo on August 23, the Republicans selected J. B. Belford as Patterson's opponent. A judge for several years and regarded as an eloquent speaker, Belford campaigned tirelessly. A vigorous campaign followed.

The election became bitterly disputed. At issue was whether the October election applied to both the unexpired term of the Forty-fourth Congress and the entire term of the Forty-fifth Congress. The constitution of the state of Colorado set the date of election for the first Tuesday in October. The temporary secretary of state, John Taffe, issued the election notices to the county sheriffs. The Republicans believed that the one October election would determine the holder of both offices; the Democrats disagreed.[16]

In later years, Tom Patterson's political enemies pictured him as having taken an ambiguous position on the legality of the situation, but the evidence indicates his position was clear.[17] He wrote to the chairman of the Democratic committee, claiming that the October election could be legitimate only for the unexpired Forty-fourth session.[18] Further, as late as September 19, 1876, Patterson sought to have the Democratic tickets that showed him as a candidate for both terms destroyed.[19]

Patterson's law partner, Charles Thomas, only added to the confusion when he ordered Democratic tickets printed to cover both terms. He later said he made the move since he knew the Republicans believed that only one election was necessary and he was confident that Patterson would win the October election.[20]

Immediately after the October election, the Colorado Democrats sent several telegrams to Samuel J. Tilden,[21] assuring the Democratic presidential candidate that a Democrat would carry Colorado. But it would be another week before the outcome became clear. Some counties reported slowly. One set of records from Las Animas County appeared to be in such confusion that a special clerical force was finally hired for the "elucidation of its mysteries."[22] Although discrepancies existed in the final tabulation, Belford clearly defeated Patterson for both terms, with the wider margin in the race for the seat in the Forty-fifth Congress.[23]

Patterson accepted defeat in regard to the Forty-fourth Congress and at no time claimed victory for that part of the contest. He even urged Belford's recognition and seating in letters to New York Republican Elbridge G. Lapham and Democratic leader Samuel J. Randall of Pennsylvania.[24] But he questioned the validity of the election to the Forty-fifth Congress, and immediately launched a campaign for a November election. The Republicans treated his move as a farce, called it "Tom Patterson's election," and even produced a song entitled "And Tommy Didn't Go."[25] By mid-October, the Republicans had withdrawn Belford's name from any projected November contest, refusing to dignify Patterson's challenge.[26]

There followed the most bizarre election in Colorado history. The Republicans, through their control of many state positions, made certain there was little machinery available for the casting and counting of ballots. In some places, the polls did not open. In others, local precinct officials gathered the votes that were cast and certified them. Since fewer than four thousand votes were cast, the state board even refused to canvass them.[27] Through it all, Patterson remained confident that he was technically in the right.

Patterson and Belford both arrived in Washington for the opening of the Forty-fifth Congress, armed with their credentials and arguments. Turmoil followed. The clerk refused to place either name on the roll and handed the problem to the House. The issue hinged on the question of whether Congress had endowed the Colorado constitutional convention with authority to fix the date of any election other than the election to the Forty-fourth Congress.

Belford, however, had signed a statement agreeing to the accuracy of Patterson's vote count in the November election, thereby giving it a semblance of legitimacy.[28] In addition, Patterson presented a legalistic brief that quoted the Republican governor of Colorado, John Routt, who admitted that in his judgment Belford was not legally elected to the Forty-fifth Congress.[29]

Finally, three reports arrived from the Committee on Elections: a majority report in favor of Tom Patterson, a minority report in favor of J. B. Belford, and a dissenting report unfavorable to both men on the grounds that no valid election had as yet been held for the Forty-fifth Congress.[30] Shortly before the determining vote, Patterson seized an opportunity to plead his case and defend himself against an attack on his personal integrity.

According to him, Representative Eugene Hale of Maine had stigmatized him as a vagrant, a mendicant, and a beggar. Patterson observed, "It is not always, sir, that 'beggars' are to blame. Men are often driven into poverty by circumstances over which they have no control. But, sir, a coward and a vilifier is always that, either from nature or his own choosing."[31] Tom reconstructed his claim to office, denounced Colorado Republicans as tools of Jerome Chaffee, and suggested that anyone worthy of manhood would have fought precisely as he had for the position. He concluded: "I leave the case, gentlemen, with you, satisfied that you will do only that which your convictions must lead you to do as law-abiding citizens. . . . In so doing you will teach these Colorado conspirators that they know neither the law, the ballot box, or the people."[32]

In a letter to Kate, he described the climax to the struggle as a severe one, lasting all day. The majority report was adopted with 116 yeas, 110 nays, and 65 abstentions.[33] A few minutes later, Thomas M. Patterson took the oath of office and became a member of the House of Representatives. Though he admitted it was a "narrow shave," he said he had been listened to with as much attention as he ever had in court and had made "a decided hit." He believed his speech had saved the day.[34]

4
Supreme Sectionalist

It is singular to me that the gentlemen who live upon the sea coast are never content to leave the central portion of this great continent the few benefits that are occasionally granted to them.

—Tom Patterson, *Congressional Record,* 45th Congress

In January of 1878 Tom Patterson took his son, James, back with him to Washington, and they set up housekeeping in a small suite of rooms at a comfortable boardinghouse at a rent of $75 a month. When James was not in school, he either came to the House with his father or was looked after by the woman who owned the boardinghouse.[1]

Meanwhile, Kate, again pregnant, was depressed over Tom's return to Washington. She claimed that his attitude toward her was cold. She believed that they could no longer be lovers but only friends. Further, she resented having to ask him for money:

> Why should you not show me the respect due to a responsible being and the prudent and careful wife that I know I try so hard to be? . . . I simply ask that you trust me enough to place at my disposal a sum of money large enough to do away with the necessity of asking constantly and deprecatingly for what I need.
> Your friend and wife, Kate.[2]

The tone of Tom's reply held a stoic quality:

> I accept the relations you seem determined to force into existence between us—that of 'friends' only coupled with the mutual obligations resting upon husband and wife. If the phrase 'friend and wife' had appeared for the first time it would not, as it does now, raise before me as a reality that the law and our individual love of our

children will keep us together in a closer relation than is befitting mere friends. . . .

I recollect during my last trip to Denver, you stated one night with a calmness that indicated reflection and determination arising therefrom that thereafter you would be 'while a wife only a friend' to me. Now a cold business letter wholly devoted to money—and between the lines an intimation that you had suffered many griev-ances in that line at my hands . . . has convinced me of my position at last and it is that position I accept.

In my supply of money to you, I shall be controlled by two con-siderations: our station in life, this includes my ability; and your reasonable wants as fixed by that station. . . .

Your faithful friend and Husband, Tom.[3]

Several more indignant and bitter letters were exchanged until, on February 2, Tom wrote a letter that concluded in this way:

Kate, I say now sincerely that I love you and have ever since we met. Business, politics, and other cares have changed my manner I suppose, but no matter what the outward show may be my heart is warm for you and its love is only yours.

Kate was overcome:

My own dear husband,

I have just read your long kind and most comforting letter of the 2nd. Its entire openness is just my ideal of what should be the char-acter of all our intercourse and I feel that I should really be ashamed to confess to you, Tom, the great joy and peace that its longed for assurances give me.[4]

By the end of the month, on February 24, 1878, their second son, Thomas, was born, seeming to bring their need for reassurance of each other's love, at least for the time, to a close. Now, finally, Tom could devote his full attention to the Congress.

Because the dispute over his election had lasted a full year, only a portion of the Forty-fifth Congress remained, and he struggled against heavy odds to compile a significant record in the House. Many Eastern Democrats, recalling how Patterson had virtually guaranteed Colorado would go Democratic, turned on him in wrath. Even before his election, the Democrats were in the majority in the House. They did not need his vote, they told him. It was a sobering rebuke.

He received only three committee assignments: Public Lands, Expenditures in the Department of the Interior, and a conference committee of little importance.[5] When measures of economy developed that might have retarded Colorado's development came up, Patterson reacted. Though he failed in his challenge to a proposal to abandon fifty-seven military forts, nearly all of them in the West,[6] he succeeded with a resolution asking the secretary of war to indicate what steps were being taken to protect residents of western Colorado from possible outbreaks by the Ute Indians.[7] And he repeatedly argued against efforts to reduce the armed forces.[8]

After noting the political realities that dictated the position of Pennsylvania representatives in their defense of high tariffs and of New England representatives whose solid support of financial legislation was beneficial to their region, Patterson called for equal justice for the West—where interests were "more important," since they concerned both property *and* life. He described the horrors of an Indian massacre and warned that some reservations were "smoldering volcanoes of murder and rapine."[9] Moreover, when Colorado appealed for troops to protect the people and allay their fears, the answer always came back that the government did not have enough troops at its disposal to meet such requests. But Patterson's passionate appeal fell on deaf ears.[10]

In matters of mining and minting, Tom Patterson introduced bills authorizing the purchase of gold dust and of gold and silver bullion at Denver. He also proposed changing the Denver storage depot for bullion into a regular United States mint.[11] When these efforts failed, he offered an amendment to the legislative appropriations bill that would have placed the Denver storage depot on the same footing as other mints.[12] During the debate over rehabilitation of the St. Louis mint, Tom argued that Denver was superior to all other points for the purpose of coinage.[13] He suggested that inasmuch as the Atlantic and Pacific coasts already had their own mints, the heart of the continent, not the "ragged edge," should receive the next consideration.[14]

He also tried to get the salaries at the Denver depot raised, and, upon being ruled out of order, attacked the East again: "It is singular to me that the gentlemen who live upon the sea coast are never content to leave the central portion of this great continent the few benefits that are occasionally granted to them. . . . They are ever grasping, ever jealous, ever opposing."[15] During the debate Patterson added that it was unpatriotic to restore the

New Orleans mint, because it would cater to South American and Mexican sources of metal.[16]

Tom's letters to Kate indicated that, while frequently discouraged, he believed he had effectively represented the state and caused the Denver mint to be elevated to the dignity of other mints.[17]

Of his other activities, he wrote:

> I have passed a busy week, perfecting legislation before the committees and passing some in the House. . . . I have also had the Committee on Public Lands recommend favorably the granting of the block of ground in Denver for a high school; also to agree to give Colorado about a million and a half acres of land for Common Schools.[18]

The last entry typified Patterson's continued interest in public land policies. When legislation proposed $20,000 to investigate trespassing on public land and depredations of timber, he exploded. Such investigators were nothing but spies. He argued that settlers might unwittingly offend under the proposal and that timber dealers would be falsely accused. Moreover, in the West few individuals owned timber lands. If a settler wanted to build, he was forced to use timber from public lands. Patterson further warned that the proposed legislation would lead to the prosecution of suits that the government would be unable to prove. Such suits, he maintained, clogged Colorado state courts. And, further, the government had not won such a case in several years.[19]

Other congressmen did not agree, pointing out that the only serious suits ever started by the government had been against railroads for the illegal use of timber for fuel and ties. Representative Charles Foster of Ohio sarcastically identified Patterson's "poor, innocent, deluded timber thieves" as the Atchison, Topeka, and Santa Fe, the Colorado Central Railroad, and the Boston and Colorado Smelting Company.[20] Patterson's arguments appeared to convince few of his colleagues, primarily because the government had not harassed settlers under previous laws.[21] But he still managed to get a bill out of the Committee on Public Lands—and passed—authorizing citizens in Colorado, Nevada, and the territories to fell and remove timber from public lands for mining and domestic purposes.[22]

In May of 1878 Tom wrote to Kate that his labors had begun to bear fruit. He confidently predicted that before the session ended he would have compiled a fine record.[23] But using his own phrase, very few of his legislative eggs hatched during his brief tenure as a representative. Near the end of his term, in response to praise from home, Tom summed up his performance and revealed some disappointment: "Thanks for your compliments as to my record. I have worked hard all winter, but with modesty. The truth is, Kate, going in after the contest, I felt reluctant to take as prominent a stand on many occasions as I otherwise would. But I did not allow any fitting occasion on local matters to pass unheeded."[24]

As for running for representative again, Tom still felt his scars from the Belford fight. In April 1878 he wrote that nothing could induce him to accept a nomination for any office.[25] And he worried about his children. Mary—or Mamie as the family called her, and who he confessed to Kate was his favorite—had a history of ear infections;[26] James was susceptible to bad influences, and little Tommy suffered from inflamed eyelids. Only Margaret (Maud) caused her parents no worry.

Nevertheless, just as he had done two years earlier, Patterson changed his mind. Back in Colorado by late summer, in time to receive the Democratic nomination and accompanied by his opponent, Belford, he toured the state in a series of joint debates. In Leadville, before an unruly crowd in a large structure called the Wigwam, Belford's speech so inflamed the audience that the chairman declared the meeting over before Patterson had a chance to speak. A large number of his followers adjourned to a nearby gambling establishment, where, according to legend, the candidate answered Belford while standing on a faro table.[27]

Democratic party leaders predicted a statewide sweep of all offices. Though Patterson joined in the optimism, the abusive aspects of the campaign irritated him. From Alma, a small mining town high in the Rocky Mountain divide, Patterson wrote to Kate, complaining that the campaign had been laborious and filled with personalities "as disgusting as they are infamous."[28]

He claimed to have conducted an honorable campaign, and looked forward to the day when, win or lose, he could turn his back on "such agony."[29] The Republicans, no longer the divided party of 1876, swept to victory in Colorado, with Tom among the losers.[30] This time he found no political or legal technicality with which to salvage his position.

Tom Patterson's brief political career as delegate and representative had exposed his intense sectional bias. He consistently agitated for legislation designed to protect or benefit the West and Colorado. He fought for home rule, increased salaries for Western officials, increased mileage allowances, and the extension of surveys. He held the Western view on the Indian problem. He resisted financial exploitation of the West by the East and indicated his allegiance to the Western position on the increasingly significant issue of bimetallism.

He also displayed an increasingly fervent allegiance to the Democratic party, only parting company with his colleagues when sectional issues cut across partisan lines. As a result of optimism or miscalculation, he frequently overestimated the political prospects of his party in Colorado. In his rhetoric and his letters, Patterson measured Republicans on a scale of corruption and tyranny.

At thirty-nine, Tom Patterson was a man of great energy, stubbornness, and well-entrenched vanity. Intensely ambitious, he tenaciously pursued office in the Belford race in the face of considerable ridicule. He could explode in a moment and speak interminably on almost any subject. He was also a man who took himself seriously. To every appearance, he was a young man "on the make."

5
The Self-Made Man

One murder yesterday and one today, both shootings and on slight
provocation in the approved Leadville style.

—Tom Patterson, to K. M. Patterson, January 27, 1882

By the late 1870s the law firm of Patterson, Markham, Thomas, and Campbell was already famous throughout Colorado. Tom Patterson had been admitted to practice before the U.S. Supreme Court in 1877.[1] He was regarded
as one of the most able criminal advocates in the state.[2] By February 1879 the
partnership had become so involved in mining litigation that Thomas opened
another office in the booming mining town of Leadville, where the courts
were jammed with mining disputes. At one point in the early 1880s, the firm's
Leadville branch alone handled four times the business done in its Denver office and averaged $10,000 monthly in cash and defaults, rather high fees for
the day.[3]

Although Tom's primary responsibility involved maintaining the office in
Denver, he frequently spent weeks at a time in Leadville. As the partners'
fame grew, Tom Patterson was obliged to travel to all corners of Colorado
and to southern Wyoming.

In Colorado in the late 1870s and 1880s, a traveling lawyer needed a rugged constitution and considerable determination. Patterson usually operated
from one of the larger communities, such as Durango, Del Norte, or Gunnison, making short but strenuous trips back into the smaller mining camps.
His letters were filled with their colorful names, and he described the difficult conditions. In a letter from Wagon Wheel Gap he told of the cold, wind,
and snow. Though he rarely drank liquor, the weather was so severe that he
was obliged to indulge in hot whiskey toddies, "reluctantly but frequently."[4]
It was after a particularly difficult coach ride in early December of 1879,
when he finally arrived in Saguache, that he wrote Kate not only about the

bone-chilling cold but of the nightmare he'd had the previous night. In his dreams, their two-year-old son, Tom, had fallen from a horrible height and been instantly killed.[5]

Six months later the child died of influenza in Denver while his father was in Leadville on legal business. Kate was left alone to bury their son. James ran away from home and started to get into trouble with the authorities. What was said between Kate and Tom during his brief stays in Denver during the stress-filled fall of 1880 must be left to speculation.

By March of the following year Kate left Denver for Europe, taking the three children with her, ostensibly to fulfill a lifetime dream. Moreover, she was determined that at the least she and Tom would be legally separated.

> I do not know how I shall stand the fatherland for a whole year, Tom. I did not sleep one instant last night thinking of you and the wrong I may be doing you by this separation.
>
> If any temptation to wrong should overcome you such as would degrade your morals, blight my life by the inevitable separation of our family, break your old mother's heart, disgrace your children's name and wreck your own career, how could I survive my error?[6]

At the base of her decision to leave was not the familiar litany of accusations but the contention made by Kate's sister, Mary, that she had seen letters written by a Mrs. Morgan that fully expressed "criminal intimacy" with Tom.[7] Kate's reaction was immediate: She wanted a divorce, or at the very least a legal separation. She asked her brother-in-law, Ernest, to arrange the details of the separation and any settlement. Understandably, Ernest declined, and Kate wrote to Charles Thomas, asking him to act on her behalf.

Tom was furious. "I have been charged, arraigned, tried, found guilty, and sentenced. Of course, it is neither expected nor would it be profitable to deny the charge and pray for mercy. You have been the jury and by your actions have shown that you deem me guilty beyond doubt," he wrote Kate.[8]

> So far as I am concerned, I want no separation not so much on my account as for the sake of our children. I have endured so much abuse during my *public* life that for myself I would not care a straw for any publicity you or your affectionate and scrupulously virtuous and conscientious sister and brother-in-law might see fit to make, but I must hesitate before I become party to putting a ban upon our children on account of either of their parents' misdeeds.[9]

Mary Campbell, he said, was "an artful, revengeful, unscrupulous and morally bad sister," and her husband, Ernest, was "still meaner and more despicable." He didn't hate them. He simply "despised them."

He refused Kate's demand for a divorce with a $100,000 settlement. He would go to court first. A separation was as far as he would go, and he demanded that Kate bring Mamie and Margaret back in two years. "To speak plainly," he concluded, "I mean that we should live a lie to our children and the public solely for the sake of the children's future."[10]

To friends and Denver society, Tom explained that he had insisted on a European education for his children. He planned to visit them when he could get away. Privately, he loathed eating his meals alone in the empty Welton Street house. His heart ached. He mourned the recent death of his father. He buried himself deeper in work.

Since many of his mining cases required a working knowledge of the mines themselves, Patterson spent much time in rugged country, deep in mine shafts. As late as 1888, when he was nearly fifty years old, he wrote: "Day before yesterday I spent going through some of the mines in which I am employed as attorney. It was hard work, as for nearly a whole day I was crawling on my belly through the drifts and levels underground making the necessary investigations to enable me to conduct the trials intelligently."[11] Patterson's firsthand experience with miners and their working conditions probably accounted for his militant defense of miners in later years.

Travel became so frequent that on those occasions when he did return to Denver for a time the routine of home and office life became "irksome."[12] His name became synonymous with careful preparation and with success. He wrote to his wife that when he became absorbed in a case he banished everything else from his mind. On one occasion when his wife was abroad, he proudly wrote her that he had not lost a case since her departure from Denver several months earlier, and sometimes he even surprised himself by winning a case he had thought hopeless.[13]

Thorough preparation, however, could not ensure victory every time. On one occasion a judge discharged a jury after one member announced publicly that there would be no verdict at all unless the jurors decided in favor of Tom Patterson's side of the case. The subsequent arrest of the juror gave rise to Kate's wry observation "Let us be protected from our friends."[14]

Patterson and Thomas frequently participated in litigation that determined the validity of conflicting mining claims. One such case, the *Iron*

Leadville, Colorado, in the early 1880s. (Courtesy Colorado Historical Society.)

Silver Mining Company v. Cheesman, resulted in three separate trials before the defendant, represented by Patterson and Thomas, was upheld by the Circuit Court of the United States for the District of Colorado.[15] The Iron Silver Mining Company had pursued a lode deep into the ground and had curved through the perpendicular of its sideline, an imaginary plane extended from the surface boundary, thus extending its claim into Cheesman's territory. The case was finally resolved in favor of Cheesman when Thomas and Patterson convinced the court that the mineral pinched out, so that it could no longer be regarded as the continuous body of mineral required under the "apex" theory. Under this theory a claimant had to fix his surface boundaries in such a way as to embrace the apex (top) of a vein. Otherwise he had no right to pursue the vein on its downward course. In order to continue following a strike to a point beneath another person's surface property, the claimant further had to establish the continuity and sufficiency of the strike.[16]

Adding to the confusion in even *identifying* the apex of a body of ore, Colorado miners frequently found "blanket" deposits. An example was the deposits at Leadville, which often lay scattered on the surface or were superficially covered by shale or debris. Such a widespread blanket of material made it nearly impossible to determine an apex, and the resulting court cases challenged the imagination and ingenuity of Colorado lawyers. Furthermore, the court was not empowered to engage experts in an advisory capacity, so the litigants paid high fees for conflicting "expert" testimony filled with obvious bias.[17] Tom Patterson, according to the *Denver Post*, had little to do with originating the Apex mining theory, but as an interpreter of these theories he received "almost fabulous" sums.[18]

In view of the violence that pervaded the mining communities, Patterson did not confine his activities to civil suits. He once reflected on the incongruity of the beautiful mountain setting's serving as an incubator for cold-blooded murder. In 1882 he described the delights of sleighing in Leadville, the streets filled with beautiful horses and jingling bells, ending with the note that there had been "one murder yesterday and one today, both shootings and on slight provocation in the approved Leadville style."[19]

From Gunnison Tom wrote that he had been defending murder suspects "all the time."[20] He once complained that, since two murder trials in Montrose had just been lost by other defense attorneys, he would have to work harder to save *his* clients.[21] In the mining areas of Colorado, murder cases sometimes hinged on the question of self-defense, following quarrels over mining claims and property rights. One such case involved Tom as defense counsel for J. J. Richey, who had owned a tunnel and mine in Boulder County. Richey had leased the property to B. E. Rhodes. When Rhodes failed to comply with all the terms of the agreement, the two men quarreled violently and then disappeared into the mine out of sight of witnesses. Richey testified that he was then assaulted by Rhodes with a rock and a knife, and that he had shot Rhodes in self-defense.

In the ensuing trial Richey was found guilty of murder, but Patterson appealed the decision, contending the jury had not been correctly instructed. The judge, said Patterson, had substituted the words "danger of enormous bodily harm" for "danger of great harm" when he had described the conditions under which a man had the right to self-defense. Patterson contended that such a deviation from the correct language of the charge to the jury had made Rhodes's attack sound like a mere assault case, thereby confusing the jury. The judgment was reversed.[22]

Another criminal case, typical of those handled by Tom Patterson, occurred on the plains of northern Colorado. When Will Avery, a Fort Collins banker, died suddenly in 1889, his widow, Mary, remarried within twelve days. The district attorney became suspicious, eventually indicting both the new husband, Frank Millington, and his sister, Dillie, for murder. Patterson,

Denver, looking south from 18th and Larimer Streets, in the 1880s. The large building is Denver's first public school, Arapahoe School. Beyond it is the Stout Street School. (Courtesy Denver Public Library, Western History Collection.)

retained by the defense, secured a change of venue to Denver, where the case was heard in the old Chamber of Commerce building on Lawrence and 14th Streets in order to accommodate the crowds. In spite of testimony by a parade of witnesses for the prosecution, Patterson, in a brilliant cross-examination, attacked the circumstantial evidence of the alleged poisoning and secured acquittal for the defendants.[23]

Because of a heavy demand for his services, Patterson could be selective. His partner, Charles Thomas, said that Tom declined retainer fees more frequently than he accepted them and would not defend "wilful criminals."[24] He tried to avoid certain types of homicides, especially those involving red-light districts. According to his friend and colleague Edward Keating, Tom Patterson enjoyed telling of an exception he had made to that rule.[25] It seems that a madam from Wyoming had traveled to Denver to beg Patterson to defend her boyfriend, a gambler nicknamed Tin Hat. The accused and a second gambler had disappeared from town on the same day, following a heated argument. A body, alleged to have been that of the second gambler, was discovered a year later in a shallow grave, and the authorities immediately charged Tin Hat with murder.

After hearing the madam's story, Tom tried to discourage her by pointing out that lawyers in one community usually resented the intrusion of foreign talent from another. When that argument failed, he tried to discourage her from hiring him by naming an unusually large retainer fee, $1,500. Retiring to another room, the madam removed the fee from the bankroll she kept in her stocking; she returned and handed it to Tom.

The evidence against Tin Hat, though largely circumstantial, was convincing. Patterson recognized that his only hope lay in proving that the year-old corpse could not be positively identified. An expert called by the prosecution had testified to having measured the decayed remains by section and having come up with figures that showed the body to be five feet, seven and a half inches, the height of the missing man. Sensing that something was wrong with the figures, Tom called upon the foreman of the jury, the local school superintendent, to recheck the calculations. The corrected figures showed the corpse was actually five feet, nine and a half inches. Once acquitted, Tin Hat immediately disappeared. Patterson admitted that he was never sure of this client's innocence; he concluded the episode proved that expert testimony could not always be trusted.[26]

On another occasion he outmaneuvered a hostile courtroom audience in southern Colorado. Convinced that his client, a Mexican, had no chance with the biased jury that had been selected, Patterson moved for a mistrial. He got it after an overenthusiastic member of the courtroom audience made the mistake of presenting the prosecutor with a bouquet of flowers during the trial.

The Denver press began to report that Tom Patterson's clients could be sure of victory. It was a reputation that greatly pleased him, and he was not above bragging to his wife about an 1883 account in the *Denver Republican* that marveled at his performance in a forgery case. After his client had been acquitted the paper concluded that it was proper to say the defendant had been exonerated as much by Tom Patterson as by the jury, since it was doubtful anyone else could have won the man's freedom for him.[27]

Tom Patterson's courtroom performances, some of which may have been embellished through repeated tellings, frequently featured touches of the dramatic. During a case in Del Norte, Patterson supposedly asked his client if he would be willing to pay possible contempt charges for what

Thomas McDonald Patterson in the 1880s.
(Courtesy Colorado Historical Society.)

Patterson planned to do in handling his case. Apparently, Tom had discovered that members of the jury were not receiving full compensation for their services because the county did not have the funds to pay at the normal rate. Told by his client to do as he thought best, the next day in court Patterson suggested to his legal adversary that they join together in making up the loss in revenue being sustained by members of the jury. Though not permitted to do so, Patterson had made his point. He was not above ingratiating himself with a jury.[28]

Yet Patterson maintained that he never resorted to perjured testimony or corrupt juries to win a case. He contended that only clumsy fools resorted to those expedients, and asserted that although he may have been the devil's advocate on occasion, he was never a "fixer."[29] Still, contemporaries accused him of putting red pepper in his handkerchief, blowing his nose loudly, and calling forth glistening tears at strategic moments. One judge, irritated by his performance, detained the lawyer on the prairies of Colorado by appointing him to defend a local drunkard, thus preventing him from pursuing his busy schedule.[30]

Whatever the truth of such stories, Patterson's letters reveal great pride in his courtroom skills. When one case called him to New York City, he delighted in being able to impress the Easterners. Obviously pleased with his performance, he wrote to Kate that he had "floored" a professional handwriting expert and had even demonstrated that the man's theories were faulty. Patterson had also led a star opposition witness into a "mass of admissions" that led to a Patterson victory.[31] Patterson's fame spread beyond Colorado, to the degree that Senator Leonard Swett of Illinois, a leader of the bar in that state, described Patterson as the most adroit, capable, and successful lawyer living west of the Mississippi.[32]

Notes of gratitude from clients attested to his effectiveness. In 1888 a Cheyenne, Wyoming, couple thanked him for having saved the husband from a "hangman's noose."[33] Another client claimed that Patterson reassured all who employed him, and that except for the hope and encouragement he inspired, clients would have been filled with despair.[34]

Patterson usually drew a large courtroom crowd, especially when he was addressing a jury at the close of a case. One contemporary observed that his success resulted from his "acute understanding" of human nature and his ability to reach the "secret depth of the souls of witnesses."[35] Observers generally regarded him as incomparable in the selection of jurors, and the *Denver Post* described him as a "searching and terrifying cross-examiner."[36] Patterson earned his fees by tireless research, attention to detail, and by his ability to analyze the strengths and weaknesses in both his adversary's case and his own. Comparing Patterson to another outstanding Colorado lawyer, Charles Hughes, the *Denver Post* called their confrontations battles between the lawyer, Hughes, and the matador, Patterson.[37]

Patterson participated in both criminal and civil cases, and the evidence points to his having undertaken an impressive number of criminal court actions involving murder charges. In 1888 one observer claimed that the general public regarded him as the greatest criminal advocate the bar of Colorado had ever produced, and deplored the fact that his success in criminal law had somewhat obscured his considerable skill as a civil lawyer.[38]

Patterson's tendency to become involved in sensational cases may have reflected his desire for attention. But while he apparently enjoyed a challenging case, he also liked to win. He probably knew that his chances for victory were greater when he opposed state district attorneys rather than highly skilled lawyers retained by corporations or men of wealth for civil-court actions. His record in criminal actions was certainly spectacularly successful. At the end of Tom Patterson's career, the *Denver Post* claimed that in sixty-two murder cases he had achieved fifty-seven clear acquittals, one pardon, and one five-year sentence; the rest of the sentences ran less than five years.[39]

Many young Colorado law students followed Patterson's cases closely and were grateful for the lawyer's time and expertise, which he gave them freely. They regarded his informal lectures on such topics as "contracts" and "evidence" as instructive and entertaining, and they became his lasting friends and supporters. One such student, George F. Dunklee, recalled the loyalty of those who served Patterson in any capacity. Without exception, Patterson treated the students with patience and kindness, and there were never any "loud words" in his office.[40]

Clearly, Patterson had reached a position of prominence as a criminal lawyer in Colorado during the 1880s. His success resulted from tenacious concentration and almost total immersion in his work. His careful preparation reinforced his skill in exploring and exploiting weaknesses in the opposition, and he mastered the art of swaying juries with emotional summations.

As Patterson's fame spread many wealthy clients sought his services, and as a consequence of his legal fees his own financial situation improved considerably. For example, when the Winfield Scott Stratton properties were sold to an English syndicate for $11 million, Stratton left $500,000 to various nephews and nieces but only $50,000 to his son, Harry. The balance of the estate went to the Stratton Home for poor children and old people.[41] Harry Stratton contested the will, hiring Senator Edward O. Wolcott as his attorney.[42] Prominent in the Republican party, Wolcott served as senator from Colorado from 1888 to 1901. Patterson, a longtime political foe of Wolcott's, led the defense of the Stratton Home.

Instead of his usual rehearsal of facts and arguments, Tom opened with an eloquent picture of the character of Winfield Scott Stratton, justifying the object of the grant and scorning the motives of a son who sought to diminish the "glory" of his father's name. Wolcott responded by suggesting an out-of-court compromise settlement of $150,000, which the Stratton Home accepted. Patterson received a "substantial" fee.[43] By 1890, when Patterson curtailed his law practice in favor of increased involvement in the newspaper business, his law partner, Charles Thomas, estimated that Patterson had abandoned a practice paying him $75,000 a year.[44]

A great part of Patterson's pyramiding affluence came from his practice of accepting property in lieu of cash fees. References to such acquisitions occur in his correspondence. In 1881 he wrote of a trip to Leadville designed to get a mine in working order; he had acquired an interest in it during the previous term in court. He purchased a new engine and pump and made other improvements in an effort to increase the mine's output, though nothing indicates that the venture resulted in a bonanza.

Though his law practice continued to allow him to live "rather extravagantly,"[45] he occasionally complained that his practice became complicated by his business dealings. His investments branched out into real estate in Denver, where, among other activities, he backed a friend in a coal business and spent $20,000 remodeling his recently acquired Grand Central Hotel.[46]

One case in particular revealed Patterson's attitude toward investments. After representing J. F. Burns against Jimmy Doyle in a dispute over possession of the Portland Mine in Cripple Creek, Patterson succeeded in getting an out-of-court settlement that pleased his client. Burns gave Patterson the option of $5,000 cash or 10,000 shares of Portland stock as a fee. Patterson took the cash. At the time of his death in 1916, the stock would have been worth $200,000.[47] But Tom Patterson liked a sure thing. He owned mining property, but he did not "plunge" into investment in uncertain stocks, preferring what he regarded as safe and surer acquisition of Denver real estate.

Tom's Denver holdings steadily increased as he followed his practice of accepting property instead of cash fees. W. W. Cox, having made a small fortune in Midland railroad contracts, built the Albany Hotel in Denver but became insolvent and died broke. Patterson, as his attorney, emerged as owner of the hotel. In another case, Patterson defended Mrs. John A. Witter against charges of murdering her husband, a wealthy liveryman, in Denver. After Mrs. Witter's acquittal, Patterson received the property of the Witter estate.[48]

Intimates quoted Patterson as saying that for every dollar he made from law he made a thousand from real estate.[49] But it was his earnings as a lawyer that gave him the capital needed for success as a real estate investor. Charles Thomas confirmed that Tom was a shrewd judge of real estate values, made no unfortunate land investments, and seldom disposed of such holdings unless unusual profits would result.[50] J. K. Mullen, president of the Colorado Milling and Elevator Company, who arrived in Denver the same year as Patterson, concurred, saying that through the years there had been no better judge of real estate values than Tom Patterson.[51]

At the time of his death, even after he had given checks to his nieces and nephews the year before in lieu of bequests, Tom Patterson possessed an estate valued at $1,611,801.60, of which $1,124,864.70 consisted of real estate and $486,936.90 of personal property. He held stocks and bonds in more than fifty companies.[52] Most significantly, he had become (after the estate of Walter S. Cheesman) the largest owner of downtown property in Denver.[53]

The Tom Patterson of the 1880s continued to display an impressive capacity for action in both his professional and public life. One contemporary, astounded at his boundless energy, marveled that he had not ruined his health.[54] He had experienced great success as a businessman, concentrating on real estate acquisition in downtown Denver. In his law practice, although opponents accused him of tricks and stratagems and complained that he led juries by means of "torrents of eloquence,"[55] he in fact prepared carefully, performed skillfully, and often won.

6
Field Marshal Patterson

> They say Patterson is endeavoring to ruin the state by getting the
> Democratic Party in power.
>
> —Tom Patterson, to Mary Patterson, November 7, 1886

At the same time that Tom Patterson was increasing his fame as a lawyer and
creating an imposing financial power base during the 1880s he was also becoming a dominant force in politics. As early as 1875 the *Denver Tribune* described him as the emerging young leader of the democracy, noting that,
inasmuch as most Colorado Democratic leaders were old men and conditioned to defeat, the door was wide open for ambitious young men.[1] In fact,
his law practice sometimes merged with his political efforts on behalf of the
Democratic party. In late 1879 he traveled to Saguache, in southwestern Colorado, to defend the position of four Democrats who were embroiled in contested elections. His performance on their behalf so demoralized the
Republican contenders that they dismissed all their claims to office, leaving
Patterson's clients as "undisputed masters of the field and offices."[2]

As a former member of the House of Representatives and the only Colorado Democrat to have achieved high national office, Patterson commanded
attention within the organization of Colorado Democrats. The party had consistently suffered defeat, and the majority Republicans so dominated Colorado in the 1880s that they controlled every state legislature. Both parties
tended to avoid major issues, devoting most of their time to resolving patronage or personality disputes within their organizations.[3] A sizable increase in
the state's population encouraged the minority Democrats to believe that their
chances were improving, on the assumption that most of the new residents
were of their party.[4] They also hoped the Republicans might founder over a
serious patronage squabble between their two senators, Henry Moore Teller
and Nathaniel P. Hill.[5]

But the Democrats faced their own internal troubles. One Colorado historian has described Tom Patterson's "bold assumption of party control" as having antagonized many of his associates, but claimed he still was in closer tune with the rank-and-file Democrats than any other party member.[6] An opportunity for Patterson to test his strength as a party leader came in 1880 at a stormy Democratic state convention at Leadville in Lake County.

The circumstances for the showdown on party leadership revolved around a popular Republican governor and the issue of martial law. Frederick W. Pitkin of Ouray, Colorado, had won the governorship in 1878 in spite of allegations that he was a recently arrived carpetbagger.[7] Pitkin quietly endeared himself in Colorado as a gentle, honest, and reliable official, and loomed as the largest single obstacle to be overcome by the Democrats.[8]

In the summer of 1880 a strike broke out in Leadville that was destined to have serious political implications. The trouble followed the usual pattern of mining labor disputes. Grievances were followed by a labor walkout designed to apply economic pressure against the owners. The mines could be reopened only by meaningful negotiation or by breaking the strike. When union leadership failed to prevent damage to property by their more extreme members management called for intervention by state troops, expecting the troops to be used as mine guards to protect strikebreakers.[9] Governor Pitkin, rarely known to act in a rash manner, reluctantly issued a martial law proclamation, and the strike collapsed.[10]

At that point, possibly feeling that by assailing Pitkin he might be able to force the Republicans to turn to a weaker candidate and in desperate need of an issue, Tom Patterson launched an attack on the martial law proclamation as a "dangerous usurpation of authority, and a clear violation of the constitution."[11]

By coincidence, the Democrats had also selected Leadville as the site for their state nominating convention. In this tense environment, Patterson faced a showdown with some Democratic delegates who challenged his wisdom in making martial law a campaign issue.[12] In response to the challenge, he delivered an impassioned speech, reminding the delegates that Democrats had previously been defeated because the party failed to face issues squarely. In Lake County, he argued, there had been no rebellion; to say otherwise would slander the good citizens of Leadville. He appealed for the delegates "not to be cowardly" and to join him in denouncing the declaration of martial law in Lake County.[13] Operating at his courtroom best, Patterson "talked to the jury," made liberal appeals to political prejudice, and used apt quotations of history to sustain his position.[14] A resolution that condemned Governor Pit-kin's use of martial law passed the convention by a vote of 225 to 90.[15]

The martial law issue dominated discussion during the campaign of 1880, and the Democrats hoped for an upset victory. Newspaper coverage clearly indicates that Patterson controlled the Colorado Democratic party. Virtually ignoring the Democratic candidates for office, opposition newspapers centered their attacks on the man they regarded as the formulator of Democratic strategy. Editorials accused Patterson of favoring mob rule and warned his philosophy held that the state had no right to protect property from destruction or to prevent labor unions from interfering with the rights of the laboring man to work where he pleased.[16] As early as July 1, 1880, the *Denver Times* declared that Patterson would seriously blunder if he pursued the anti–martial law issue.

As the campaign progressed, the Republican-oriented *Times* claimed the Democrats had accepted Patterson's campaign issue without enthusiasm and were putting up a feeble fight.[17] Another Republican paper, the *Denver Tribune,* asserted that many Democrats had refused to contribute to "Tom Patterson's glory" in any way. Accusing Patterson of having pushed a "distracting and irrelevant" issue on the Democratic Party, the *Tribune* coined the phrase "Tompattersonism" and wondered if the Democrats of Colorado would allow him to carry them about in his pocket forever. Still, the *Tribune* grudgingly conceded that Patterson was an indefatigable party worker as he stumped the state in September.[18]

Alone of the Denver newspapers, the *Rocky Mountain News,* whose editor, W. H. Loveland, generally defended the principles of the Democratic party, defended Patterson and called him a gallant counsel for the people.[19] But the *Times* declared that Patterson was no real friend of the *News* or Loveland but had duped him for his own political purposes. The most extreme attacks on Patterson accused him of being a nihilist and a communist.[20]

Two days before the election, an incident occurred that spelled certain defeat for the Democrats. Democratic spokesmen and the *Rocky Mountain News,* in line with widespread national resentment against competition from cheap Chinese labor, had attacked the Chinese immigration policy as a threat to the welfare of American laborers. Blaming the problem on Republican legislation, the Democrats claimed that once in office their party would limit or halt Chinese immigration. After an emotional final Democratic rally, a group of Denver citizens rioted, burning what the

News subsequently called dens of opium and prostitution. One Chinese man died.[21]

The Republicans, who had been making the most of the law-and-order issue throughout the campaign, quickly exploited the situation. Republican officials arrested twenty-four men on riot and murder charges. When aroused Democrats suggested breaking the men out of jail, Tom managed to dissuade them. The *Times* blamed the riot on appeals to passion and violence, and sarcastically congratulated Patterson for his role in manufacturing the "murder-our sentiment."[22] The *Tribune* contributed the politically damaging accusation that Democratic party leaders had tried to control the crowd by appealing to them as "Democrats."[23]

The Republicans swept to victory in 1880. Governor Pitkin won comfortably, and the Republicans elected forty-six out of the sixty-two members of the state legislature.[24] The *Tribune* reported that Tom Patterson led his party to the worst defeat it had ever received in the state.[25] The *Times* gloated, "By all means let Mr. Patterson make up the issues for the Democracy two years hence."[26]

The picture of Tom Patterson that emerged from the election of 1880 emphasized a combative spirit capable of resorting to demagogic appeals that frequently seemed to be born of desperation. Stung by the opposition's criticism of the election-eve riot, he developed a strategy and displayed leadership that certainly were subject to question, given the results of the election. Still, no serious challengers to his dominance emerged during the following two years. Perhaps the seemingly hopeless task of guiding a minority party to success discouraged competition.

Under Patterson's guidance, the Democrats did rally to pose a serious threat to the Republicans in 1882. Because political issues had failed to win in the past, Patterson shifted his campaign strategy to emphasize recruiting popular candidates. Opposition newspapers warned that with his shrewd insight into political affairs he had spotted the weak link of Republicanism in the county legislative tickets. Further, said the *Denver Times,* Patterson had recruited exceptionally good Democratic candidates, persuading previously reluctant Democrats to form the foundation of a strong ticket.[27]

The *Times* gave full credit to Patterson for mounting the first genuine threat to Republican domination and began to refer to him as the "Boss" of the Democratic party in Colorado.[28] The Democratic state convention, this time meeting in "perfect harmony," selected Patterson's law partner, Charles

Thomas, as chairman of the state central committee and endorsed the Patterson candidates.[29]

Fortunately for the Democrats, in 1882 the Republicans again became embroiled in a patronage fight, this time between Nathaniel P. Hill and Jerome Chaffee. Bitter factionalism placed the party's dominance in jeopardy. When the dust settled, Patterson's brother-in-law, Ernest L. Campbell, emerged as the Republican candidate for governor. Never backed by the Hill faction with enthusiasm, Campbell was said by his opponents to be a thinly disguised Democrat; that they misunderstood his testy relationship with Tom Patterson and contended that if Campbell were elected the administration would fall under Patterson's control.[30]

Ernest Campbell's decision to become a Republican candidate was undoubtedly influenced by his extremely tense relationship with Patterson. In turn, Tom's loathing for Campbell, whom he believed to be the cause of his marital problems, only increased his determination to defeat the entire Republican ticket, including his brother-in-law.[31]

He ranged across the state on a series of strenuous speaking tours. Climaxing a week of speeches in the Arkansas River Valley and southern Colorado, he scheduled eight speeches in one day at Trinidad.[32] Back from Europe for a visit, Kate complained that her husband was rarely at home before two in the morning and that he frequently was absent in spirit, "being much absorbed by political affairs."[33]

In the heat of the campaign, the *Denver Times* chided Patterson for not rejecting some of the slanders directed against Campbell during the race, and warned that Patterson was harming his own good name by hiring mudslinging pamphleteers. Much of the abuse came from disgruntled factions in Campbell's own Republican party. He was accused of being a romancer and one who never told the truth when there was something else to tell.[34] At the same time, it also suggested that a conspiracy existed to defeat Republican candidates through the pages of the *Denver Republican* and *Denver Tribune*. But on the eve of the election, the newspaper admitted that Patterson had conducted a brilliant campaign to defeat Campbell.[35] As a result of that campaign, the Democrats finally captured the governorship when James Grant defeated Campbell. But they failed to win control of the state legislature, essential if Tom Patterson were to realize his ambition of becoming United States senator from Colorado.[36]

Both friendly and opposition newspapers had taken note of Patterson's emerging ambition for the senate. The *Central City Post,* which described itself as the only Democratic newspaper in key Gilpin County, applauded Patterson's goal and called him Colorado's "most talented citizen."[37] The *Silver Cliff Weekly Herald* observed that Patterson was working "with terrible earnestness" to elect a Democratic legislature and suggested that he might be using party funds earmarked for the election of legislators to advance his own political preferment.[38] Shortly after the election, the *Denver Times* referred to his well-known senatorial ambitions.[39]

When the Republican legislature divided in a lengthy wrangle over the senatorship, the *Denver Republican* noted that Democrats still held the "absurd" notion that the Republican dissension might allow them a chance at the position. The true picture, said the *Republican,* was that "Field Marshal Patterson has received the empty honor of a nomination for the Senate by a Democratic caucus."[40] The *Times* sarcastically discounted the rumor that "Prince Tomasio Patterson" would issue a manifesto, denounce the legislature, set aside the right of Republican candidates, and take the senatorship by right of his "divine inheritance."[41]

The evidence indicates that Patterson became so committed to seeking the senatorship that he was unable to withdraw gracefully as his party's nominee, even when it became apparent that the Democrats could not control the legislature. When the Republicans finally settled on Thomas M. Bowen as their candidate, Patterson lost to Bowen on a straight party vote.[42]

Kate, who had come to accept Tom's terms regarding their private life, never lost interest in her husband's career and predicted his future success. The Republicans "were becoming spoiled" by their long lease of power and no aspirant stood near her husband on the Democratic side.[43] A temporarily discouraged Tom indicated his public concerns were waning because "as one grows older the spirit tames and the ambitions of a worldly character are blunted."[44] Yet in the election two years later, Patterson displayed his usual resiliency and maintained his control of the party.

In June of 1884 the Republican convention was held in Chicago. On the fourth ballot, James Blaine was nominated for the presidency. A month later, the Democrats nominated Grover Cleveland.

At the Colorado Democratic state convention meeting to nominate candidates, Patterson was the chairman and received praise from several speakers as the man who had finally made the party a formidable force in the state.[45] When Governor Grant declined to seek a second term, Patterson recruited the popular Alva Adams of Pueblo. The *Times* sourly observed that the entire slate had again been prepared by "Lord Patterson."

The paper further suggested that Patterson had killed efforts on behalf of a challenger to Adams when Patterson let it be known that if Adams were not selected he would refuse to stump the state.[46] Once again it was evident that the Democratic party depended on Patterson's speaking skills.

With his slate of candidates in the field, Patterson traveled across the state as part of a team consisting of Charles Thomas and Alva Adams. At Silverton, Gunnison, and Castleton, on the western slope of the Rockies, he held audiences "spellbound" with speeches usually lasting two hours.[47] From Crested Butte he wrote that meetings in the San Juan area had never been so well attended. Democratic enthusiasm was at a high pitch. He rode forty miles over the mountains to speak at Aspen and Leadville,[48] arriving east of the mountains in Pueblo "sanguine as to a Democratic triumph." In Colorado Springs, the chairman of the political rally introduced him as "Little Giant of the Rockies."[49]

Patterson's speeches and letters from this period reflect his approval of Grover Cleveland's candidacy, and he predicted Cleveland's election. His fire was directed against "corrupt" Republicans.[50] The *Denver Times* lamented that Patterson regularly concentrated on the difference in purity between the Democrats and Republicans, and Democratic speakers steadily denounced Republicans for introducing scab labor into Colorado.[51]

Tom Patterson's personal stake in the outcome of the election again drew attention from newspapers representing both parties. The Republican *Pueblo Chieftain* happily reminded its readers that a vote for Democratic legislators meant a vote for Tom Patterson for U.S. senator.[52] The Democratic *Georgetown Miner* agreed, and also thought it was a good idea. The *Times* anticipated that Grover Cleveland might have a chance to defeat James G. Blaine but added, "What does it profit Tom Patterson if the Democrats gain the whole nation and he lose the legislature?"[53] Unfortunately for Patterson, while the election races tended to be very close, the Republicans maintained their control over the legislature and recaptured the governorship.[54]

When 1886 rolled around, the *Denver Times* reminded its readers that once again Patterson had arranged the entire program of the Democratic state convention and accused him of being a "syndicate" all by himself. As temporary chairman of the convention, Patterson praised the honesty of President Cleveland and keynoted the issue of Republican corruption. But an ominous note crept into the speech when he indicated that Colorado Democrats disagreed with the president on the issue of bimetallism.

Nevertheless, Democratic optimism seemed to be at a peak and Republican papers expressed some gloom about election prospects. The *Denver Times* sounded the alarm that Patterson was again probing weak spots among Republican legislative candidates. By staying with Alva Adams for a second try for governor, the paper contended, Patterson had strengthened Democratic appeal in southern Colorado.[55]

In the age before the secret ballot, Republican papers seriously considered the possibility of Democratic "vote buying."[56] Such attacks seemed to indicate that Patterson had succeeded in attracting more campaign money than ever before. One paper declared that the Democratic candidate for lieutenant governor had been selected strictly on the basis that a large monetary donation had been acquired from him. Democratic leaders, according to the *Denver Times,* having tasted the spoils of office, were eager for more and were "bleeding everybody."[57] The *Denver Tribune,* purchased by the Nathaniel Hill faction of the Republicans, changed its name to the *Denver Republican,* and attacked the Democratic campaign as a "conspiracy for spoils." If the Patterson people succeeded at the polls, argued the *Republican,* no fair vote would ever be possible in Colorado again.[58]

Sensing that Democratic chances had reached a new high, Patterson ranged across the state, stressing the superiority of the Democratic candidates.[59] The Republican *Grand Junction News* sought to expose Patterson's political techniques and complained that when he spoke about the enormous increase of state expenses under Republicanism, he conveniently omitted mentioning that Colorado citizens had voted to lengthen the legislative session from forty to ninety days and to increase legislative salaries from four to seven dollars a day. Colorado, countered the *News,* was a growing state, and governmental affairs would normally increase in expense proportionately.[60] As election day approached, Tom Patterson reflected a degree of vanity, taking pleasure that, as usual, Republican papers were roundly abusing him by saying he was "endeavoring to ruin the state by getting the Democratic Party into power."[61]

Tom's campaign brought the Democrats closer to total victory than ever before. Democrat Alva Adams was elected governor. Highly popular, Adams was an eloquent speaker and had extensive business connections in southern Colorado. His magnetic personality helped break through Republican strongholds in all parts of the state, with the result that Democrats nearly gained control of the state legislature.[62] In trying to explain the loss of many Republican legislative seats, the *Denver Republican* blamed too many stay-at-home Republicans.[63]

At a victory celebration for Adams in Pueblo, Patterson attributed the Democratic gains to the high caliber of Democratic candidates, which had convinced many good Republicans to lay aside party prejudice and vote for Democrats. Predicting even greater successes in the future, he claimed the party would soon be in a position to exert effective influence against many existing evils. He denounced Rockefeller's Pueblo-based Colorado Coal and Iron Company for its labor practices, called for regulation of railroad abuses, and supported the concept of lowered tariffs.[64]

Thus, the history of Colorado politics in the 1880s reflected a simultaneous rise in the fortunes of Tom Patterson and the Democratic party. From the disaster of 1880, he and the Democrats had steadily cut into the Republican legislative majority and won two governorships. The issue of integrity in public positions dominated the strategy of the minority party, with favorable results. There seemed to be no question that Tom Patterson played a key role in engineering the rise of the Democrats to respectability by carefully orchestrating policy and candidates.

During this period, Tom's private life continued to be filled with frustration and loneliness. After Kate's initial departure for Europe in 1881, she returned with the children only periodically.

"I am very lonesome and feel far less like allowing you to stay this time than I did on your first trip," he wrote to Kate in June of 1883. "But when you come, I want all the children with you and I'll leave it to you to say whether or not it will be for their interests to return this fall or next spring."[65]

The tone of the frequent letters exchanged within the family was now warm and affectionate. Mary (Mamie) and Margaret attended a French convent school, and chafed under the restricted life they were forced to lead. Tom missed them sorely, especially Mamie. But it was James who was his central concern. In school in Halle, James had stolen a keepsake from the man with whom he was boarding. He injured his eye, which was slow to respond to treatment. And in 1883 James was eighteen but weighed only one hundred pounds, a fact that convinced his father that his son needed "careful attention and wise direction."[66] Worried about the boy's weak resolve, Tom and Kate continued to place their hope in Germany's tradition of stern discipline.

In the summer of 1884 a cholera scare broke out in Paris and Tom decided to go to Europe, perhaps to bring the children home. But he returned with only Mary, leaving Margaret and James in France for another year. Whether it was

James McDonald Patterson, nineteen years old, at school in Halle, Germany, in 1884. (Courtesy Archives, University of Colorado at Boulder Libraries, Patterson collection. Bx 8, Fd 3.)

Mary Grafton Patterson, standing, and Margaret Mountjoy Patterson
in 1883 at convent school outside Paris, 1884. (Courtesy Archives,
University of Colorado at Boulder Libraries, Patterson collection,
Bx 8, Fd 3.)

then that Tom and Kate became reconciled can only be speculated upon. But
when Kate finally returned for good in 1885 she and Tom were on friendly
terms and apparently had come to an amicable understanding about their future together. Whatever their differences, they shared delight and dismay
over their children's successes and failures.

Kate's health took a turn for the worse at this time, and she began what
would become her habit of making extended visits to friends in the East.

Mary and Margaret enrolled in Bryn Mawr College for Women and spent the Christmas of 1886 with James, who was attending Johns Hopkins University in Baltimore. A month later, in a chemistry laboratory explosion, James sustained a serious injury to his hand and he was given codeine for the pain. The following spring he became engaged to Josie Coleman, only seventeen, whom Kate considered a social climber and an inappropriate mate for her son. The romance waned. By 1888, despite continuing poor health, James entered the University of Virginia Law School, planning to take two years in one.

Mary graduated from Bryn Mawr College. Margaret (Maud) talked to her father about studying medicine. Tom felt closer than ever to his family and the signs seemed favorable that he could persuade them all to spend the summer in the lodge he had built the previous year in Grand Lake. But, as had become her practice, Kate took the children with her to Atlantic City. Tom's mother, Margaret Patterson, who had lived with her daughter in Boulder, Colorado, since her husband's death, was in poor health, suffering chronic heart problems; she would die by the end of the year. But in early summer Tom still hoped for the best, and he turned his full attention to politics.[67]

In June of 1888 the *Grand Junction News* acknowledged Patterson's continued influence by referring to "Tom Patterson and his crowd." The Western Slope paper also predicted that he would once again receive the nomination of the Democratic legislative caucus following the fall elections.[68] At the Democratic state convention in Denver, Governor Alva Adams ended speculation as to his own plans by placing Patterson's name in nomination for governor. The endorsement caused the convention to rise to its feet with a roar, followed by a fifteen-minute demonstration. Patterson, in accepting the nomination, declared that the Democrats always had an uphill fight against the moneyed interests in Colorado. Although corporations would oppose him, he would "move among the people," seeking their support.[69]

Privately, Patterson called himself a "monumental idiot" for accepting the nomination, though he believed his candidacy was "unavoidable."[70] His comments raise an interesting question. Why had Patterson, who identified himself with the common man and possessed the power to control his party, tended to avoid running for elective office? Perhaps he realized that as party leader he had made decisions that might unite his opponents in a way not possible with such previous Democratic candidates as Governors Grant and

Adams. The Republicans had never let the public forget 1876, when Tom became a member of the United States House of Representatives by "stealing" the position on a "technicality." Mary Campbell, his sister-in-law, was amazed that he accepted the nomination, inasmuch as he had earlier said he would avoid any repetition of the abuse he had suffered during and after his 1878 race for the House.[71]

A contemporary political observer, Fitzjames McCarthy, observed that Patterson's reputation as a great courtroom defender of criminals would work against him in a contest before the people. McCarthy argued that taking advantage of technicalities of the law in defense of a client, a perfectly proper thing to do in an adversary position, nevertheless gave the successful criminal lawyer the reputation of being "tricky." While McCarthy personally believed Patterson's honor to be unimpeachable, he declared that, unfortunately, Patterson's reputation was one of a trickster and a demagogue.[72] Perhaps, as Patterson considered his reputation and recalled the abuse he had received in his last campaign, he believed his best hope for political office lay in avoiding the direct route, by means of selection as U.S. senator by a vote of the state legislature.

By 1888 Colorado Democrats were generally dissatisfied with Cleveland's monetary policies and did not campaign with their usual fervor.[73] The Republicans, no longer fighting among themselves, launched a well-organized blitz under the astute direction of party organizer Wolfe Londoner. A grocer turned politician, Londoner had been elected mayor of Denver and enjoyed popularity among newspapermen because of his well-stocked wine cellar.[74]

The national campaigns stressed the tariff issue, and the subject also dominated the speeches of Patterson and his opponent, Job A. Cooper. Cooper and his supporters emphasized the need for a "business" administration. They conceded that Cooper's oratory failed to match Patterson's "pyrotechnics," but suggested that the Republican candidate might be more effective with his "plain and businesslike" arguments.[75] The Republicans also made extensive use of the speaking talents of popular Representative Hosea Townsend, and all Republican speakers hammered away at the need for tariff protection. In Leadville, Cooper said the issue boiled down to what might happen to Colorado wool, iron, and other mining products.[76]

In October Patterson took his campaign to Colorado Springs, long a Republican stronghold. When it became evident that he would attract an overflow crowd, the city's Democrats shifted the meeting from the court house hall to the opera hall. There, after a concert by the Firemen's Band, the mayor introduced Tom Patterson by referring to his name as a "household word" in Colorado. Though his voice was hoarse from previous campaigning, Tom nevertheless spoke for two and a half hours. He stressed the need for reform in state government offices controlled by Republicans. He accused the Republican state treasurers of having used public funds for private loans, thereby reaping a harvest of $160,000.[77] He deplored the Republican tactic of "waving the bloody shirt" of the Civil War, noting that he, a Democrat, had served in the Union Army. And he read portions of an article by Terence Powderly, national leader of the Knights of Labor, concerning the unhappy condition of some of the working class.

The focus of his speech, however, was the issue of the protective tariff. He ridiculed a Republican-proposed "free list," sarcastically noting that very little protection was needed for such things as bed feathers and acorns, two "typical" items on the list. Contrary to Republican propaganda, Patterson argued, placing an important item like wool on a free list would not destroy the industry. He cited the history of the hide industry, which had been placed on the free list in 1873 when it had been in decline. Nevertheless, Patterson said, he was willing to bet that there was not a pair of foreign boots in the house.[78]

During his campaign, Tom Patterson denied Republican charges that the Democratic party stood for free trade. He insisted that the party did favor tariffs, but only those necessary to meet current needs. He called for articles used by the laboring class to be placed on the free list, or the tariff on them to be reduced to the lowest possible figure. Such a policy, said Patterson, would help to "close the gap" between capital and labor, something that must occur in order for the country to avoid a drift toward revolution.[79] Yet his opponents accused him of a "straddle" on the tariff issue.[80] In October the *Silver Cliff Rustler* dubbed him "Too Much" Patterson during his wildcat tour of the state, and observed that, although he ostensibly was working for the governorship, "he gives away that what he really wants is to go to the Senate."[81] And the *Pueblo Chieftain* argued that though Patterson would like to be governor he would be less than disappointed if he lost—as long as the Democrats won the legislature and rewarded him for his party service with the senatorship.[82]

Although Patterson attracted huge crowds with his oratory, he failed to cut into the solidarity of the Republicans, who swept all offices in a landslide.[83] He took only meager consolation from the fact that he had run well ahead of the rest of the Democratic ticket, wryly observing that he had gone down in the "Democratic wreck."[84]

As a politician, Tom Patterson emerged as a man of tremendous resiliency. His talents as an organizer, fund-raiser, party worker, and orator were considerable. But it was Tom Patterson's seemingly autocratic will that led him to assume responsibility and to enforce obedience. His preeminence in his party during the 1880s seems beyond dispute. He succeeded in maintaining control through tenacity of purpose, charisma, and a capacity for leadership unequalled by any other Colorado Democrat of the time. He led a discouraged and disorganized minority party to respectability and made it a sometimes formidable adversary to a majority party accustomed to success, amply supplied with money, and entrenched in the official patronage of state and national governments. He alertly capitalized on the blunders or disaffections of the Republicans to snatch partial victories. He did not relish losing, but when he did he renewed his efforts with undiminished energy.

7
The Fusionist

Patterson has so burned his bridges he can never return to the Democratic Party.

—*Denver Times,* November 28, 1892

In early 1890 Thomas Patterson bought into Denver's oldest newspaper, the *Rocky Mountain News,* a decision that would influence the rest of his career.

His private life was on a relatively even keel. Both daughters had graduated from Bryn Mawr College, and his son, James, had become a partner of the firm the previous year. Only the family's health—his wife's, his oldest daughter's, his son's—remained a problem. In fact, his son's condition was enough of a worry to induce Tom to send James to Hot Springs, Arkansas, for a "cure" in March of 1890. To his mother James wrote, "My own desire since beginning to realize that I am a confirmed invalid with rheumatism and dyspepsia is to regain my health so that I may at last be of some use to my long suffering father and my patient mother."[1] But the same day James wrote to his sister Maud, telling of his depression and that he saw little improvement. Tom, however, was hopeful as always about his son's erratic health.

In 1892 Patterson bought a house on the corner of East Eleventh Avenue at Pennsylvania Street from Thomas B. Croke, who had built it the previous year but never lived in it. It was an adaptation of the architecture of France's Loire Valley, particularly that of the Chateau d'Azay-le-Rideau, constructed in 1520. The imposing three-story house had a parlor, library, dining room, pantry, and kitchen on the first floor, five bedrooms and two baths on the second. On the third floor were a playroom that would later be used by Patterson's grandchildren, three bedrooms, and a bath for servants. A billiard room was in the basement.[2] A carriage house in the same architectural style was on the west edge of the property. Tom was pleased at Kate's favorable reaction to the house. With family worries behind him, he hurled

himself and the *News* into the battle for free silver, the issue that had dominated Colorado politics for ten years. By 1892 Patterson held controlling
interest in the newspaper. Because he and his partner, John Arkins, generally agreed in their political and economic philosophy, Patterson wrote
most of the editorials.[3]

In Nevada, Utah, and Colorado in the 1870s mine owners had put enough
pressure on Congress to finally result in the passage in 1877 of the Bland-
Allison Act, which provided for government purchase of between two and
four million dollars' worth of silver each month. The act thus furnished a
market for silver, although still falling short of making silver legal tender.
Because of the tremendous flow of the metal from mines in the west and
elsewhere around the world, however, the move failed to halt a steady decline in silver prices.

By 1890, with North and South Dakota, Montana, Wyoming, Washington,
and Idaho joining the ranks of the other western silver states, a compromise
was struck trading support for high tariffs in return for the passage of the
Sherman Silver Purchase Act, which provided for the acquisition of a limited
amount of silver by the government each month. Yet none of the silver purchase acts changed the fact that the United States remained exclusively on the
gold standard and that silver prices continued to fall, a fact that seriously concerned Coloradans, who were keenly aware that the silver industry was one
of the state's largest sources of revenue.

Ironically, a national economic dilemma linked the fortunes of silver producers with those of debt-ridden farmers. The inflation that had occurred during the war, with the adoption of a paper standard not backed by precious
metals, had been an advantage to all debtors, many of them farmers. But
specie payment based on gold was reinstated after the war, and the postwar
appreciation had continued unchecked because of the scarcity of gold relative
to the needs of industry. Efforts to restore greenbacks and revive the inflation
of the war years failed during the 1870s, and the debtors of the country faced
the continuing inequity of an appreciating dollar. So, for different reasons,
farmers and silver men joined forces to call for a free and unlimited coinage
of silver. Rural debtors sought another way to cheapen the dollar, while silver
producers hoped to boost the price of the metal.[4]

Patterson had carefully considered the money issue. Public and private
statements of his position reveal his conviction that the economic problems
of the day could be solved through bimetallism. A respectable theory in use
for years in most countries of the world, bimetallism was based on the

Thomas Patterson home. East Eleventh Avenue at Pennsylvania, Denver. Carriage passengers are Margaret Patterson Campbell and son Tom. (Courtesy Archives, University of Colorado at Boulder Libraries, Patterson collection. Bx 8, Fd 3.)

premise that, by using two metals, when a difference in their established values occurred the one with the lower value became the temporary standard and came into greater demand, thus bringing the values back to something like the ratio originally set.[5]

Early in his political career, while a territorial delegate to the House of Representatives in 1876, Patterson had expressed deep concerns over the exploitation of the West, citing high interest rates on venture capital and the unequal freight rates charged by Eastern money men. He had condemned the "Crime of '73." He hoped that the Democratic party could be won over to the crusade for silver, but if that failed he had vowed to "ride on ahead until the procession caught up" with him.[6]

By 1892, with the Eastern "gold wing" in control of the Democratic party, Patterson reluctantly faced the issue of reconsidering his lifelong association. By blending his correspondence with articles in the *News* and the opposition papers, it is possible to unfold the dramatic story of his struggle over that momentous decision.

Personal tragedy also gripped his life that spring. James's health was worse. He was addicted to codeine, originally administered for pain after the accident to his hand when he was at Johns Hopkins University. He had sunk into a deep depression. By mid-February, Tom and Kate decided to hire a male nurse and to send James to Pasadena with his two sisters in the hope that the warm climate and a change of setting would help. But on February 24 Tom received a letter from James, written in a nearly illegible scrawl. "I wake up trembling all over and have not since that time passed a quiet moment except under the influence of codeine. I am getting over one of the worst spells I've had. . . . Since arriving here have been continually depressed."[7] A few days passed and James began to send Tom telegrams, pleading with him to dismiss Davis, the male nurse, and to let him return home.

His son was straining his patience. On March 7 Tom wrote, "I am angry and disappointed at the telegrams. Though my love is untouched, I continually ask myself has he the qualities in him that will yet make him a man? The answer comes back doubtful but it is tinged with hope. . . . I write as gloomily as I do in the face of assurances from Davis that you have not touched the drug at all."[8] James never received his father's letter, for in the early hours of the following day he killed himself with an overdose of codeine. Tom answered Maud's frantic telegram, instructing her to have the body immediately embalmed and to start with it on the train the next day. He would take the next train out of Denver and meet Maud, Mary, and the coffin somewhere along the route from Pasadena.

With so many hopes and dreams shattered, perhaps believing he had nothing more to lose—or so he thought at the time—Tom decided to throw political caution to the winds and to "go for broke." That very month, in late March, the *News,* normally happy to cheer Democrats and flail Republicans, applauded the "courageous" stand taken by Republican Senator Henry Moore Teller in opposing incumbent President Benjamin Harrison on the issue of free silver.[9] Patterson hoped that the forces favoring unlimited coinage would be able to exert sufficient pressure to obtain some concessions. In his opinion, the West needed to convince the party establishments that it stood united, regardless of party affiliations.

The *News* endorsed the formation of nonpartisan 'silver clubs' in several counties. According to one historian it actually helped organize the clubs, which by July numbered fifty thousand members.[10] At the same time, the paper attacked other Denver newspapers for deserting free silver.[11]

The next month, April of 1892, the *News* supported both Colorado Republican senators, Teller and Edward O. Wolcott, in their "declaration of independence" from their party's antisilver position. In answer to a subscriber's complaint that a Democratic newspaper should never support Republicans, the *News* quoted Gladstone's position that while it was the duty of the minority to find fault with the majority, party aims should be laid aside to unite in the face of a "great threatening public danger."[12] Later in the month Patterson wrote to his wife, Kate, that not only was the support for silver growing steadily, but the controversial issue had also increased the circulation of the *News*.[13]

The *News* heartily endorsed the scheduling of a national silver convention prior to the major-party conventions. The paper hoped the convention might influence the selection of candidates and platforms, although it predicted that heroic action would be necessary to defeat gold-party plans "for enslaving the masses."[14] At the state convention, amid cheers, Tom Patterson accepted designation as a delegate to the national silver convention, asserting that if the major parties disappointed Colorado with their silver platforms the men of Colorado must meet to decide what to do. Denver's very existence, he said, depended on the cause of free silver.[15]

When the Republican Arapahoe County convention endorsed Harrison, the *News* blasted the gathering for "undermining" Senators Teller and Wolcott, who were of the same party. When the Republican state convention also endorsed Harrison, the *News* took comfort in reporting that more than six hundred Republicans at the meeting had refused to commend any act of the Harrison administration and had hissed Nathaniel P. Hill, editor of the *Denver Republican,* when he hewed to the "goldbug" line.[16]

An early indication of Patterson's belief that party lines might be obliterated by the silver issue appeared in a long letter to his wife in early May. He admitted some fear that he had helped to unleash "a beast" that might prove uncontrollable. Democrats and Republicans by the thousands declared they would no longer vote with the old parties if candidates were nominated who displeased them. What would happen if both Grover Cleveland and Benjamin Harrison were nominated? What would Teller and Wolcott do? Most important, what would the *Rocky Mountain News* do?[17] Tom, at least privately, still harbored doubt about his own willingness to sever his connections with the Democratic party.

Yet the *News* did endorse a state silver platform denouncing the silver act of 1873, defended the concept of free silver, and claimed that the interests of wheat and cotton growers were the same as those of the miners.[18] At the national silver convention, however, Patterson discovered a general state of depression among other delegates, who freely predicted that they would be buried trying to stop either Harrison or Cleveland.[19] These fears were partially realized when in June the Republican national convention in Minneapolis renominated Harrison and adopted a weak and confusing plank it hoped would allow silver men in most places to support the party.

The Democratic national convention in Chicago remained the only hope for the silverites. Even so, on June 17, 1892, the *News* editorially expressed a fear that to obtain votes in support of tariff protection some delegates would sacrifice the proposed silver plank.[20]

Accompanied by his daughter Margaret (Maud), Patterson headed the Colorado delegation to the convention, where he automatically gained a place on the Democratic national platform committee. His first contribution to the silver cause occurred when the silver caucus nearly disintegrated over the selection of a presidential candidate. The *News,* with Arkins at home interpreting the activities of his colleague, described Patterson as one of the "cooler heads" who had preserved unity.[21] Even the opposition *Denver Republican* expressed admiration for Patterson's skill at harmonizing the caucus and gave a detailed account of his "dulcet eloquence and quick intelligence."[22]

Deliberately avoiding the problem of agreement on a presidential candidate, Patterson diverted the antagonism of Colorado's forty-two delegates by leading an earnest discussion of the silver plank. After indicating his own change of heart about a silver candidate, Patterson led the group to a unanimous endorsement of Senator Albert P. Gorman of Maryland.[23] Moreover, he designed the phraseology of the silver plank and helped steer it through a hostile platform committee.[24]

Patterson personally presented the silver plan to an openly antagonistic convention. Displaying great patience and determination, the Coloradan endured almost continuous interruptions from the floor and galleries. He tried to impress upon the delegates the dangers involved if they rejected the silver position. He warned that while he might have only a few supporters in the convention, millions in the country stood with him.[25] Yet when the final votes were cast, the convention had rejected the plank and nominated Cleveland as the candidate for president.

In spite of the abuse heaped upon him during his speech and the complete repudiation of his position by the convention, Tom could not yet bring himself to bolt his party. His newspaper partner, John Arkins, was not so encumbered.

Patterson wired Arkins that he wanted the *News* to take a "wait and see" attitude. Arkins answered that a paper never got anywhere waiting for whatever was going to happen next. Patterson countered by demanding that nothing be done until he returned to Denver. Arkins replied that now was the time to act, and that the paper should announce for the leading Populist contender, James Weaver of Iowa, the next morning. The exchange concluded with Patterson still protesting and pleading for time.[26]

By the time Patterson arrived back in Denver, however, the *News* had come out strongly against Cleveland and for Weaver in the forthcoming Populist convention. Tom's decision had been made for him. And to his surprise, he discovered that, thanks to Arkins's initiative, his own popularity in Denver and Colorado was at an all-time high. Subscriptions to the *News* increased sharply and congratulations poured in for his Chicago performance and for the stand he actually had been reluctant to make.[27]

Among opposition newspapers, the normally Republican *Aspen Sun* congratulated Patterson for his "able and gallant" fight for free silver and for the "bold and courageous" stand he had taken after his defeat at Chicago. The *Denver Republican,* however, accused Patterson of "grandstanding" in Chicago, and advised him to stick by the "crazy" program mapped out by his "wicked partner." The paper confidently predicted that the *News* would try to "creep back under the Cleveland tent at the earliest possible moment."[28]

Writing to Kate, Tom admitted that initially he had been "disgusted" with the problems Arkins had created but had changed his mind. Repudiation of Cleveland by the *News,* he admitted, was right and had had to come. His goal would be to carry Colorado against both Harrison and Cleveland and thus obtain a clear verdict for silver.[29] When the Populist national convention in Omaha adopted a straight silver plank, the *News* endorsed Weaver as the only candidate standing for the "constitutional rights of silver."[30]

Yet in what proved to be another far-reaching decision, Patterson refused to sever all connections with the Colorado Democratic party and made plans to preserve his own leadership in the party by steering it in a new direction. He called for the "fusion" of silver men of all parties, arguing that silver advocates could and should control the state government. He urged voters to support the Populist presidential electors and to elect silver sympathizers to state offices, irrespective of party.

To those who accused him of being a traitor to the Democratic party, Patterson replied that he believed in reversing an unsound course. He accused critics of holding to a mistaken belief that endorsement of free silver could ever be secured in the national Democratic party as long as it was still dominated by Cleveland and the "moneyed forces."[31]

Clearly, Patterson hoped to be able to maintain the Democratic state organization while rebuking the national party position, and he followed that difficult path with great determination. The first political reaction came from Democrats who refused to continue to recognize the *News* as the semiofficial party newspaper. On July 3, 1892, a mass meeting of loyalist Denver Democrats publicly denounced Patterson,[32] and El Paso County Democrats talked of boycotting the *Rocky Mountain News*.[33] Populist leaders, intent on sweeping control of state positions and also on electing Weaver, reacted negatively to Patterson's fusion suggestion.[34] In this atmosphere, Tom Patterson faced the enormous problem of convincing the various factions of the wisdom of his position.

The first crisis occurred on July 28, 1892, when the Colorado Silver League and the state Populist convention met simultaneously. Both conventions appointed committees to confer on a joint slate of candidates. At this point, Patterson's "friends" made an unsuccessful effort to obtain adjournments in order to prevent the naming of a state ticket by the two groups before they could be combined with fusionist-minded Democrats. Tom personally argued his case in a dramatic appeal to the delegates of the conventions but lost. Silverites and Populists combined to nominate a full state ticket, headed by Davis H. Waite for governor.[35]

Patterson stubbornly refused to abandon his fusionist plan. On August 8, 1892, the *News* began daily masthead publication of the silver ticket of Weaver, his running mate, James G. Field of Virginia, and the names of the Populist presidential electors. Faced with such a commitment by the paper that had always been the unofficial organ of the Democrats, nonfusionist Democrats collected $50,000 and launched the *Denver Post*.[36] The *Post* proclaimed that silver must not override other problems, endorsed party loyalty, and attacked Patterson.[37]

In the stormiest political convention in Colorado history, fusionists and loyalists collided at Pueblo in a battle for control of the Colorado Democratic party. The Weaver-Patterson supporters arrived with control of a majority of the delegates, sporting purple badges. The Cleveland regulars displayed their "white wing" badges of purity.

Fighting repeatedly threatened to break out on the convention floor, and the threat of police eviction was made against the outraged Cleveland delegates. Repeated efforts by the regulars to get on the floor were ignored by the chairman, Thomas Jefferson O'Donnell, a Patterson man.[38] Speakers on both sides were hooted and jeered. A minority report was heard only through Patterson's personal intervention. At length, while the majority report was being adopted, Cleveland delegates roared in anger as Cleveland's portrait was torn down and removed from the hall. The regulars finally stalked out of the meeting, reassembled nearby, and nominated their own straight party ticket.[39]

When the furor died after one of the most remarkable political gatherings ever held in Colorado, the result was a Democratic convention that had adjourned as an auxiliary to the Populist national ticket. Patterson continued to urge the public to support state candidates of the Silver Democrats, but to reject Grover Cleveland in favor of James Weaver.[40]

The Republicans viewed the Democratic split with undisguised pleasure and predicted the failure of fusion efforts. Meeting in Pueblo on September 8, 1892, Republican party regulars defeated a silver challenge within their own ranks and confidently predicted victory for Harrison.[41]

At this point, Patterson's allegiance to the free silver movement clearly involved both an intellectual and a practical commitment. He had defended the sectional interests of his mining state throughout his public career, and had found those interests compatible with his avowed interest in improving the conditions of the common people. His driving personal ambition to lead and to receive recognition, however, remained. To what degree did he really believe he could reroute the direction of the Democratic party and still maintain his control of it? To what degree did he believe he could insert himself as a leader of the Populists? The answer appears to be that Tom Patterson, historically so successful within the Democratic party, had almost unbounded confidence in his capacity to sway colleagues by the strength of his reasoned arguments and skillful oratory. He also believed he was right. He might be in error, but he was never in doubt. Convinced that the only way to defeat the Republicans in Colorado was through a coalition of silver factions, he dedicated himself to that goal.

As a result, Patterson's principles and convictions merged with his personal ambition. His bid for leadership in the Populist party, however, collided with that of Davis Hanson Waite, the Populist candidate for governor. Waite was a man whose energy and iron will were as strong as Tom Patterson's. He, too, claimed to speak for the common people.

Certainly Patterson had little reason to reject Waite's candidacy for governor on grounds of philosophical differences.[42] Both championed the cause of labor unions and supported the concept of compulsory arbitration. Both believed that gambling and saloons constituted a major cause of political corruption at the local level. Above all, both men believed that corporate power exploited the people, both argued for government regulation of those who abused power, and both looked with favor on government ownership of the transportation and communication industries.[43]

The central question for both men apparently was the problem of monopoly versus the people. Each assumed a position compatible with the two fundamental propositions of Populist philosophy, as identified by historian John D. Hicks: Government must restrain the selfish tendencies of those who profit at the expense of the less fortunate, and the people, not the plutocrats, must control the government.[44]

The two political leaders disagreed, however, on the solution to the money question. Waite essentially favored fiat money (greenbacks), although he was willing to use silver as an issue to educate the people to the virtues of inflationary paper money. Conversely, Patterson believed that free coinage of silver could solve the debtor's problem without resorting to what he regarded as the questionable use of fiat paper currency.[45] Waite also emphasized the need for the total list of Populist reforms in 1892, including such issues as the direct election of senators and the levy of an income tax. Patterson believed that only the silver issue could bring victory in Colorado.[46] To Patterson, the ultimate objective lay in breaking the control of Republicanism, which he identified as the most dangerous vehicle of the moneyed powers.

The antipathy between the men was undoubtedly exacerbated by Patterson's jealousy over Waite's rapid rise to popularity. Given his pride and vanity, Tom probably regarded Waite as a usurper of his own standing among the disgruntled labor and farm elements in Colorado. With his lengthy training in Colorado politics Patterson belittled Waite's credentials and temperament, although Waite had served terms in the state legislatures of both Wisconsin and Kansas. Tom Patterson also may have been smarting from his own unsuccessful bid for the governorship in 1888, and, given his antipathy for "carpetbaggers," he undoubtedly was aware of Waite's relatively recent arrival in Colorado.

In the pages of the *Rocky Mountain News* Tom Patterson characterized Waite as opinionated and conceited, lacking in caliber and judgment, breadth of mind, tolerance of spirit, and the depth of character required to be governor of Colorado.[47] Curiously, he said nothing about Waite's reputation as an anti-Catholic.[48] When Tom Patterson failed to persuade the Populists to choose a candidate other than Waite to head the state ticket, he faced a dilemma. Should he refuse to support Waite or should he accept him on the grounds that a state fusion victory and the resulting Republican defeat were more important than the choice of governor?

The *News* followed an interesting course throughout most of the campaign. While praising the national ticket headed by Weaver and commenting favorably on state silver candidates of all parties, it virtually ignored Waite's candidacy. Such lack of support for the Populist leader understandably antagonized Waite's advisors, who subsequently resisted Patterson's efforts to cement fusion by mixing Silver Democrats into the Populist slate of candidates.

Waite's own *Aspen Union Era* declared flatly that the Populists would not fuse in Colorado or anywhere.[49] Some Populists even accused Patterson of trying to trade Davis Waite for Democratic control of the state legislature.[50] Several times, Patterson and his followers conferred with the Populists in order to prevent them from completely repudiating the shaky alliance.

Though the demands of the Silver Democrats steadily diminished as the campaign progressed,[51] the Republican-oriented *Denver Times* reported great dissatisfaction among Populist leaders over the "high-handed" manner in which Patterson was trying to "run" the Populist campaign. Of particular irritation to the Populist leaders was the fact that some of their own candidates, friendly to Patterson, informed the *News* of their campaign plans before informing Populist committeemen. One committeeman raged that he would rather be a hopeless minority than a cat's paw at the hands of Tom Patterson.[52]

Waite's position and that of his advisors seemed clear. They sincerely believed that the purity and vigor of the new party would be undermined by any concessions to the Silver Democrats. Waite feared that the Populists would be devitalized amid the intrigues of the older party, and he wanted the silver issue to be subordinated to what he regarded as the more fundamental reforms of the Populist program.[53] It also is possible that he thought the Populists could win without the support of the Silver Democrats.

Toward the end of the campaign, Waite's strong performance caused the *News* to change its position. Claiming that the character and qualifications of the Populist leader had been misunderstood at the beginning of the race, the

Davis H. Waite, Populist Governor of Colorado, 1893–1895.
(Courtesy Colorado Historical Society.)

paper finally endorsed Waite as a friend of silver who did grasp the danger of class legislation perpetuated by the wealthy.[54] The only plausible interpretation of Patterson's reversal is that, once he saw Waite would probably win, his practical and opportunistic side came into play.

Meanwhile, regular Democrats challenged the right of Patterson's Silver Democratic electors, committed to Weaver, to appear on the ballot. The Republican secretary of state, E. J. Eaton, upheld the challenge and refused to certify the Silver Democratic ticket. Complex and time-consuming litigation followed, occupying both wings of the Democrats, until the issue made its way to the Colorado Supreme Court, which finally ruled that both slates had to be certified.

In late October, the Democratic national committee tried to mediate the struggle dividing the Democrats. Fearing the loss of Colorado's electoral votes to Harrison and writing off Cleveland's chances, the committee persuaded a majority of the regular Democrats to withdraw their electors and substitute Weaver electors. In effect, the national committee, though making no known contact with Patterson, actually vindicated his original strategy.

Patterson's former law partner, Charles Thomas, was among those Democrats who had never strayed from working to take the state from the Republicans in order to help Cleveland. Unlike Patterson, Thomas wanted no fusion with Populists at the state level. Ultimately, the Republicans faced a coalition of Populists, Silver Republican defectors, Silver Democrats, and regular Democrats who voted for Weaver simply to help Cleveland.[55]

Thus Tom Patterson found himself in a strange and frustrating position. Through personal influence and political skill he had hoped to turn the bulk of the Colorado Democratic party to support the Populist presidential candidate, a commitment that caused Democratic regulars to view him as a traitor and the Populists generally to exclude him from any party deliberations. Yet Patterson grimly adhered to the goal of breaking the majority Republican grip on state politics. The support of free silver was the only way to bring that about. Day after day the *News* pounded away on the silver theme, supplementing the attack with charges of Republican corruption at the state and local levels. *News* editorials increasingly sympathized with the "peaceful" revolution of the Populists, ultimately describing the campaign as an armageddon against privilege and greed.[56]

Caught up in a highly emotional campaign, pro-Harrison and pro-Weaver newspapers engaged in inflammatory journalism. Reputations were assassinated; both Republican senators, even though they had worked for silver, were denounced as enemies of the people. Populists were urged to refuse to listen to opposition speakers and to regard Republican meetings as treasonable. Spurred by such appeals to prejudice, mobs, especially in the mining towns, took possession of halls engaged for Republican meetings and howled speakers from the platform.[57]

As usual, Patterson delighted in being assailed by opposition newspapers, and accepted numerous invitations to speak in communities across Colorado. In two trips to Loveland, Patterson "converted some Republicans."[58] He also took time for a trip to Helena, Montana, to convince Democratic and Republican party leaders that not all silver men were "political anarchists."[59]

As election day drew near, the *News* predicted a Populist victory and a remarkable revolution in political sentiment. Even the great body of the business community, according to the paper, was in accord with the fight for "our central industry." In the week preceding the election, the *News* used the political "bandwagon" technique by asserting that the Republican state central committee had informed every county organization that the fight for Harrison was hopeless. Patterson even hoped that Weaver might hold the balance of power in the electoral college if the Harrison-Cleveland race proved close.[60]

Patterson accurately predicted a major triumph for Populism in Colorado. Weaver electors ran fourteen thousand votes ahead of Harrison, and Colorado sent two Populists, Lafe Pence and John C. Bell, to the U.S. House of Representatives. Waite won the governorship by a margin of six thousand votes and Populists captured many of the state offices. The new Colorado Senate contained a combination of twenty Populists and Democrats to fifteen Republicans, and the normally large Republican majority in the House was cut to a single vote.[61] Writing about the election in later years, Patterson's law partner, Charles Thomas, recalled the jubilation of finally defeating the Republican ticket "in toto" for the first time.[62]

While Colorado historians generally agree that Tom Patterson and the *Rocky Mountain News* played major roles in the Populist success,[63] one article contends that the impact of the *News* had been exaggerated because it was concentrated in the Denver area where the coalition of the fusionists received only 6 percent more votes than the Democrats alone had received in 1890.[64] Of more importance is the question of how many Democrats were converted to the Populists or found reinforcement of their decision in

Patterson's example. The official totals indicate a marked defection among the regular Democrats.[65]

Opposition newspapers did credit Patterson and the *News* with having had a significant impact, the *Denver Times* declaring that he had delivered 90 percent of the Democratic party to support Populism. Yet given Patterson's established popularity as a speaker, it becomes difficult to separate his influence as orator and party leader from his influence as editor. Moreover, the opinions of the *News,* especially considering Patterson's statewide reputation, were hardly limited to Denver. Colorado newspapers of the time made a practice of using articles and editorials from the pages of the Denver press.[66]

There can be little doubt that without the support of a sizable number of Silver Democrats, the Populists would have failed. Subsequent developments verified that the greater part of the Populist vote had come from disaffected elements of both major parties who did not accept the total Populist program, a fact that Patterson recognized by concentrating on the silver issue. There is also the intriguing fact that Weaver, supported enthusiastically by the *News,* ran some eight thousand votes ahead of Waite, whom the *News* ignored for most of the campaign.

Tom and his family certainly believed that the *News* had played a major role in the victory. From Boston, his wife and daughters reported that papers there were filled with the wonderful "victory of the people" in Colorado, and they speculated as to what the results might mean for Patterson's political future. Mary suggested that her father must feel encouraged to seek new worlds to conquer now that he was a real power in the land.[67]

Patterson conceded that he now enjoyed greater national prominence than ever, and he reported that the election was universally referred to as "my victory."[68] The *Denver Times* even speculated that he might be the Populist presidential candidate in 1896.[69]

When the *St. Louis Republic* and the *New York Sun* suggested his name as a possible member of Cleveland's cabinet, Patterson concluded that Easterners apparently thought that what he had done was for Cleveland, preventing the Colorado electoral votes from going to Harrison. Obviously they did not understand the nature of his fight, he wrote, and he pledged to remain consistent on the money issues, though still treating Cleveland "fairly but fearlessly."[70]

In the months after the election, Patterson reaffirmed his support of Populism as the only party favoring free coinage of silver, and attacked those

Democrats who "sold their souls" for patronage benefits from the Democratic administration. He suggested the old parties had outlived their usefulness and urged young men entering political careers to join the Populists.[71] Not surprisingly, the Democratic party's social organization in Denver, the Greystone Club, dropped him from its board of directors. Patterson, asserted the *Denver Times,* had so thoroughly burned his bridges that he could never return to the Democratic party.[72]

8
Bloody Bridles

There are not enough Populists left in the state to flag a handcar.

—*Denver Times,* May 9, 11, 1900

Though the *News* was tardy in its support of Populist gubernatorial candidate Davis Waite during the campaign of 1892, after his election the paper commended him as "fearlessly incorruptible and uncompromising."[1] Patterson's newspaper associate Ed Keating claimed that only the *News* among the major Denver newspapers had refrained from ridiculing him in the early months of his administration. Yet a review of the *Denver Republican* and the *Denver Times* during the period reveals only moderate criticism of Waite prior to the summer of 1893. Even those who had feared Waite's "anarchistic" tendencies found them less prominent than anticipated.

But during the spring, when the Populists rebuffed Patterson's suggestion for a fusion campaign at the local level, Waite's uncompromising nature seemed less appealing to him. As he had feared, the subsequent Denver city elections in May resulted in a Republican sweep of the public offices, with the Populist candidate for mayor running a distant third behind both Republican and Democratic candidates.[2] Clearly, the Populists could not stand alone, and Patterson privately criticized the inflexibility of the governor.[3]

That June, India closed its mints to coinage of silver, precipitating a new crisis for the silver-producing states.[4] The next week the price of silver fell from 83 cents an ounce to 62 cents an ounce. Many Denverites withdrew their savings from banks, and on July 18 six banks shut their doors.[5] Thousands of miners who had been laid off drifted into Denver. A tent and shack city sprang up at Riverfront Park along the South Platte River.[6] Within two months, forty-five thousand men lost their jobs in Colorado alone.[7] Waite, in a speech to a special state silver convention, climaxed a wrathful attack against Eastern creditors by saying that it was infinitely better "that blood should flow to the horses' bridles, rather than our national liberties should be destroyed."[8] Though Waite gained the nickname of "Bloody Bridles" from the speech, his biographer has pointed out that little consideration was given to such moderate statements in the speech as the governor's observation that "our weapons are argument and the ballot."[9]

Before the summer of 1893 had ended, the repeal of the Sherman Silver Act further enraged Colorado silver men. In December Waite suggested that Colorado coin its own money supply. Under his proposal Colorado would ship its silver to Mexico, where it could be coined and returned to Colorado.[10] Quite likely the governor did not really expect passage of the measure by the Colorado legislature, but he made the proposal to dramatize the seriousness of the problem and condition the public to the use of fiat money in the future.[11]

The *News* joined a general outcry against Waite's suggestion, calling the scheme dishonest and unconstitutional and saying it would lead Colorado into using ten cents' worth of silver in coin supposedly worth a dollar.[12] Patterson said that Waite's proposal implied that Colorado had the power to declare the English shilling and the French franc legal tender.[13] Other opponents ridiculed the proposed money as "Fandango Dollars."[14] Patterson obviously feared the proposal was a threat to the welfare of the silver industry. In the first major public break with Waite, he rejected unlimited expansion of the money supply through the use of greenbacks.[15]

The *News* went on to express disappointment with Waite in other areas. In January 1894 the paper's editorials expressed fear that the governor's appointments represented an effort to turn the police into a wing of a partisan political machine. When Waite requested a special session of the legislature to consider several reform proposals, one of them a million-dollar appropriation for the construction of a state canal to give work to unemployed labor, the *News* complained that the governor had defied public opinion and public interests.[16] Though he agreed to the need for reforms and internal improvements, Patterson declared Waite's timing to be unfortunate and inappropriate because no money was available and the special session would cost the taxpayers $30,000.

Furthermore, said the *News,* a special session would be a waste of public money, because it was impossible to get any legislation through the hopelessly divided Colorado Senate. On January 3, 1894, the *News* carried a front-page political cartoon showing Waite whipping a horse (labeled the legislature) toward a "reform" creek, with the caption saying that one could drive a horse to water but could not make him drink.

Stung by Patterson's criticism, Waite announced that in the absence of an effective Populist voice he would start his own Denver newspaper. Patterson treated the idea with sarcasm and attacked the governor for pursuing his "pet" notions while at the same time adopting a dictatorial attitude toward the legislature and mismanaging the state in general.[17]

Fearing the flow of events might leave the public somewhat confused as to the position of the *News* in regard to Populism and reform, Tom Patterson declared it was a true Populist paper, representing the masses, and free from the corrupting influence of the moneyed powers. The *News* consistently supported efforts for social and economic reform, but Patterson insisted that he would reject reckless and impractical Populist leaders who, by their irresponsibility, endangered the ultimate success of the party.[18]

Of all the reform measures adopted by Colorado during the Waite administration, one of the most significant—women's suffrage—did receive support in the pages of the *News,* although the paper stopped short of a full editorial commitment. Patterson battled his partner, Arkins, on this issue. According to Ellis Meredith, the daughter of the managing editor and a contributing journalist, Tom wanted to "bring the paper out for suffrage" but Arkins was "adamant against it."[19] She noted that, as on many issues, she "never thought that Patterson got the credit that was coming to him."[20]

Tom Patterson's position on this issue was consistent with his view on equality of opportunity, and his views probably reflected the influence of the Patterson women. According to Meredith, his wife and daughters were "ardent and effective suffragists."[21]

As early as 1877 Kate Patterson had spoken publicly for women's suffrage, and she served as the corresponding secretary for the Women's Suffrage Association's annual convention in February of that year. In 1890 she headed a substantial subscription list at a public meeting to generate support for the women's vote. She and her daughters had taken an active part in the formation of the Colorado Equal Suffrage Association, as had Ellis Meredith. Mary and Margaret helped organize a Young Women's League auxiliary.[22] Tom opened the door for Meredith to write articles from "a woman's point of view," and she credited Arkins with tolerance in allowing her to go on writing suffrage articles "over my own name."[23]

In January 1894 Patterson privately expressed his conviction that Waite could not possibly be re-elected,[24] and he embarked on a determined effort to prevent Waite's renomination for governor. Claiming to speak more in sorrow than in anger, the *News* asserted that if the Populists wanted to save the ship, they must pitch Waite overboard.[25]

In the spring and summer Governor Waite took action that further discredited him with some voters and reinforced his image as one who acted rashly. On two occasions he called out the state militia, in what the *News* castigated him for as heavy-handed actions that left the public uneasy and wasted the taxpayers' money.[26] The first of these, the "city hall war," began when, discovering that his own appointees to the police and fire commission were subject to underworld influence and had failed to clean up gambling, red-light districts, and law-violating saloons, he attempted to remove them from office.[27] The commissioners, having been confirmed by the Colorado Senate, claimed they could be removed only by impeachment. Refusing to vacate their offices, they asked that the issue be settled by a decision of the state's supreme court.

Faced by such defiance, Waite summoned the state militia, armed with artillery, and ordered it to surround city hall. The commissioners added four hundred loyal Denver police, special deputies, and assorted underworld friends to their excellent defensive position. Thousands of Denver citizens gathered at the scene, waiting for the action to start. Finally, after cooler heads assured the governor that a decision would be reached quickly, Waite agreed to let the court settle the matter.[28] The state supreme court ruled against the commissioners, who reluctantly abandoned their positions.

A reading of the *News* from the time of the controversy gives the distinct impression that the paper was struggling to find fault with Waite. At first defending his right to oust the commissioners, it went on to deplore his extreme action in proclaiming martial law. Underworld elements did influence the police and fire board, said the *News,* but the governor's reckless response had brought an unhappy notoriety to Colorado. Ultimately, the paper agreed the court decision had been correct and must be accepted, but claimed that Waite had exceeded his powers by calling out the state militia.[29] Though such an interpretation has been questioned on the grounds that the commissioners were clearly guilty of insurrection against the executive branch of government,[30] the "city hall war" did make Waite the butt of many a Denver joke.[31]

When Waite later summoned the state militia during a strike in 1894 at the gold camp in Cripple Creek, Patterson again found himself in an awkward position. The miners' demand for an eight-hour day had been refused. When

Governor Waite attempted to effect a peaceful settlement, Patterson, also in sympathy with the workers, nevertheless found it difficult to give the governor any credit for his efforts to work out a solution. Virtually ignoring Waite's role in the eventual settlement, the *News* took Waite to task for being too eager to call out troops.

As the fall campaign approached, the *News* repeatedly accused Waite of exceeding his power as chief executive and, through his poor judgment, of agitating routine matters into difficult situations. Patterson's editorials characterized the administration as constantly involved in some childish squabble, thus dividing and destroying the hopes of the Populists.[32] While praising the Populists as a great and noble party, he argued that the renomination of Waite would spell certain defeat.

On the eve of the Populist state convention in Pueblo, Patterson was still pressing the party delegates to reject the governor. In a futile effort to provide a substitute candidate, the *News* cultivated support for Lafe Pence, a Populist congressional representative from the first district and a personal friend of Patterson's.[33] But with Waite supporters in firm control of the convention, Patterson underwent the type of abuse he had suffered two years earlier at Chicago, this time being hooted even by those he had helped to elect in 1892. Ignored by the convention chairman, he strode up to the stage and stood with arms folded while a debate raged as to whether he should be heard. When he refused an order to leave the platform, the noise became deafening.

After a plea from the Las Animas delegation for civil treatment of the editor, Patterson received five minutes to speak. Noting that five minutes failed to allow him to make his point, he recalled that even in Chicago the minority had been given the right to be heard. In a brief statement he defied the hostile crowd, saying, "Now, as ever, I will stand defending the right of a minority against the tyranny of the majority."[34]

When the Populists renominated Waite, Patterson announced that the *News* would be an independent paper. It would support all Populist candidates except Waite. Democrat Charles Thomas was a far better choice for governor, wrote Patterson. Again, he admonished the Democrats and Populists to unite, and launched another strenuous speaking tour for Populist candidates all over the state.[35] As the campaign progressed Patterson said as little as possible about Waite, but when pressed on the subject, in Cripple Creek, he said simply that Waite was not corrupt. During a November debate in Montrose an opponent quoted from the *News* his negative comments concerning Waite, and Patterson replied that he had nothing to recant, that he had been guided by the course of the logic of events.[36]

Meanwhile, the *News* continued to criticize the two major parties and cheer any weakening of old party ties. It attacked the Republican argument that increased tariff protection would solve industrial distress. But it was the Cleveland administration that received the brunt of the paper's assault. Patterson accused the president of treachery to silver, of condoning business conspiracies, and of following an inadequate tariff reform policy. The administration, he said, had sunk to a depth of popular contempt unequaled in American history.[37] Still, Tom held no illusions about the chances of liberating the Democratic party from the control of the "goldbugs," and he remained committed to the Populists as the only party that offered a solution to the money problem.

As Tom Patterson had predicted, the Republicans elected nearly their entire state ticket by comfortable pluralities, they regained complete control of the state legislature, and Waite lost by nearly eighteen thousand votes to Republican A. W. McIntire.[38] Tom's prophecies materialized in part because Waite had been discredited in the minds of many Coloradans, causing some observers to note that the attacks on the governor by the *News* had weakened Populist solidarity.[39]

In reporting the defeat, the *News* defiantly called for fusionists to get together for 1896. To survive as a party in Colorado, it said the Democrats must abandon the moneyed powers and favor the people. Nationally, Populist prospects had improved, said the paper. The party had doubled the number of its votes in 1892 to two million, with a predicted eight million votes by 1896.[40]

The many possible motives for Patterson's actions make an evaluation of his relationship with Waite difficult. He would have been less than human not to resent Waite's rise as a leader of the common people, but he also seems sincerely to have feared that the governor lacked the temperament and capability to establish the Populist party as a permanent force in Colorado politics. Waite and others regarded themselves as the only true Populists dedicated to the complete list of reforms, although Patterson—the practical politician—believed that by concentrating on the single issue of silver the party would gain broad enough appeal to topple the traditional Republican control of Colorado. Thus, he became the leading example of the internal split developing in the Populist party between the fusionists and the Populists who sided with Waite. Believing most voters were not prepared to accept broad radical change, the fusionists looked upon free silver as a lever with which to raise the possibility of other reforms.

With Waite discredited at the polls and with Patterson impressing Populists around the state with his unstinting efforts in their behalf, the *News* steadily established itself as the unofficial voice of the party. Patterson's political fortunes seemed to be on the rise, but during 1894 another factor appeared that would seriously affect his future commitments.

On March 13 William Jennings Bryan visited Denver to speak at the Democratic Greystone Club. Elected to Congress from Nebraska in 1890, he was already well known for his staunch and articulate support of free silver. The *News* wrote of his Denver appearance in enthusiastic words, describing Bryan as probably the most able champion of bimetallism. Calling Bryan's visit an education and an inspiration, the paper carefully labeled the Nebraskan as a Populist-Democrat.[41]

In his private life at this time, Tom Patterson had little cause for rejoicing. Mary, the oldest and his favorite among his children, had died after years of ill health at the age of twenty seven on November 26, 1894. Devastated, Tom and Kate went into seclusion, leaving Margaret to run the household and receive callers. If there was a bright side to those dark days in the Patterson house on 11th and Pennsylvania Streets, it was the appearance of a distant cousin from an influential Wheeling, West Virginia, family, Richard Campbell. A reporter for the *New York Sun,* he was on his way to an assignment in the Far East. Family legend describes his meeting with Margaret as love at first sight. In deference to her parents' state of mourning, particularly her mother's, Margaret and Richard waited a year to marry.

Kate gradually returned to her custom of spending a good portion of each year in Boston or Rhode Island with friends. Margaret and Richard made their home with Tom; in 1896 their first child, Thomas Patterson Campbell, was born. From that day and until his death Tom Patterson would feel a special kinship with his grandson. The child brought new light into his life, and once more Tom Patterson was able to turn his full attention back to politics.

Though enthusiastic about Bryan, Patterson's first choice for a presidential candidate in 1896 was Henry Moore Teller. He undoubtedly recognized the political wisdom of supporting a Colorado man, and he also calculated that if the nominee were a Colorado Republican the Republican party in the state might collapse in the face of a three-party fusion of Silver Republicans, Silver

Margaret Patterson on her wedding day, 1895, with her mother, Kate. (Courtesy Archives, University of Colorado at Boulder Libraries, Patterson collection, Bx 8, Fd 4.)

Democrats, and Populists. Republican Senator Teller had increasingly defied his party on the silver issue, and thus had attracted the support of the *News* as early as January 1896.[42]

In May 1896 Patterson called upon the Democratic party to give serious consideration to the nomination of the maverick Republican, and claimed that the *News* had been the first newspaper to suggest such an unusual eventuality. But two things would have to happen for this remarkable political development to occur. First, Teller would have to make a clean break with the party he had ably represented for over two decades. Second, the militant free-silverites would have to secure a working majority at the Democratic national convention. The *News* concluded that the only hope for a Democratic victory lay in a candidate and a platform that would unite all the disaffected elements under one banner.[43]

That summer, when the Republican national convention endorsed a platform vague enough to allow some bimetallists to remain in the party, Teller emotionally rejected the weak silver plank and renounced his allegiance to the party. Amid the jeers of the delegates, Teller led twenty-three other Republicans from the St. Louis convention.[44]

The *News* greeted Teller's fateful decision with a mammoth front-page drawing depicting the disintegration of the Republican party and a rare seven-column headline: "The First Gun in the Campaign for President Henry Moore Teller."[45] Because he had already addressed the issue of what the Populists should do if the Democrats happened to decide in favor of free silver, he reasoned that the Populists should graciously support the Democratic candidate.[46]

The *News* consistently supported Teller's candidacy. Prior to the Democratic national convention in Chicago, a silver delegation made up of Patterson, Charles S. Hartman of Montana, and Charles A. Towne of Minnesota had had an informal meeting with the thirty-six-year-old William Jennings Bryan to seek his support for Teller's candidacy. Bryan rejected the suggestion, arguing instead that Silver Republicans and Populists must join in luring Republicans to the Democrats. Besides, he said, he had as good a chance to win as anyone.[47] An unknown member of the delegation leaving the meeting reacted to Bryan's contention by saying that "the young man was nutty."[48] When Bryan did indeed win the nomination, Patterson reminded his readers that the *News,* while supporting Teller to the final vote, had endorsed Bryan's flawless devotion to silver and had labeled him a good selection "if a straight out Democrat is nominated." Patterson's enthusiasm grew daily, his editorials predicting that Bryan would draw Populists and Democrats to-gether and praising the Nebraskan as the "most eloquent and powerful as-sailant of official oppression now living."[49]

At the same time, the *Denver Times* observed that Patterson had assumed complete control of the Populists, pushing Waite, the "war" governor, to the rear by winning a state credentials committee vote by 29 to 9.[50] When the Populist national convention met in St. Louis, Patterson, as chairman of the Colorado delegation, helped secure the Populist presidential nomination for Bryan over the objections of those delegates who feared that such action would constitute a sellout to the Democrats and would be a signing of their own party's death warrant.[51]

When it came to naming the Populist vice-presidential candidate, however, Tom Patterson and the other fusionists lost a struggle with the "middle of the road" faction. The fusionists wanted to endorse Arthur Sewall, Bryan's Dem-ocratic running mate, but determined opposition succeeded in naming Tho-mas Watson, thus leaving Bryan with two vice-presidential candidates.[52] The *News* played down this evidence of internal division among the Populists, fearing the Populist move might prove confusing to voters and thus damage Bryan's chances in the election.[53]

During the election campaign of 1896 Patterson spent several weeks tour-ing and speaking on behalf of Bryan, concentrating on his old home state of Indiana but also stumping the states of Illinois, Michigan, Kansas, and Ne-braska.[54] Though Bryan was narrowly defeated, Kate Patterson headed a del-egation to prepare a reception for the Bryans in Denver.[55]

Bryan's political appeal seemed to vindicate Patterson's stubborn argu-ment for fusion and strengthened his position as leader of the Colorado Pop-ulists. Patterson resisted any temptation to resume his long association with the Democratic party, arguing that the Populists must remain in the field as a formally organized party in order to stand guard over its principles and to be a coercive force upon the conscience of the Democrats, lest the moneyed powers reassert control of that body.[56]

Between 1896 and 1900 the *News* steadily supported free coinage of silver, and in 1898 encouraged its readers to support the Silver-Union ticket of Sen-ator Teller and Charles Thomas, the latter campaigning successfully for the governorship of Colorado.[57] The Waite "middle of the road" element virtually disappeared, enabling the fusionists to consolidate their control of the Popu-list party in Colorado and also to increase their working relationship with the Democrats.[58]

Henry Moore Teller, U.S. senator, 1876–1908. (Courtesy Colorado Historical Society.)

In 1900 the *News* once more championed Bryan's candidacy. Bryan himself called for more fusion of all friends of silver, regardless of party.[59] En route to the Populist national convention at Sioux Falls, South Dakota, Patterson spoke at a banquet in Omaha, Nebraska, amid rousing cheers for himself, for Jerry Simpson of Kansas, and for Bryan.[60] The *Denver Republican* predicted that the big tent at Sioux Falls would bulge like a balloon when Patterson lifted his "ceaseless tenor voice."[61]

The Populists honored Tom Patterson by making him permanent chairman of the national convention. In accepting the chairmanship he recalled that his original break with the Democrats had reflected his disappointment with that party on the silver issue, but said he had come to appreciate more fully the total reform program of the Populists. He concluded that the Populists had not nominated Bryan to please the Democrats, but because Bryan stood for Populist principles.[62]

Reacting to Patterson's speech, the *Denver Times* sourly observed that there were not enough Populists left in the state to flag a handcar and predicted that Patterson would be in the Democratic fold by July.[63] But Patterson remained firmly in the Populist camp, traveling across Colorado and through other states in support of Bryan.[64]

The Bryan and Patterson families had become such close friends that Bryan frequently visited the Patterson home when he was in Denver, often dropping by at the spur of the moment, and sometimes showing up early enough to take breakfast.[65] Years later, Patterson's grandson and namesake recalled Bryan's questionable table manners and his general air of self-righteousness. But at the time nothing so mundane interfered with Bryan's and Patterson's friendship, or with Bryan's daughter, Ruth, spending time at the Patterson summer lodge at Grand Lake.[66] Bryan carried Colorado in all three of his losing tries for the presidency, and Patterson served as his host when the Democratic national convention of 1907 convened in Denver's new city auditorium.[67]

As with Bryan's, Patterson's dream of national victory through fusion never quite materialized.Although he contributed significantly to an era marked by important political realignment. While the Democratic party absorbed most of the Populists, the latter group could take some satisfaction, as had Patterson at Sioux Falls in 1900, in the fact that the absorbing party had embraced many Populist principles and reforms.

Although Patterson was genuinely sympathetic to the concept of general reform on behalf of the people, his primary motivation in championing fusion can be traced to his notion of what was good for Colorado. Essentially a sectionalist, he sincerely believed that any success in his battle for free silver would accrue to the benefit of the entire country. And his hopes of developing an effective opposition to Republican party control in Colorado finally materialized with the erosion of traditional party loyalties and realignment during the 1890s.

Patterson himself realized the highest goal of his personal political ambitions. In 1901 a coalition of Democrats, Silver Republicans, and Populists in the Colorado legislature rewarded him, for his constant efforts on behalf of silver, with a seat in the U.S. Senate. In his acceptance speech he announced that he would work with the Democratic party and join the Democratic senatorial caucus.[68] In pursuit of his goal of fusion, Tom Patterson had come full circle back to the Democratic party.

9
The Violence of Good Men

There is no limit to the aggressions of privileged wealth impelled by human avarice.

—Tom Patterson, *Rocky Mountain News,* July 8, 1892

Throughout Thomas Patterson's career, his opponents and admirers alike agreed that he consistently identified with the working man and gave steady support to the cause of organized labor. Critics questioned his motives, charging him with demagoguery designed to advance his own political and financial ambitions. The more extreme attacks accused him of fomenting class warfare and of advocating socialism and anarchy. But Patterson's friends stressed his loyalty to causes intended to improve the social and financial condition of the working man, and praised him for stubbornly maintaining his position in the face of contrary public opinion and downright intimidation.

Overall, the record seems to indicate that Patterson, while deploring the use of violence as a tactic, urged labor to make use of its numerical strength to achieve peaceful progress within existing political and legal systems. Almost alone of the Denver newspapers during the 1890s, Patterson's *Rocky Mountain News* supported the cause of labor unions and presented a favorable version of the character of union members as they struggled with owners and managers of capital.[1]

By the 1870s industrialization had both changed the process of production and created important alterations in the relationship between labor and management. The United States rapidly surged to the level of a world power, producing ever greater quantities of consumer goods for domestic and world consumption. But Americans paid a price for industrial progress. Workers in many industries believed that they were denied what they regarded as a "fair share" in the exploding economy. Realizing they possessed little bargaining power as individuals, they collectively began to challenge conditions arbitrarily prescribed by the employer.

Patterson observed that capital claimed the right to buy labor in the cheapest market, while simultaneously depressing the market price of labor by encouraging the existence of a large surplus of unemployed workers. That could only be accomplished, he asserted, through the existence of business conspiracies that controlled and curtailed production. He declared flatly that only unions could check the exploitation of the worker.[2]

He believed that, there being no limit to "the aggressions of privileged wealth impelled by human avarice,"[3] political organizations must exist to curb corporate rapacity. Furthermore, he feared that the displacement of labor by new machinery would increase the number of the unemployed and further depress wages.

Contending that production needed to be regulated, Patterson called for an equitable system of distributing profits between worker and owner. The very safety of society, he wrote, "cried out" for such a system. He reasoned that workers toiling for a pittance could not rear intelligent, "high-thinking" children, and observed that when hungry men became desperate they would break the bounds of law and society in riot.[4] He warned that the remedy for labor's problems did not lie in resistance to existing laws or in rebellion against constituted authority, but rather that labor would profit from better organization and intelligent, concerted action at the polls. Condemning extreme methods, he suggested that, inasmuch as working men "had the votes," they should operate within the system, no matter how inequitable it might be.[5]

Patterson assumed the role of a morally obligated guardian of society's underprivileged workers. While willing to champion unpopular causes, he deplored labor strategies that might alienate the rest of society. He feared the consequences of an increasing dichotomy between social classes, and believed that labor's best hope lay in convincing concerned citizens of the justice of labor's cause. Further, he believed that capitalism would eventually be modified into something better, though he lacked any specific vision. He simply believed that a government by and for the people was incompatible with an economic system under which the natural resources of the country were allowed to be monopolized by a few individuals.[6]

Patterson's position raises a question about his political and economic philosophy. To what extent did he really challenge the validity of the existing economic structure? His most complete answer appears in a series of editorials he wrote when he assumed control of the *Denver Times* in 1902.

His acquisition of the *Times* coincided with an apparent drive by the Socialist party to become a factor in Colorado politics. During the summer of 1902 rumors suggested that Socialist leader Eugene V. Debs might be planning to make his home in Denver.[7] In his inaugural editorials, Patterson answered accusations that he had embraced socialist doctrine by firmly endorsing ownership of private property as "man's second nature," which could never be abolished by a revolution.

He pointed out, however, that the public concept of private property had undergone a significant change when it accepted the idea that no man should be permitted to use his property to the material injury of society or his neighbor. He conceded that this was a socialist principle, but argued it had not been established by Socialists. Patterson accused the Socialists of having made propaganda out of "humanitarianism," and insisted that any party could subscribe to such a concept. He argued that every piece of humane legislation, such as child labor laws and the ventilation of mines, had been put into operation by the very parties that would oppose socialism to the bitter end. Moreover, he said, some adherents of the major parties themselves had already accepted municipal ownership of such industries as heating and lighting, believing that government could manage better than individuals. Such changes, though still in their infancy, demanded the active support of every true reformer.[8]

Patterson complained that the Socialists apparently didn't want any progress—if they could not reach their goals in one jump. He argued that the only function of the Colorado Socialist party was to antagonize the "healthful humane" sentiment widely diffused in both the Democratic and Republican parties. As one who had seen fusion bring about a measure of political success in Colorado, Patterson deplored the tendency of the Socialists to stay to themselves and suggested they had become "drones in the beehive of reform." How much better, he reasoned, to mingle with other parties and gain the support of those who, although not yet ready to abandon private ownership, stood prepared to push for many needed reforms.

Essentially, Tom Patterson maintained that as long as the Socialists refused to enter the mainstream of the political arena they would remain powerless to secure a single reform.[9] He argued that the socialist attitude defeated practical results and undid the work of such responsible labor leaders as Samuel Gompers of the American Federation of Labor and John Mitchell of the

United Mine Workers. Patterson particularly admired John Mitchell's faithful observance of contract obligations.[10]

Clearly, Patterson rejected the Colorado Socialist party more on pragmatic than on idealistic grounds. To him, positive labor reform would come within the framework of the established political parties. He did not reject the idea of eventual acceptance of the Socialists' goals, but he criticized the "dreamer" aspect of their plans, believing them to be wasteful, futile, and even counterproductive. Although he regarded socialism as a "heresy," Patterson argued for the right to believe in it. But by 1916 he had become more critical, calling Socialists cranks who "embrace too much self-subjugation, abandonment of individuality, and reward that belong to real effort."[11]

Though Patterson rarely referred to sources for his ideas, he occasionally quoted the English leader William E. Gladstone, whom he obviously admired. Observing that the English statesman fought against entrenched aristocratic privilege in such matters as franchise reform, Patterson believed that, just like his own statements of belief, Gladstone's reflected a strong moral fervor. He easily substituted "combinations of wealthy" in the United States for Gladstone's "aristocratic privilege" in England. Yet Patterson's commitment seemed to carry beyond social reform and to touch a vague spirit of collectivism grounded in a selective, pragmatic approach to the problems of the developing urban society.[12]

During the 1890s, attacks by the *News* on abuse of labor by management were far ranging. The paper blasted the Philadelphia and Reading Railroad for ignoring the laws of supply and demand everywhere but in the labor market. It deplored efforts in the Senate to defeat an employer's liability bill, and it hailed the organization of a "Loyal Labor League" as a Populist auxiliary.[13] The paper cheered unionization of Denver Tramway Company employees and accused the company's management of irrational and unjustifiable prejudice against lawful cooperation among working men for their mutual benefit.[14] And the *News* insisted that unbiased facts about labor unrest and its causes were nearly impossible to secure, because the telegraph's channels of communication were controlled by capital and used for its own self-interest.[15]

When the Pennsylvania Homestead strike occurred in 1893, the *News* charged that violence had been precipitated by a private army of hired detectives, an example that loomed as a "dire menace" to the laboring people of the entire country. Patterson personally deplored the intervention of the Pinkerton detective organization in labor affairs and called for prohibition of such activity. He urged Governor John Routt to withdraw permits that allowed Pinkerton agencies to operate in Colorado in order to make the state an example for others.[16]

When the Panic of 1893 ripened into the depression of 1894, *News* editorials sympathized with the increased misery of the unemployed. The paper condemned police pressure on "criminal vagrants," insisting that the unemployed were honest men entitled to respect. Patterson's concern deepened when Jacob Coxey, seeking a solution to unemployment through government work-relief programs, launched his "petition in boots" toward Washington, D.C. In support of Coxey's action, Tom suggested that, instead of condemning the excesses of Coxey's group, the administration of Grover Cleveland should inquire into the causes leading up to the march.[17]

The *News* also gave editorial support to the Colorado wing of "Coxey's army," led by a Denver electrician named G. S. Sanders. Sanders's group of unemployed Coloradans commandeered a Missouri Pacific freight train bound for Kansas City but only got as far as Scott City in western Kansas before surrendering to a marshal supported by a hundred armed men.

When the Colorado "army" arrived in Topeka for arraignment on charges of obstructing and delaying the United States mail, Patterson challenged the legitimacy of the charges. He argued that if any mail trains had been delayed it was because the company ditched engines and cars across tracks and even tore up rails in order to thwart Sanders.[18] In supporting the actions of the Coloradans, Patterson was clearly deviating from his preachments against violence. Yet Patterson was opposed to extreme actions by labor. During the early stages of the Pullman strike in Illinois, his paper praised Eugene Debs for managing to avoid violence. When lawlessness broke out among the strikers, the *News* expressed Patterson's familiar theme that only when strikes were conducted within the law would they be effective in advancing labor.[19] When the anthracite coal field disturbances of 1902 brought a collision between President Theodore Roosevelt and the coal operators, the *News* applauded what it regarded as a victory for John Mitchell's United Mine Workers. Pleased that Roosevelt had helped force recognition of the union, Patterson praised the actions of the Republican president.[20]

While the editorial columns of the *News* spoke favorably of such leading figures as Roosevelt, Gompers, Mitchell, and William Jennings Bryan, it denounced men like Andrew Carnegie as a menace to labor. It condemned Whitelaw Reid, editor of the *New York Tribune* and the Republican vice-presidential candidate in 1892, as an autocrat and a persistent and determined opponent of organized labor who replaced union workers with scabs or "rats."[21]

The broad-based positions on labor adopted by Patterson's newspapers take on added significance when measured against his actions during major labor upheavals in Colorado, several of which drew national attention to the state between 1893 and 1894. In 1893 a dispute broke out in the Cripple Creek mining district, closely followed by a confrontation at Leadville in 1896. Between 1902 and 1904 almost simultaneous eruptions involved Cripple Creek and the southern coal mines of Colorado. In all such instances, Patterson and the *Rocky Mountain News* became targets for criticism by more conservative groups, and in 1903 he suffered direct reprisal by owners and managers of capital.

During the early days of the Panic of 1893 the mining town of Cripple Creek became an oasis for many unemployed miners who sought work there in the gold mines. Jobs and good pay abounded during the summer, but by the end of the year Cripple Creek had far more applicants than available jobs. That fact was noted and acted upon by some mine owners. Taking advantage of the situation, operators announced that as of February 1, 1894, the normal work shift would be increased from eight to ten hours a day with no increase in the daily wage. In response, the miners organized and affiliated with the Western Federation of Miners (WFM) and promised to go out on strike on February 7, 1894.[22]

As the February deadline approached, the *News* noted increasing tensions in the Cripple Creek area. Patterson warned the miners that, though their cause was just, moral force was the only legitimate weapon in a strike and violence to person or property always redounded against the strikers.[23] Experience in other parts of the country showed that the use of violence by labor only alienated public opinion.

He had great faith in public opinion as the agent of change and favored tactics by labor that would rally public pressure to its side.[24] Such views formed the basis for his commitment to compulsory arbitration as the best hope for improving labor's position in society. Fearing that any violence would convince the public that maintaining law and order was more important than social reform, he tried to maintain a favorable image of the strikers. He insisted that if they resorted to extreme measures it was not because they were anarchists or criminals, but because they had been goaded into such action. It was the "violence of good men." He recognized that if the strikers appeared to precipitate violence they would lose the sympathy of the public, which would in turn condone such repressive measures as the use of state militia for strike-breaking.[25]

When the strike began in Cripple Creek on February 7, 1894, the miners had a relief fund already organized and they promised to stage a lengthy walkout. By March 14 the mine operators had secured an injunction to prevent interference with their mines, which continued to function with imported "scab" labor. Two of the large owners, however, James Burns and Winfield Stratton, expressed sympathy for the miners' right to bargain collectively, and Stratton worked out a compromise contract with union president Calderwood. The contract called for a nine-hour workday but increased wages from $3.00 to $3.25 a day.[26]

Six El Paso County deputies from Colorado Springs, trying to enforce the injunction, fled the mining district when confronted by a posse of miners that claimed to be the local police force. El Paso County Sheriff Frank Powers telephoned Governor Davis H. Waite, who responded by sending three hundred militiamen. When local union president John Calderwood and twenty miners submitted to arrest, the troops withdrew.[27]

At this point, aware that the intervention by state militia historically had worked against the interests of the miners,[28] Tom Patterson supported the court injunction, which he interpreted as dictating to neither side while restraining "outside parties" from interfering by force or intimidation. Though he carefully avoided any direct mention of the radical fringe of the Western Federation of Miners in his editorials, he obviously had that group in mind when he warned the local miners of the bad public relations that would result from any assault on sheriffs' officers. He emphasized that any organized resistance to the injunction probably would give mine owners an excuse to request militia support once again.[29]

In the early stages of the strike, the miners maintained a high degree of discipline and gained considerable sympathy across the state.[30] But when the operators subsidized deputies to protect strike-breaking workers, the situation deteriorated. The union miners reacted by fortifying a promontory called Bull Hill and frightening off additional deputies being brought in on two flatcars, by setting off dynamite explosions. Sheriff Bowers immediately recruited twelve hundred additional deputies in Colorado Springs, many of whom were former Denver policemen. Governor Waite ordered the deputies to disband, told the strikers to disperse from Bull Hill, and again alerted the militia.

When neither side complied and an arbitration effort on the campus of Colorado College in Colorado Springs broke up under a lynch threat against Calderwood and Waite, the meeting adjourned to Denver. There, a notable victory for the union occurred in an agreement that called for eight hours of work at the old rate of three dollars a day and no discrimination between union and nonunion men.

Waite, whose support of the union had never wavered, dispatched a militia that arrived just in time to prevent the Colorado Springs deputies from attacking Bull Hill.[31] Eventually, the military shipped the deputies back to Colorado Springs by rail, the mines resumed operation on eight-hour shifts, and three hundred miners submitted to arrest on charges ranging from disorderly conduct to homicide.[32]

Throughout the episode, Patterson's *News* continually praised labor's efforts to improve its condition. Just as steadily, it condemned any hint of violence. On May 28 Patterson criticized the "unlawful resistance" of the Bull Hill miners and their penchant for military-like organization. He also warned both strikers and the public against the dangers of exchanging law for anarchy. Patterson continued to fear the consequences of the use of state troops; after Waite had made his first withdrawal of the militia, the *News* said that the governor learned slowly but surely that the use of troops was not the proper way to operate.[33]

Given Waite's sympathy for the strikers, his deployment of the militia was designed to combat the threat of the hired deputies. Further, the probability of continued militia activity undoubtedly helped the governor to bring about a favorable settlement with the mine owners.[34] In June the *News* reversed its position on the use of state troops. Patterson wrote that, as he approved of the "just" terms of the Denver settlement and there was no longer any need for the militia to take sides, use of the militia to enforce the agreement was now legitimate. When Sheriff Bowers subsequently lost control of some of his deputies, the *News* advocated the continued use of the troops to support the terms of the settlement.[35]

On the basis of the evidence, Patterson seems to have had difficulty juggling his enthusiasm for the immediate improvement of the workers' condition and his conviction that progress should be made in the courts, at the polls, and through the principle of arbitration. Patterson sincerely feared any further precedent-setting recourse to military intervention. He probably also believed that no matter who was governor, state troops would sooner or later be used to defeat a strike. Yet knowing of Waite's bias on behalf of the miners and being so immersed in his fusion ideas and his efforts to eliminate Waite as the head of the Populist ticket, Patterson found it difficult to give the governor the credit due him for helping to resolve the dispute.

Even if Patterson appeared to be inconsistent in regard to Waite's handling of the situation, he steadfastly kept a favorable view of the strikers, many Italian immigrants, before the public. The *News* became the voice of hope and encouragement for them. The *Denver Times* criticized the *News* for defending men who had inverted the American flag and had flown the Italian flag over it.[36] Colorado Springs was the home of many wealthy mining investors, and emotions ran solidly against the strikers. Not surprisingly, the *Colorado Springs Weekly Gazette* accused the *News* of advocating anarchy during the "emergency," and labeled the Denver paper "the vilest sheet that ever disgraced a civilized community."[37]

Patterson's "moderate" approach to labor problems also failed to impress other newspapers that claimed to be speaking for a populace alarmed over the efforts of radical and anarchistic labor. For its part, the *News* constantly emphasized the hardships endured by the miners and virtually ignored the presence of more militant labor officials, an approach that seemed to be vindicated when both operators and miners observed the settlement both in letter and spirit. The Cripple Creek camp boomed as business conditions improved, and the labor surplus diminished. The Cripple Creek disturbance of 1894 left behind it none of the great bitterness that characterized later confrontations in Colorado.[38]

In contrast to the general good will at Cripple Creek after the strike, an intensely hostile atmosphere against labor existed in Colorado Springs, where the arrested miners went on trial. Patterson displayed his twin commitments to labor and the legal process. He agreed to defend the union men after the original defense attorney had been tarred and feathered by night riders,[39] in spite of receiving threats of similar treatment.[40]

The Bull Hill trials, conducted during the spring of 1895, had been postponed from the previous year. The *Colorado Springs Weekly Gazette* had accused Patterson of delaying the trial in order to have the defendants in jail during the fall election campaign. Patterson, wrote the *Gazette,* aimed at arousing sympathy for the strikers in an effort to encourage a large election turnout by indignant Populists. Patterson claimed he could not possibly attend to the matter until after the election, and his associate in the trials, J. K. Vanatta of Colorado Springs, called such allegations "bosh."[41] Patterson may have been capable of such a maneuver, but no evidence proves the point. It was more likely that the Populist campaign so monopolized his energies that he placed the legal action at a lower priority.

From February to June of 1895, Patterson spent much of his time in Colorado Springs defending the Cripple Creek miners.[42] Although losing an appeal for a change in venue, he challenged prospective jurors with "rigid" examinations and eliminated such prejudiced individuals as a member of the American Protective Association, an organization that included among its goals the destruction of unions.[43] In addition to the likelihood that members of the Protective Association participated in the tarring of Patterson's predecessor, the organization (the forerunner of the Ku Klux Klan in Colorado) was strongly anti-Catholic.

Tom Patterson complained of sensational stories in Colorado Springs newspapers that had worked the public mind "into a fever" against the miners. While even his opponents conceded Tom's skill and energy on behalf of the defendants, he expressed "much disappointment" when a few of the miners were found guilty.[44] Given the tense atmosphere, the later evaluations judging his efforts successful seem warranted.[45] Of the thirty seven indictments against the strikers, all but three were dismissed, one man was convicted of stage robbery but later released by the Colorado Supreme Court, and two miners, sentenced to seven years' prison for blowing up the Strong Mine in Cripple Creek, were pardoned before their sentences expired.[46]

Even as Patterson concluded his defense of the Cripple Creek miners, more labor trouble erupted at Leadville, where the depression of 1893 and 1894 had seriously affected the economy.[47] In May of 1895 the WFM organized a union in Leadville under the title of Cloud City Miners' Union Number 33. The new union steadily increased its membership and in the summer of 1895 struck for a wage increase.

When rumors spread that the mine operators would soon import strikebreakers, local union members armed themselves and union pickets called "regulators" tried to discourage newcomers to Leadville. In response to the miners' activities, the mine operators asked Governor Albert W. McIntyre, Waite's successor, to dispatch national guard troops.

Sheriff M. H. Newman assured the governor that he could maintain order without troops.[48] But on September 21, 1896, a dynamite attack on the Coronado Mine triggered fires and casualties that caused militia to be sent and martial law declared in Lake County. While the destruction appeared to be the work of a small group of militants acting without authority, the union position suffered severely.[49]

With military protection assured, the operators imported large numbers of scabs from the lead districts in Missouri and began to reopen the local mines amid a tense atmosphere. A special grand jury investigating the Leadville violence indicted ten men for murder, two for assault, thirteen for arson, and twenty-three for conspiracy.[50]

As the months dragged by the mines continued to function under the supervision of the National Guard, and the union position grew increasingly futile. On March 9, 1897, the miners gathered to hear the advice of Edward Boyce, president of the WFM, and labor leader Eugene V. Debs. Debs and Boyce suggested that the strike effort, although magnificent, was hopeless in the face of existing odds, and advised men to return to work. In an emotion-packed vote, the union reluctantly ended the nearly nine-month-old strike, basically on the operators' terms.[51]

During the Leadville strike Patterson occupied two roles, one as a pro-labor advocate in the pages of the *News* and another as a defense lawyer for the union leaders charged with murder and arson. In November of 1896 he summarized the background of the Lake County disturbance in a lengthy editorial. He declared that prior to the use of the National Guard, the miners had been law-abiding, industrious working men. In fact, however, troops had arrived only in response to the September dynamiting, and Tom Patterson's position exemplifies how his bias in favor of the miners influenced *News* coverage of Colorado labor problems.

While he questioned the wisdom of the strike, Tom Patterson argued that the workers were not the criminals that the owners and general public had branded them as. Moreover, he asserted that no government had the right to coerce strikers through the use of the national guard.[52] Just as he had done in the Cripple Creek strike, Patterson again accused the owners of intractability, blamed them for goading strikers into extreme actions, and supported the workers throughout the strike.

The *Denver Republican* accused Patterson of trying to aggravate and prolong the strike. The *News* had done "everything in its power," it maintained, to encourage the strikers to believe that they had a chance to win. Since various state corporations had retained Patterson on occasion, the *Republican* questioned his claim to be a great friend of the working man, even as it conceded his role as "boss criminal defender" of the WFM.[53]

In mid-November Patterson again extolled the virtues of arbitration as a means of solving labor disputes. He insisted that when large bodies of industrious men complained there must be something to discuss, and employers had the responsibility to consider the complaint. Instead, the owners treated the strikers and their complaints with "contemptuous arrogance."[54]

He argued that two thousand good men had been goaded into violations of the law by owners who planned to crush the union through a combination of using scab labor, sending discharged miners out of state, importing police forces, and using the militia. Only a healthy public sentiment could force the owners to arbitrate, and the *News* urged the state legislature to pass laws forcing arbitration.[55] In response, the Colorado General Assembly, while passing no legislation on the subject, did assign a special committee to suggest a proposal for ending the strike. The special committee, in turn, recommended and secured an arbitration committee that formed the base for the eventual settlement.[56]

Although the more militant labor leaders objected to the no-wage-increase part of the eventual agreement, and even though the terms appeared to represent a defeat for the union, Patterson tried to convince his readers that the very acceptance of arbitration by the owners constituted a victory for labor. The operators, he wrote, had in effect recognized labor's right to organize, thus abandoning their refusal to admit the existence of the union.[57]

Patterson's stance raises the question of why he was ready to make the Leadville settlement seem like a victory when the operators apparently received much the better of the settlement. The answer seems to be that he tried to save face for the miners and to bolster their morale. More significantly, he firmly believed that even though the arbitration principle failed to help the strikers in this instance, the use of arbitration as a technique for solving labor disputes carried more importance in the long run than did getting a favorable settlement for the Leadville miners. Moreover, the episode raises the additional question of Patterson's credibility as a spokesman for labor when the union came to see arbitration as removing the one weapon labor had, the strike.[58]

Patterson's support for arbitration reflected his high regard for the adversarial techniques associated with his law career. He wanted labor to take its chances with a jury made up of participants and concerned citizens. He recognized that the major difficulty lay in getting any hearing at all. With strong convictions on this issue and always his own man, Tom Patterson saw no inconsistency in his position. He certainly regarded himself as solidly pro-labor in pursuing a goal he regarded as the best hope for labor organizations, no matter what position the union assumed.[59]

As he had for the Cripple Creek defendants, Patterson participated in much of the legal work on behalf of the Leadville labor leaders—with positive results. The defense, believing a prompt trial would be to the miners' advantage because of the great number of unemployed miners in the community, watched anxiously as the prosecution exhausted efforts for a continuance. Finally the assistant district attorney presented a motion for nolle prosequi, which would merely have dropped the charges temporarily, leaving the possibility that the defendants could be reindicted at a later date.

Tom Patterson and his partner, E. R. Richardson, attacked the proposal vigorously. The judge denied the prosecution motion and scheduled the trial for January 27, 1897. Meanwhile, the prosecution arranged for the state attorney general to file application for a writ with the Colorado Supreme Court prohibiting the district judge, who it feared sympathized with the miners, from proceeding with the case.[60] But the court refused to make the writ of prohibition a permanent one, and directed the judge and the district attorney's office to reach an agreement acceptable to all parties. As a result, not one indictment developed and no further charges were ever brought against members of an organization regarded by many Coloradans as anarchistic.[61]

Shortly after the resolution of the Leadville disturbance, Tom Patterson proclaimed that a compulsory arbitration bill would soon be passed by the General Assembly, thus making the Leadville strike the "last important labor trouble in Colorado."[62] He was wrong.

10
Mile-High Armageddon

Patterson is an unscrupulous old scoundrel, rotten to the core, who should be placed in a strait jacket and sent to the mental asylum in Pueblo.

— *George's Weekly,* September 25, 1903

In spite of Tom Patterson's hopes, no compulsory arbitration measure had been passed by 1903, when the WFM members voted to strike the Cripple Creek mines in support of the union's attempt to organize smelter workers in nearby Colorado City.[1] As the confrontation escalated, the WFM became convinced that it faced a well-organized effort by the Mine Owners Association to drive the unions from the state.[2]

With the cooperation of Republican Governor James H. Peabody, the mine owners obtained the use of several hundred state guardsmen and also subsidized a number of deputies. The Mine Owners Association agreed to supplement state funding for the militia. It also declined to deal with the WFM, and thus established the major issue: the miners' right to have a union.[3]

According to historian George G. Suggs, Patterson personally wrote the *Rocky Mountain News* editorial of October 4, deploring the strike but deploring even more the use of the national guard to destroy the WFM. He called the move "tantamount to prostituting that great arm of the state's defense to a revolutionary and criminal purpose." He argued that the use of troops was "unnecessary and provocative."[4]

As the mines resumed production using strikebreakers, civil rights vanished in Cripple Creek. Criminal libel charges closed a miners' newspaper and troops searched homes for weapons. On November 21, 1903, a dynamite explosion rocked the Vindicator Mines, killing two men. Governor Peabody declared Teller County to be in a state of insurrection and rebellion;

he suspended the writ of habeas corpus, leading Adjutant-General Sherman Bell to observe that "the military is the whole works at Cripple Creek now."[5]

When the military stepped up its practice of placing miners in bull pens without lodging any formal charges, Patterson's law partners, E. F. Richardson and Horace Hawkins, sought assistance for the miners in the federal courts. Though judges in the lower state courts of Colorado occasionally ruled in favor of the civil rights of miners, the state supreme court, under the leadership of Chief Justice William H. Gabbert, either ruled against the miners or delayed action by reserving its opinion. When Richardson succeeded in getting a writ of habeas corpus from Judge Amos M. Thayer of the U.S. Circuit Court of the Eighth District in St. Louis, the governor released all the military prisoners to civil authorities.[6]

At this point, a second explosion occurred at Independence railroad station killing thirteen nonunion miners. The bull pens filled again as Mine Owners Association representatives seized civil positions of authority and, supported by the militia, shipped "undesirable" miners to the plains of western Kansas. In addition, the association adopted a card system under which discharged miners could not recover their card, without which they could not find employment elsewhere.[7] Governor Peabody wired President Theodore Roosevelt for aid in the "emergency." But the president replied that aid could be sent only if an insurrection against state authority existed. Following an investigation, no federal troops were sent,[8] the strike was broken, and the WFM never really recovered in Colorado.[9]

Though Patterson had turned the union's defense over to his partner, Richardson, he played a major role in the congressional decision to investigate the situation. On December 11, 1903, in his role as a U.S. senator from Colorado, he moved for an inquiry into the causes and the handling of the labor troubles in Colorado. Asserting that the inquiry was needed to check the high-handed tactics being used by mine owners and state officials, Patterson also presented petitions from labor organizations requesting a rapid investigation.[10]

As a result of his stand, Patterson engaged Senator Nathan B. Scott of West Virginia, a spokesman for mine owners in general, in a bitter debate. Scott, as an absentee owner, was a member of the Colorado Mine Owners Association, a group "furnishing the money that pays the troops that are being used for the extermination of labor unions in Colorado."[11] In Colorado, charged Patterson, the writ of habeas corpus had been suspended, military authorities confined strikers to bull pens, and the right of trial was denied. One military proclamation declared that unemployed persons were vagabonds to be expelled from the country. And, never one to overlook an opportunity to needle an opponent, Patterson chided Scott for maligning members of great labor organizations. Such members, he said, had just had lunch at the White House on the invitation of President Theodore Roosevelt.[12]

In 1902 Patterson had bought the afternoon *Denver Times*. He now committed both his newspapers to keeping the miners' case before the people. A day seldom passed without editorials and news stories arguing that the Mine Owners Association, the governor, the militia, and the Colorado Supreme Court had refused to follow the processes of the civil courts. *Miners Magazine,* the official journal of the Western Federation of Miners, frequently reprinted *News* editorials and occasionally purchased multiple copies of key issues for distribution.[13]

In addition, the *News* purchased the only advertising space held by a newspaper in the *Miners Magazine* and used it to quote Edward Bryce, a former WFM president, who had observed at the 1897 union convention that the *News* was the only daily newspaper of any note from coast to coast that was friendly to labor.[14]

Strategically, Patterson followed the practice of referring to the labor movement as a mass of honest, exploited men, while playing down the role of radical elements within the union. Because union officials Charles A. Moyer and William Haywood were perceived to be extremists by many Coloradans, Patterson's editorials rarely referred to the leaders by name. One exception to this practice followed an incident at Ouray, where officers arrested Moyer for desecrating the United States flag by listing union grievances across the stripes of the flag, reproduced on a poster. A few weeks later Patterson, stating the philosophy of the *News,* presented a list of principles. Though strikingly similar to Moyer's, it contained an antiviolence clause missing from the union list.[15]

In spite of all the apparent rapport and the community of interest between Patterson and union leaders, their relationship seems to have been a guarded one. Patterson's rejection of violence as a tactic and his open dedication to the inviolability of contracts and the principle of arbitration probably did not sit well with the more militant unionists. That may explain why the *Miners Magazine* reprinted supportive editorials from the *News* yet did not credit Patterson personally for his papers' assistance, or for his performance on labor's behalf in the courtroom.

When the union purchased his services as legal counsel, nothing indicated that they did so for any reason other than his skill and reputation. Among WFM ledger entries, "legal expenses" included payments to Patterson until September of 1903. After that date the payments went exclusively to his law partners, Richardson and Hawkins, as Tom Patterson had retired from active practice. Nevertheless, an opposition newspaper, *George's Weekly,* continued referring to Patterson after this date as "attorney-in-chief" for the WFM and claimed he was receiving an exorbitant fee, despite the fact that the last payment Patterson received in August 1903 was $1,000, a figure typical of payments in other months during the height of the disputes.[16]

Patterson's withdrawal from the union's case was motivated not only by the pressures of his responsibilities as senator, but also by his struggle to maintain leadership of the Democratic party in Denver and the state, and by his efforts to resist a determined attack by mine owners and other large businessmen to destroy his newspapers. The first warning of an effort to put economic pressure on the *News* and the *Times* came from a relatively small Denver newspaper, *George's Weekly.* Founded in 1884, this paper represented the personal journalism of Herbert George, owner of a small smelter, and had consistently presented anti-union views. In 1901 and 1902, George had argued that the developing smelter trust would mean higher silver prices and consequently higher wages, and he had attacked unions as "combinations of ignorance to fleece the public." He went on to attack Patterson for creating strife and dissension between capital and labor.[17]

The following year, in 1903, the newspaper proudly announced that it had become the official organ of the newly formed Citizens Alliance. The alliance represented an effort by the Mine Owners Association to broaden the base of the fight against unionism by appealing to businessmen and any other Colorado citizens concerned over the "threat to a stable society" posed by labor. Although *George's Weekly* had attacked the *Denver Post* for its mildly favorable attitude toward labor during the second Cripple Creek strike,[18] it directed a major assault against Patterson and his newspapers, referring to them as the "*News-Times* Riot Breeder," and calling the union the "Western Federation of Murderers."

The *Weekly* complained that "skate" Patterson's papers gave page after page of coverage to the union and none to the Citizens Alliance. The paper also condemned the editor of the *News* at the time, a belligerent Irishman named Thomas McKenna.[19] The solution to eliminating these papers, wrote

Home of Patterson's *Rocky Mountain News,* 17th and Welton Streets, Denver, Colorado, in the early 1900s. (Courtesy Colorado Historical Society.)

George, was simply to call for a business and advertising boycott of both the *News* and the *Times.*[20] Since *George's Weekly* spoke for the Citizens Alliance, Patterson could not have been too surprised when the alliance finally did try to destroy him financially.

Patterson alerted the readers of the *News* and the *Times* to the assault. According to the *News,* its chief advertisers announced that they were cutting back on their patronage of the paper and that they planned to maintain only the minimal amount of advertising required under existing contracts.[21] Denver's four largest department stores—Daniels and Fisher, Joslin's, A. T. Lewis and Sons, and the Denver Dry Goods Company—headed the defections. Seven lesser firms followed their lead. As most of the large advertisements withered and some disappeared entirely, Tom Patterson's business manager and son-in-law, Richard C. Campbell, warned him that he would be ruined if the boycott continued.[22]

Edward Keating, editor of the afternoon *Times,* described Patterson's reaction to the boycott. Pacing in his office, the senator decided it was time for a showdown to see whether he or the Citizens Alliance controlled his newspapers. Advising Keating to reduce expenses, as it might be a long fight, Patterson announced that he had $250,000 he could put his hands on within twenty-four hours. After that, other arrangements would be needed. One way or another, he would see it through.[23]

Without big advertisements the *News* and the *Times* became rather thin, and Patterson used the front page of each paper to explain the situation. In place of the columns normally filled by the large advertisers, Patterson energetically cultivated small stores in Denver and began a front-page feature called "A Roll of Business Honor" that listed loyal firms defying the boycott.

Meanwhile, the *News* continued to print pro-labor accounts of the strike, and editorials continued to uphold the right of labor to organize. Some articles contained highly emotional appeals. At least twice the *News* featured pathos-ridden stories of workers, exiled from their families, who reportedly had been driven to commit suicide. Group pictures of deported miners ran side by side with pictures of their desolate wives and children. The military received constant attention, with headlines such as "General Bell deports another lot of men from Cripple Creek without the semblance of a trial."[24]

Support for Tom Patterson quickly appeared. The Denver Trade Assembly understandably endorsed his position and condemned the boycott. He personally received a thunderous ovation after explaining his position to an admittedly sympathetic audience of seven thousand at a labor picnic at Rocky Mountain Lake. The *News* and the *Times* printed letters of support and sympathy daily, including a strong message from Tom Patterson's senatorial colleague, Henry Moore Teller. Teller denounced the boycott and argued that no paper in the West had been so consistently and earnestly loyal to the best interests of the state as had the *News*. Teller described the paper as fearless, honest, and intelligently conducted.[25]

Patterson admitted that the department store "octopus" had caused severe hardships for his newspapers, but he remained defiant. Addressing the "plain people," he announced that the business loss to the *News* from declining advertisements amounted to about $8,000 per month, or virtually $100,000 if the boycott continued for a year. To help balance this loss, he suggested that the citizens of Denver could best show their sympathy for his cause by subscribing to the *News*. Within days of his announcement, the paper reported that, since the boycott had begun, *News* circulation had increased at a faster rate than ever before—and it offered to open its books to anyone seeking proof.[26]

Quite logically, Tom Patterson played up the attack on his newspapers as a threat to their very life. Although Citizens Alliance hoped that they might fail, Patterson, by his own estimates to Keating, could probably have kept the newspapers going for several years. Nevertheless, even a short-term boycott undoubtedly worked a severe hardship. Patterson struggled along for nearly a year without patronage from the boycotting stores. And when the boycott continued even after the labor disturbance had quieted, he concluded that the Citizens Alliance was continuing the pressure against the *News* as part of an effort to re-elect Governor Peabody in 1904 and ultimately to exterminate the union.

Eventually the advertisers returned. Doggedly, *George's Weekly* continued its vituperative attacks on Patterson. Between 1903 and 1905, the paper blamed Patterson for nearly every labor problem, large and small, in the state of Colorado and coupled his name in headlines with those of Moyer and Haywood. A hysterical climax was reached in early 1905, when the paper called him an "unscrupulous old scoundrel, rotten to the core, who should be placed in a strait jacket and sent to the state mental asylum in Pueblo."[27]

Summarizing Patterson's actions during this tense period is easier than correctly identifying his motives. The evidence indicates that he continued his consistent support of the working man and his right to organize. He led the protest against restrictions on civil liberties, a protest no doubt arising from his fundamental fear of military usurpation of civil authority. Indeed, his concern for freedom of speech caused him to defend union leaders publicly, a practice he had previously avoided on the grounds that those leaders were thought of as extremists by many Coloradans.

Patterson believed that he was the most effective voice for the common man in the state. Although he was willing to be called a demagogue by his opponents—and he certainly recognized the potential voting strength of the workers and cultivated their political support—his sincerity and commitment to improving labor's condition seem to be beyond question, even when he disagreed with labor's tactics. In the end, the interest generated by his confrontation with the Citizens Alliance did have a favorable impact on the circulation of the *News,* a fact not lost on Patterson, whose newspapers at the time were engaged in a strenuous circulation battle with the other Denver papers, particularly the *Denver Post.*

Patterson's consistency in support of labor weighs heavily against suggestions of opportunism on his part. That he gained by his fight against the boycott was not the reason behind his decision to fight. Rather, in a city generally hostile to his views, and with several powerful factions combined against him, Patterson faced the challenge to the independence of his newspapers with courage, stubbornness, and a flair for making the most of the drama. Ultimately, although he certainly believed he was right on the labor issue, he felt even more deeply that he had a right to express his views fully on any issue.

Was his motivation political? The fact that Tom Patterson already had attained the highest political position to which someone not native born could aspire makes the possibility unlikely. Was he looking toward a second term as senator? Was it possible that he believed the security of his political future depended on a demagogic appeal? On both counts the answer is probably no, for by 1904 Patterson already realized that serious divisions within his own Democratic party weakened his chances for a second term in the Senate. He had been disclaiming any future political ambitions as early as 1902. Now, whatever aspirations he might have had seemed virtually nonexistent. Instead, the situation suggests that his efforts for labor found their roots more in principle than in personal ambition.

During his tenure in the United States Senate, Patterson spoke frequently on behalf of labor measures. He supported Senator Robert M. LaFollette's Hours of Service Act, designed to protect railroad passengers from accidents caused by weary employees. While many of its supporters regarded the act as a public safety measure, Patterson viewed the legislation as primarily a labor measure. His colleague, Senator Teller, also recognized that the real significance of the bill lay in its prohibiting railroads from working their men for too many hours without a break.[28]

The two Colorado senators helped pass the measure over the protests of such conservatives as Joseph B. Foraker, Henry Cabot Lodge, and Porter J. McCumber. Patterson even forced some rewording of the bill by eliminating a section that he believed could have been interpreted as calling for a sixteen-hour day without time and a half for overtime. After a supporting speech from Senator Albert Beveridge, Patterson's corrective wording was adopted.[29] When LaFollette became ill, Patterson claimed to be his spokesman for the final draft of the measure; after Senate approval, the House passed the bill unanimously.[30]

Patterson also worked to secure an eight-hour workday for laborers digging the Panama Canal. He argued that alien laborers should be accorded the same protections as American workers, and he appealed to the humanitarian instincts of his colleagues. At the same time, he appeared to be equally motivated by a fear, that under the contract system, unprotected alien workers would be preferred by the "corporate employers" and thus drive American workers from the scene.[31]

When Congress considered an "anarchy bill" after the assassination of President William McKinley, Patterson warned of the possible anti-labor effects in the measure. One clause in the bill provided for the punishment of persons who gave "advice and counsel" that might lead to acts of violence. Patterson objected, pointing out that such a provision might open the door to persecutions "that come nearer creating anarchy than any body of anarchists can create." He added:

> We cannot bridle men's tongues so that the words they utter will be measured by our ideas of propriety. We cannot erect a standard of moral conduct and force every citizen to reach that standard or suffer from legal penalty. We must submit to evil, we must realize that we are in the midst of evils, but to revoke them we must not fly to evils that are of far greater moment.[32]

Such pronouncements encouraged Patterson's enemies to denounce him as a radical, especially during his support of strikers during labor disturbances. Yet, on examination, his statements actually reveal a *fear* of anarchy.

Patterson viewed as suspect almost any legislation he thought might ultimately be construed in such a manner as to punish labor unfairly. In 1903 he pointed out that a section of a bill purporting to punish robbers of mail trains possessed language broad enough to include unions. Perhaps recalling the federal government's use of the injunction during the turbulent 1890s, he argued that under the existing wording strikers also could be accused of obstructing a train's passage.[33]

After leaving the Senate, Patterson continued to speak out for organized labor. In 1913 trouble developed in the coalfields of southern Colorado, climaxed by the "Ludlow Massacre." The miners struck for improved working conditions and union recognition, but essentially they were challenging despotic rule by the mine owners. The strikers claimed that the Colorado Fuel and Iron Company, controlled by interests connected to John D. Rockefeller, dominated political, economic, and social matters. Widespread use was made of the blacklists, armed guards, company spies, venal politicians, summary discharges, strikebreakers, and the suppression of free speech, free press, and free assembly.[34] Patterson, having sold the *News* and the *Times,* joined the discussions as a prominent elder statesman. At the request of Governor E. M. Ammons, he spent three days and nights at the state-house trying to help end the strike. In his view the strike leaders had proved they were reasonable by accepting the possibility of intervention by federal troops. The operators, however, declined to talk with the labor leaders, calling them murderers and interlopers.[35]

The representative from the third congressional district in Colorado, Harry Seldomridge of Colorado Springs, inserted into the *Congressional Record* what he called a "lucid" version of the strike, as written by Patterson. The former senator stated that the real issue lay in the means of settling the dispute, and that both parties should consider their obligation to society. The miners, Patterson wrote, had been willing to abide by the decision of any reputable and distinguished group of men; the operators adamantly said that there was nothing to arbitrate. Tom criticized the operators as "blind to the march of public sentiment," and called for a state constitutional amendment requiring compulsory arbitration.[36] At seventy-five, two years before his death, Tom Patterson continued to emphasize his favorite solution to the turbulence brought on by industrial strife.

Primarily in response to the situation and in the belief that he could quiet confrontations between labor and management, Patterson emerged from retirement in 1914 to make an ill-advised race for governor.[37] With Ben Lindsey, another reform candidate in the contest, Patterson succeeded only in dividing the reform vote, with the result that a conservative Republican was elected.

Patterson's relationship with labor also is revealed on a more personal level. During the financially grim summer of 1894, members of the International Typographical Union asked the newspaper owners in Denver for a meeting to discuss a proposed pay cut, which the owners defended as a measure necessary to enable them to weather the hard times. Among the proprietors, only Tom Patterson and his *News* partner, John Arkins, agreed to attend the meeting. He pleaded for a voluntary and temporary reduction in wages during the economic crisis—and the workers voted to accept a 10 percent reduction for a sixty-day period. Though Patterson thanked the union for its aid, he regretted they had rejected his full request.[38]

As a by-product of the negotiations Patterson did lose some reporters from the *News;* they were hired away by competitors at higher salaries. Generally, however, when dealing with collective labor, he apparently met existing wage rates. In one of his rare land acquisitions outside of Denver, he became involved in a small coal-mining operation near Louisville, Colorado. According to his law partner, Horace Hawkins, he always operated with union labor, always paid union scale, and never suffered a strike in his mine.[39]

At the time of Tom Patterson's death, John McLennan, president of the Colorado Federation of Labor, praised him as "the most aggressive advocate of the rights of the people that the state of Colorado has ever known." Noting that labor had lost a good friend, McLennan added that Patterson had always stood for a square deal for labor and had supported labor even when he considered the cause lost.[40]

Throughout his public and private career, a fundamental faith in the legal process was the foundation of Tom Patterson's reasoning. In his opinion, the solution of labor's problems lay in the arbitration of disputes by distinguished citizens. In that way labor could at least receive a fair hearing; at best, fair-minded individuals would be won to labor's point of view.

The use of arbitration, however, did not preclude stopping production through collective action. Strikes were the most effective means of getting a problem before the people, but to avoid alienating the public they must represent moral force applied within the limits of the law. He rejected violence on principle as well as on the grounds that it made for bad public relations. Yet when he thought that unions had been goaded into extreme action by the injustice of management, he became the leading apologist for labor excesses. He consistently criticized "illegal" corporate pressure, as well as state and military pressure brought to bear on unions by the influence of corporations. He feared that when military force superseded use of the civil court system, it could be used to support corporations and to crush unions. Unions, according to Patterson, represented the only effective check on the exploitation of the worker, given corporate control of prices and production.

How much of Patterson's position represented a demagogic appeal to workers? Certainly, many stories in his papers carried a bias that appealed to the workingman. He argued that they had the votes to redress industrial evils. But the unions did not control Colorado politics. Moreover, Patterson alienated many Denver citizens by his defense of unionism, and he showed a willingness, even an eagerness, to face vilification by his enemies.

His sense of collectivism, however, stopped short of embracing socialism. He preferred the "legalism" of working through established political parties. In his stubborn stand against the boycott of his newspapers, Patterson pictured himself as the small entrepreneur struggling against the heavy odds of an organized large-business conspiracy. Such a view made him sympathetic to the trustbusting rhetoric of Theodore Roosevelt, and in his last years he supported Woodrow Wilson.[41]

The evidence indicates that Tom Patterson was a man dedicated to private enterprise. He detested any combination of wealth or power that might block him, or block others, from proving their worth. Paradoxically, he both endorsed collective action and remained dedicated to individualism.

11
Showdown for the Senate

Tommy will rattle around like a marble in a bass drum.

—*George's Weekly,* January 12, 1901

In 1901 Republican Edward O. Wolcott was up for re-election to the U.S. Senate. He had served with Henry Teller, a fellow Republican, since 1886. Though he had spoken out against the repeal of the Sherman Silver Purchase Act in 1893, he had also launched an oratorical attack against Jacob Coxey's army, which had sought relief from unemployment. Rather than ally himself with the Silver Republicans, Wolcott remained with the regular Republican party. He served as temporary chairman of the 1900 Republican convention and renominated William McKinley for president, with Theodore Roosevelt as his running mate.[1]

The Democrats saw their chance to capture the seat. Though nearly every party leader in the state was eager to throw his hat into the ring, Governor Charles Thomas—a staunch supporter of goldbug Grover Cleveland—appeared to be the leading contender. To succeed, however, he had to prevent the fusionists from endorsing Tom Patterson at the state Democratic convention.[2]

Patterson was foreign-born, and the office of senator was the highest position he could legally hold. As early as 1882 Kate had naively confided to their daughter Mary that, because of her father's service as the first Democratic representative from Colorado in 1876, his efforts for statehood and his work in reducing the number of Republicans in the state legislature to a slim majority, she was certain that "Papa will be one of Colorado's two Senators."[3] But the Republicans maintained party discipline and in 1882 denied him the position on a straight party vote.[4]

The years passed. Patterson continued to focus his energies on bimetallism, and throughout the 1890s he worked feverishly to fuse the Populists with the Silverites of both major parties. But when he went so far as to bolt his party for the Populists, some elements of the Democratic party could not forgive him.

In the summer of 1900 the conventions of the Populists, the Democrats, and the Republicans met simultaneously in Denver. Certain that a strong fusion ticket would result in Patterson's eventual election to the U.S. Senate, the Democratic conference committee held out for fusion on its own terms. The Populists and the Silver Republicans refused to go along. In an unprecedented move, Patterson and Senator Teller appeared together at the state Democratic convention, demanded recognition, and pleaded for fusion on a basis fair to the smaller parties. Remarkably, the delegates disavowed their own leaders and agreed to accept the terms that the smaller parties offered.

The fusion ticket won in Colorado, re-electing Silver Republican John F. Shafroth and Populist John C. Bell to Congress. It also brought a safe majority into the state legislature, which would select a senator for the open seat.[5] Patterson had spent twenty years preparing for this opportunity. He confidently threw his hat into the ring. Former governor Alva Adams was the dark horse candidate. But Patterson's chief opponent was Charles S. Thomas, his former law partner.

The senate seat was also a long-held dream for Thomas. Born near Darien, Georgia, in 1849, Charles Thomas had experienced firsthand the bitter privations of life in the Civil War South. He had briefly served with troops from Georgia. By 1871 he had graduated from the University of Michigan Law School. Like Patterson, he brimmed with ambition. Believing his best prospects to be in the West, Thomas had decided on Denver, arriving in December of the same year.[6]

From the earliest days of their relationship, Patterson and Thomas had worked together for the election of Democrats. They were law partners until 1889 when Patterson's son, James, joined the firm. Yet by 1892 they had taken different paths. While Patterson led the Silver Democrats and his *Rocky Mountain News* supported the Populist Davis Waite for governor, Charles Thomas was among the Democrats who were solidly behind the election of Cleveland and who wanted no fusion with the Populists at the state level.[7] Yet it was the *News* that encouraged its readers to support the Silver-Union ticket of Senator Teller and Charles Thomas when Thomas ran for and was elected governor in 1898.[8]

Unlike Tom Patterson, Charley was basically a loyal team player. Though always dubious about William Jennings Bryan's chances to win the presidency, he campaigned diligently on his behalf each time Bryan was the

Democratic candidate. In contrast, Patterson willingly explored new territory to achieve the triumph of silver and his own ambitions.[9]

As the day approached for the election of the junior U.S. senator from Colorado, Patterson believed that he had the support of the fusionists who dominated the legislature. His well-known long association with former Silver-Republican-now-Democrat Henry Teller was an added bonus. Thomas, who still served as governor, controlled Denver's fire and police board and the board of public works, giving him tremendous political influence. The president of the fire and police board, Robert Speer, was the other half of the Thomas-Speer "machine."[10] In addition to the straight-line Democratic votes, Thomas was certain of the influence of the incoming governor, James Orman, whose candidacy Thomas had supported.[11] The extent to which each man could "collect the markers" he had accumulated over the years would decide the outcome.

But if Charles Thomas thought he could carry out his campaign for the senate seat out of sight of public eyes and behind the traditional political curtain, he underestimated Tom Patterson. On Thursday, January 10, on the front page of the *Rocky Mountain News* there appeared the full text of a letter to Patterson from Thomas. The letter was first sent to the Albany Hotel, owned by Patterson and being used as his headquarters, then delivered by messenger to his home. Alongside was printed Tom Patterson's reply. Thomas proposed there be a caucus of fusion members of the legislature, that the vote be made by ballot, and—perhaps most significantly—that, should no decision be made, the vote not be attempted again until the next session of the legislature. Patterson penned the following reply:

> Hon. Chas. S. Thomas, City:
> My Dear Sir—Your letter of even date herewith was handed me tonight at 11:15 o'clock. It would have been more in keeping with the importance of the subject had you sent it to me earlier so that I might have prepared my answer in time for publication of both your letter and my answer in the same issue of the morning papers.
> . . .
> I heartily concur in your suggestion, indeed I request that you agree that the fusion members of the legislature meet in caucus to agree upon a candidate for the United States senate—the person receiving a majority of the votes in the caucus to be voted for in the legislature by all the fusion members. But I venture to suggest this Monday night at 8 o'clock is too late for the convening of the caucus. The voting in the legislature must commence the next day at

Charles Sewell Thomas, Patterson's law partner, governor of Colorado 1899–1901, and U.S. senator 1913–1921. (Courtesy Colorado Historical Society.)

noon. I would prefer that the caucus first convene upon Saturday next at 2 o'clock.

[I]nstead of the voting in caucus being by ballot, it be on roll call, each member expressing his choice for senator in caucus as his or her name is called. I am convinced that no member of the legislature will hesitate to publicly announce his choice for senator in caucus. . . .

I cannot comprehend why you propose that should the caucus adjourn at any time without choice, it shall be arranged that no choice be made or attempted in the ensuing joint session of the legislature or until another session of the caucus. To enter in such an agreement would be to arrange to violate the act of congress providing for the election of United States senators. . . . To act upon such an agreement would be so palpable a violation of the letter and spirit of the law that I cannot consent to do it. [12]

The following day, January 11, the front page on the *News* carried the following:

In reply to Mr. Patterson's letter of Wednesday night Mr. C. S. Thomas yesterday morning sent a note which is printed below. Mr. Patterson did not reply to it yesterday because he desired to submit it to a caucus of his friends in order that his reply might have their sanction.

Thomas argued that Patterson's proposal to move up the date of the caucus did not jibe with the customary time for such a meeting. Further, some members were ill or came from a distance. At this late date, to expect them to come sooner would be an inconvenience. Like the proper time for the caucus, he defended casting a ballot because it was the custom. He left it up to the members of the caucus to decide the matter themselves.[13]

On January 12, the next day, Patterson replied:

I thought it proper to submit all our correspondence touching a legislative caucus to a meeting of my friends and supporters in the legislature. Their unanimous opinion was that the matter of a caucus concern the fusion members of the legislature alone, and that, as candidates for their suffrages, it was not ours but their province to determine all matter connected with it. I unhesitantly acquiesce.

Thomas, in turn, replied rather indignantly, "My Dear Sir—My suggestion of a caucus can in no way be construed as dictating to members of the general assembly. Some had to propose it and I presume from the contents of your letter of the 9th I merely anticipated you in doing so." The January 13 edition of the *News* carried a front-page story headlined: "Majority Sign Call for Fusion Caucus." Of the ninety-one fusion members of the legislature, fifty-seven, or eleven more than a clear majority, signed the agreement to enter a fusion caucus for Monday night at 8 o'clock in the House chamber of the state capitol to determine who would succeed Senator E. O. Wolcott as the next United States senator from Colorado.

The afternoon prior to the vote, Patterson's supporters, fifty-two of them members of the legislature, met at the Albany Hotel. Governor Thomas and his supporters conferred at the Brown Palace. They knew that to receive a majority in the fusion caucus required forty-six votes. Fifty-two members were presently meeting in Patterson's headquarters. Earlier, Alva Adams had advised Thomas that he was withdrawing from the contest in order to limit the possibility of a drawn-out struggle in the legislature.[14] In the face of growing Patterson strength, Governor Orman withdrew his support.[15] Robert Speer and Thomas concluded that the fight was over. They sent word to Patterson, asking that he meet with Governor Thomas. In a room at the Brown, Charley Thomas told Tom he had decided to withdraw. He announced his decision in tears.[16]

That evening in the caucus, on the only ballot taken, Patterson received seventy-four of the eighty-seven votes cast, with seven going as a compliment to Justice Charles J. Hughes, five to James H. Blood, and one to Congressman Shafroth. The choice of Tom Patterson was then made unanimous.

The following day, in a joint session of the legislature, Tom Patterson won the senate seat by an overwhelming 91 to 9 vote.[17] But the struggle had engendered such bitter feelings that it threatened to drive a permanent wedge between the one-time friends and law partners. The rift so concerned William Jennings Bryan that he expressed the hope that the future success of the Democratic party in Colorado would not be jeopardized.[18] He need not have worried, for when Patterson stood before the joint session of the legislature to give his acceptance speech—his wife, daughter Margaret, and her husband seated in the front row—he announced his decision to work with the Democratic party and he praised William Jennings Bryan as "the father of us all."[19]

Reaction to Patterson's election varied among Colorado newspapers according to their editorial philosophies. Those favoring him stressed his record as a friend of the masses and praised his abilities as an organizer, fighter, and orator.[20] Patterson's friend and political associate, Thomas Jefferson O'Donnell, expected Patterson to become an important figure in the Senate.[21] Opponents commented primarily on his ambition and opportunism; and while many newspapers were willing to reserve judgment, several freely predicted that he would be a cipher in the Senate, with one suggesting that "Tommy will rattle around like a marble in a base drum."[22]

Outside Colorado, the *St. Louis Globe-Democrat* predicted that Patterson would shine as an orator. The *Salt Lake City Daily Herald* praised him as a man of conscience and a fighter, while the *Chicago-American* credited much of his success to his wife, who was "prominent in good works" and would be a social asset.[23]

More than twenty years after he had served as Colorado's first Democratic member of the United States House of Representatives, Patterson returned to Washington as a U.S. senator. His leadership of Colorado fusionists raised some confusion concerning his party identification. As late as 1900 he had been chairman of the National Populist convention. Yet in an early Senate speech—in which Patterson enthusiastically proclaimed the virtues of the Democratic party and referred to it as "the party of the people"— the doubt was resolved.[24]

Upon his arrival in Washington, Patterson took up residence in the Shoreham Hotel, which enabled Kate to hold frequent receptions for members of Washington society and for constituents from Colorado.[25] Like her husband, Kate had harbored dreams about the day her husband would become a senator. From the earliest years in Denver she had enjoyed being a hostess to the best society. Now that her husband was a U.S. senator, the ultimate opportunity had arrived. A year later, on July 16, 1902, she was dead of unknown causes.

In spite of her fragile health, Kate had been a person of accomplishment in her own right. She had led or been part of many causes: early efforts to obtain women's suffrage, promotion of art in the public schools, the founding of the Woman's Home Club and the Denver Orphans' Home, the YWCA, the Fortnightly Club, the Association of Collegiate Alumnae, and the Ladies' Relief Society.[26] The years when Tom was seldom home had not been spent idly.

Above all, through good times and bad, the U.S. Senate seat was a dream Kate and Tom had shared. At last it was a reality. The endless separations and

Tom's compulsion for work and politics had strained their marriage. Yet it was Kate who first joined him on his journey toward the greatness for which he longed, and now she was gone.

12
The Anti-Imperialist

> If the Filipinos ever did achieve independence, the islands would be
> simply a sucked orange.
>
> —Tom Patterson, *Congressional Record,* 57th Congress

After his wife's death, Tom Patterson moved to the more modest quarters
of the Willard Hotel. From his office in the Senate Annex Building he directed the operation of a small staff, relying primarily on the assistance of
his nephew, Arthur C. Johnson, who had worked as a reporter for the *Rocky
Mountain News.*

Patterson hated to write, preferring to dictate nearly all his correspondence. Under the pressure of Patterson's demands, Johnson improved his
skills at a shorthand school in Washington, until eventually he could take dic-
tation.[1] Apparently Patterson stressed the need for economy, and he also expected Johnson to assist in research and the management of the office. He
quickly developed a systematic schedule, arising not later than seven for exercise, breakfast, and some reading, including the Washington newspapers.
He arrived at the Capitol by ten to attend committee meetings, going to the
Senate at noon. Sessions there usually lasted until five or six o'clock, at which
time he would to return to his office to attend to correspondence.[2]

After dinner, he prepared speeches he proposed to make and gave thought
to the examination of witnesses who would appear before committees the
next day. He normally went to bed anywhere between midnight and two in
the morning.[3] Visitors and those seeking favors frequently interrupted the
schedule, causing Tom to observe that although his life in Denver had been a
busy one, "the life of a zealous Senator as compared with it is perpetual motion to society in [L]ent." He switched from coffee and tea at dinner to claret,
"in the manner of the Portuguese attache," with the result that he went to bed
a little earlier and awakened at six o'clock "fresh and active."[4]

But no amount of work Patterson did could change the political conditions that militated against his becoming an effective force for change in the Senate. In 1901 Republican conservatives held a comfortable majority, with leadership like Senators Nelson W. Aldrich of Rhode Island, John C. Spooner of Wisconsin, Orville H. Platt of Connecticut, and William B. Allison of Iowa. Other senators of influence were Henry Cabot Lodge of Massachusetts, Eugene Hale of Maine, and Joseph B. Foraker of Ohio.

Republicans like Senators Jonathan P. Dolliver of Iowa and Albert J. Beveridge of Indiana, who later would voice discontent with conservative policies, seemed content in 1901.[5] The man destined to become the leader for progressive reform, Robert M. LaFollette, did not arrive in the Senate until 1905. Senate legislation resulted primarily from Republican caucus action, relegating the function of the minority Democrats almost entirely to one of criticism.[6]

In addition to being outnumbered by the Republicans, Patterson's Democratic party also lacked cohesion. That, in turn, added to its inability to muster effective opposition on most issues.[7] Many of the Southern Democrats, such as Senator John L. McLaurin of South Carolina, generally reflected a conservative viewpoint on domestic matters. And the struggle continued for control of the party between the followers of William Jennings Bryan and Grover Cleveland.[8]

Because reformers in the Congress did not exist in significant numbers in either party, little consistent opposition to conservative measures could be expected. The chief pressure for reform during the first half of the decade came during the administration of President Theodore Roosevelt, and expediency made even Roosevelt appear too willing to compromise during much of his first administration.[9]

In this milieu, Tom Patterson soon became one of the most vocal members of a small group of combative Democrats. He was consistently supported by Teller and by Senator Edward W. Carmack of Tennessee.[10] It also was not unusual for Patterson to vote in the company of Senators Charles A. Culberson of Texas, Fred T. Dubois of Idaho, and Joseph W. Bailey of Texas.

Alluding to the unwritten law that a senator must not "open his head" as a freshman, Arthur Johnson wrote that Patterson very wisely was taking no part in any of the debates.[11] Yet Johnson also knew of Patterson's energy and ambition to become a senator of stature. With great difficulty, Tom restrained himself from active participation on the Senate floor during the first two months of the session.

In February, however, Patterson "broke out early." Upon entering the Senate chamber, Arthur Johnson was stunned to find Patterson engaged in a heated exchange with Senator Foraker over the Philippine question. Although his colleagues usually looked with disapproval on any new man who asserted himself offensively, Tom Patterson apparently made a favorable impression during his first debates. The *Washington Post* commented that his first extended speech drew a careful, attentive, and appreciative hearing.[12] After one early effort Patterson received hearty handshakes from nearly all the Democrats; he cited as proof of his impact that his arguments had been taken up and disputed by the Republicans.[13]

Patterson soon developed the reputation of being fearless. And although he occasionally got in the way of a "pretty hard smash," Johnson noted that his uncle always moved to the next round bright and smiling, usually scoring points himself before the exchanges ended. As the session drew to a close, Johnson was surprised whenever Tom failed to participate in a discussion, and he observed that the senator was thriving on the "cordial roastings" he received from those whose policies he opposed.[14] The *Indianapolis Journal* described him as a fighting Irishman whose greatest delight in Washington was "making someone squirm."[15]

The *New York Sun* attacked Patterson by comparing his performance with that of another freshman senator, John F. Dryden of New Jersey. While Dryden had spoken only twice during a four-month period, the Colorado senator's 517 times had set a record never approached by any new member.[16] The *Sun* complained that Patterson instructed veterans in senatorial procedure, interrupted speakers, persistently cross-examined his opponents, and even presumed to make suggestions to his own people as to the proper course of the arguments. Patterson, said the *Sun,* could not shed his defense-lawyer tactics, had no concept of dignity and courtesy in the Senate, and ultimately would be rated below Senator Tillman in that regard.[17]

Certainly Patterson's aggressiveness involved him in some petty exchanges and occasional discourtesies, but he generally adhered to the rules, and both he and his adversaries used the forms of address customary in the Senate. At one point, though, he engaged in an embarrassing exchange with Senator Foraker concerning which of them interrupted the most. Senator Platt once vowed to remain on his feet until "the Senator from Colorado ceases to be in a state of eruption."[18] Senator Beveridge criticized Patterson's tendency to be redundant. But Senator Chauncy M. Depew of New York appeared more tolerant when he simply noted that lawyers with leanings toward Populism had the gift of words.[19]

Tom Patterson's willingness to give procedural advice, even as a freshman senator, did prove useful at least on the occasion of Senator Tillman's physical assault on his colleague from South Carolina, John L. McLaurin. Tillman stated that McLaurin's vote for the treaty with Spain had been bought by an administration promise of patronage control in South Carolina. McLaurin called Tillman a liar, whereupon Tillman leaped across Henry Teller's desk to strike McLaurin. The stunned Senate was on the verge of remanding both men to custody when Patterson suggested that the Senate, sitting in executive session, could handle the situation with less notoriety by disposing of the case as a contempt-of-court proceeding. After a supporting statement from Senator Aldrich, the Senate concurred. When McLaurin nearly reopened the furor during his apology to Tillman, Patterson saved the day by catching his attention and begging him to desist, and the matter was resolved.[20]

Patterson had settled in. He was attracting the attention of his colleagues. He was primed to do battle.

Tom Patterson's two chief interests in the Senate were anti-imperialism and antitrust regulation. He felt especially fortunate in being assigned to the Committee on the Philippines and the Committee on Interstate Commerce. During his first session in the Senate he became most prominent as an anti-imperialist, and he devoted nearly all of his time and energy to the issue of the Philippines.[21]

In 1899, following the annexation of the Philippines in the Treaty of Paris at the end of the Spanish American War, the U.S. Senate adopted a resolution declaring that the islands would not become a permanent possession. When an 1899 commission argued against immediate self-government, however, a bloody three-year revolt began under the leadership of Emilio Aguinaldo, who rejected trading Spanish masters for American ones. By 1902 the uprising was crushed by methods that aroused criticism from anti-imperialists in the United States. Patterson arrived in Washington ready to join the assault against prolonging this experiment in empire.

The proceedings of the Committee on the Philippines quickly developed into an openly partisan duel between the Republican members, led by Senators Spooner and Beveridge, and the Democrats, led by Patterson, Carmack, and Culberson of Texas—a trio soon labeled the "syndicate of vituperation" by the opposition press.[22]

Thomas McDonald Patterson in 1902. (Courtesy Colorado Historical Society.)

The imperialists argued that expansion in the Far East held the key to solving a growing national surplus of investment capital. The minority Democrats, with Patterson and Carmack the leading spokesmen, challenged American commitment to imperialism on ideological grounds. They questioned witnesses who came before the committee about the propriety of American actions during the war, and during the insurrection and occupation that followed. The *Washington Post* observed that Patterson's arguments reflected sound preparation and were the most responsibly presented.[23]

Claude G. Bowers, biographer of Senator Beveridge, concluded that Tom Patterson performed as a vigorous and resourceful prosecutor when he and his allies cross-examined a distinguished list of witnesses regarding United States policy and the ruthless manner in which the Filipino insurrection had been quelled.[24] Patterson also became the chief spokesman for the minority members of the Philippine Committee in carrying the fight to the full Senate, where he and Teller jointly attacked United States policy and performance.[25]

On the Senate floor, Patterson pointed out the eventualities if the United States became involved in the Philippines on a permanent basis. He argued that either the Islands must become a territory and subsequently a state; otherwise, they would revert to anarchy, causing more armies to be sent to bring about complete subjugation. He strongly suggested that the Filipino resistance to American rule was well founded, declaring: "This country should be frank with the Filipinos. They should know whether they are intended for statehood . . . under the protection of the Constitution, or whether they are to resort to the last avenue that is open to those who aspire for liberty and love independence."[26] Concerned over newspaper reports that civil liberties were being denied the Filipinos, and having read disturbing communications from the Federal party of the Philippine Islands, Patterson challenged the authority of the Philippines Commission. He asserted that the commission had exceeded its power in trying Filipinos without worrying about such Constitutional safeguards as trial by jury.[27]

Noting that the commission's law followed old Spanish statutes rather than United States law, Patterson singled out a clause calling for punishment for "giving aid and comfort" to any person engaged in insurrection. Such a measure, he said, outlawed even "Good Samaritanism." Compared with commission law, he said, the sedition laws of 1798 were a "beacon light of liberty." He predicted that Filipinos would be prosecuted for mere offenses of the mind by some government satrap eight thousand miles from constitutional relief, and he suggested that the hangman's noose would be in "merry demand."[28]

During the debates, Senator Knute Nelson of Minnesota defended the administration's support for the Philippine Commission's actions. Inasmuch as Congress had not yet established *any* government in the Philippines, he argued, the commission was correct in acting as an agency of the executive department.[29]

Patterson became increasingly opposed to retaining the Philippines, under any circumstances. He and Carmack exploited every opportunity to expose the questionable results of the American occupation—such as the use of water torture by American troops and allegations of rape and violence directed toward helpless Filipinos. Patterson brought the results of the testimony taken in committee to the floor of the Senate, and he recounted the brutalities involved in the "pacification" of the islands.[30]

He complained that the capture of the rebel chief, Aguinaldo, had violated rules of war and international law, and he urged that Aguinaldo be asked to present his side of the case to the committee in person.[31] Patterson consistently defended the right of Filipinos to fight for their own independence, a position that once led to a heated exchange with General Arthur MacArthur. When MacArthur said that he had ordered one military thrust after he determined that friendly relations could not be restored, Tom Patterson suggested that the important result was the three thousand Filipinos killed or wounded. To which MacArthur testily replied, "Fortunately with the result that a great victory was won by the American Army."[32] Even with the appearance of MacArthur and Taft, Tom Patterson and Carmack repeatedly accused the Philippines Committee of refusing to summon many crucial witnesses.[33]

The *Denver Republican* insisted on calling both Patterson and Teller "modern copperheads," no better than those who had given aid and comfort to the enemy during the Civil War. It tried to promote mass meetings in Colorado to protest their "despicable" conduct.[34] The *Post,* archrival of Patterson's *Rocky Mountain News,* admitted that Democratic questioning had revealed information pointing out the outrageous use of "torture and torch" by elements of the American occupational forces.[35]

The *Post* went on to say, however, that Patterson's tendency to view everything with alarm caused Americans to appear to be a "dreadful and unholy" people; it advised him to "cheer up a bit."[36] Upon completion of a particularly vigorous interrogation of Admiral George Dewey by Patterson and Carmack, the *Washington Post* wryly observed that the two senators at least had not made Dewey seem contemptible for having defeated the Spanish fleet.[37]

As the witness bearing ultimate responsibility for occupational policy in the Philippine Islands, Secretary of War William Howard Taft received such sharp questioning that Senator Spooner accused Patterson of harming basic American interests and of adding to Taft's problems in the Philippines.[38] Taft himself, though depressed and irritated by the attitude of the Democratic members of the Philippines Committee,[39] maintained his composure and insisted that unfortunate events in the islands, such as incidents of cruelty, were isolated and did not represent United States policy toward the Filipinos.

At times tension ran high in the Philippines Committee meetings, and Patterson engaged in many sharp exchanges with fellow senators who opposed his views. When he accused Chairman Henry Cabot Lodge of Massachusetts of taking a menacing attitude toward a witness, Lodge responded, "No more than you in defense of him." Later Patterson privately expressed satisfaction over the exchange, having "talked back" to the powerful Lodge on this and other occasions.[40] Arthur Johnson observed that Patterson was camping hard on the trail of the Republicans; he believed that a number of them felt sorry Patterson had ever been appointed to the Philippines Committee.[41]

Republican Senator Foraker tried to embarrass and discredit Patterson on the floor of the Senate by charging that he was inconsistent and insincere in his anti-imperialistic beliefs. Quoting editorials from the *Rocky Mountain News,* Foraker asserted that Patterson had not always spoken for independence for the Philippines.[42] Knowing in advance of Foraker's plan to embarrass him, Patterson carefully prepared his rebuttal.[43]

The *News,* under his direction, had indeed reversed its position as of December 1898, because of the way in which the United States had acted after taking control of the islands. The shift, he explained, represented a change of honest conviction, not of political expediency. He noted that the policy change had occurred immediately after the November elections of 1898 and thus could not be attributed to campaign rhetoric. Moreover, it represented no bid for patronage benefits, as no Democrat was president.[44] He charged that the government had misrepresented what was actually happening in the Far East by implying that the Filipinos were yearning for the care and protection of the American nation, and he quoted at length from *News* editorials explaining his reversal of position.

Tom Patterson also noted that Foraker himself had shifted from his original position of advocating only temporary control of the islands.[45] With support from Senators Teller, Carmack, and Hoar, Patterson strongly denounced the proposed Civil Government bill for the Philippines and stressed his fear of corporate influence in the Islands. He argued that the bill was simply a scheme to facilitate exploitation of the area by American capital, and he indicated that if the Filipinos ever did achieve independence the Islands would be simply "a sucked orange."[46] In response to a challenge by Senator Dietrich that the rebel leader, Aguinaldo, had promised up to fifteen thousand acres of land to his future cabinet members although the Civil Government bill allowed only twenty-five hundred acres to each U.S. corporation, Patterson argued that the twenty-five hundred acres would mark only the first step to much larger consolidations by U.S. investors.[47]

In addition to objecting to provisions in the bill concerning landholdings, Patterson also attacked the sections of the bill providing for a legislature, judiciary, and for educational curriculum. Popular assembly would be impossible, said Patterson, and there could be no appeal in the Philippines from a decision of a United States court. Furthermore, although the Filipinos would be paying taxes for the support of schools, they would have no part in determining what should be taught. He feared that compulsory teaching of English might crush out native languages, a "cruel" consequence of U.S. policy.[48]

Patterson's position as an anti-imperialist revealed the strain of racism that ran through the arguments of both expansionists and anti-imperialists. He apparently shared the views on the races characteristic of his time, asserting that no amount of assimilation could ever bring the Anglo-Saxon and the Filipino to a plane of equality.[49] Though Tom Patterson would battle to secure legal rights for oppressed peoples, he was not necessarily disposed to accept them as political equals. His hopes for the freedom of the Philippines may possibly have been influenced by a reluctance to see the islands of brown-skinned people elevated to American statehood.[50]

Patterson's voting record on the Philippine Civil Government bill consistently matched the anti-imperialist tone of his speeches, as was true also for Carmack, Tillman, Culberson, Dubois, and Teller. His own amendment to repeal the Sedition Act lost by a vote of 47 to 28. He supported Teller's two amendments that would have extended constitutional law to the islands and let the world know of America's intention to deprive the Philippines of liberty and self-government. Both failed by a margin of two to one. The Coloradans secured a minor victory in a close 38 to 34 vote, ensuring that no immediate relative of an insurrectionist could be punished for failing to give information against his kinsman. When Patterson and his allies opposed the bill in its final form, however, they lost by 45 to 26.[51]

The evidence seems clear that Patterson and Teller—supported primarily by Carmack, Culberson, and Hoar—attacked nearly every provision of the proposed legislation for civil government in the Philippines. Patterson feared that even temporary occupation of the Islands would inevitably lead to permanent occupation as the economic stakes became more pronounced. Basing his argument essentially on inherent dangers to the freedom and rights of the Filipinos, he stressed the traditional American commitment to the democratic principles of self-determination.

In a time of feverish commercial enterprise, he believed that all interests except those of a materialistic nature would be obliterated. He knew his position was not popular in Colorado. The *Denver Post* claimed that Patterson's stand varied so greatly from public sentiment that his party would certainly suffer for it in the November elections.[52] Though he realized the anti-imperialist cause was doomed, he held to his position.

Still, he succeeded in causing many embarrassing moments for the defenders of imperialism. His primary accomplishment lay in helping lodge a protest, in raising moral questions, and in reminding a changing society to remember its founding principles. According to two historians, such anti-imperialist attacks on exploitative economics and defense of civil rights for Filipinos helped keep alive the cause of Philippine independence.[53]

Patterson also succeeded in attracting marked attention as one of the chief spokesmen of the anti-imperialists. Senator Beveridge observed that not even Holy Writ could sway the senator from Colorado and those "who follow in his wake."[54] The *Denver Post* complained that because of his apparent leadership, Patterson had become saturated with his own importance.[55] During the summer of 1902, while vacationing in Colorado, Beveridge invited Carmack to join him, facetiously pointing out that, while in Colorado, Carmack could also see Patterson and plan "more diabolical schemes against us on the Philippines Committee."[56] Instead, convinced that he could accomplish nothing more by his presence on the Philippines Committee, Patterson transferred to the Committee on the Judiciary for the next session of Congress.[57]

In 1904 both Colorado senators renewed their attack on administration foreign policy when President Roosevelt orchestrated his famous "seizure" of Panama from Columbia. Once again, Patterson and Teller were in the minority.[58] The country still burst with enthusiasm for imperialistic adventure, and constituents were pressuring their senators, of both parties, to ratify the Panama Treaty. Patterson had so little popular support in the matter of Panama, suggested the *Denver Post,* that if recall were available he would be removed from office.[59]

Spirited debates concerning the justice and morality of the administration's actions occupied the Senate during much of January 1904. The bulk of the criticism was presented by the Coloradans and Senator Bailey. Against them were the formidable Senators Lodge, Platt, Fairbanks, and Spooner. After Teller had destroyed Lodge's defense of the legality of Roosevelt's action, clearly exposing it as an act of aggression, Patterson engaged administration apologists on nearly every major point. Roosevelt, he said, had abandoned Nicaragua, flouted Colombia, revolutionized Panama, abetted a secession movement, and negotiated an agreement with a "mushroom" republic.[60] The *Washington Post* commented that the fencing between Patterson and Spooner was particularly entertaining.[61]

When Senator Spooner tried to use the Treaty of 1846 with Colombia as the legal basis for United States intervention in Colombian affairs, Patterson countered with a well-documented rebuttal, stating that no violations of the treaty had occurred that warranted U.S. action. Quoting previous government figures, he illustrated how Roosevelt had deviated from past interpretation of the treaty.[62]

Senator Fairbanks challenged Patterson's assertion that the United States had tried to bully the Colombian Congress into accepting the Hay-Herran Treaty. In answer, Patterson quoted from a communication from Secretary of State John Hay to the Colombian Congress that contained an obvious threat: "If Colombia should now reject the treaty or unduly delay its ratification, the friendly understanding between the two countries would be so seriously compromised that action might be taken . . . next winter which every friend of Colombia would regret."[63]

Colombia, argued Patterson, had every right to resent coercion by the rich and strong; rejection of the treaty could be traced to the deliberate threats of the United States. In an exchange over whether the United States had been hasty in recognizing the New Panama Canal Company's secessionist government, Patterson provoked the blunt statement from Senator Dolliver that ancient rules of recognition must give way to the desires of the United States government.[64]

Patterson's arguments triggered lengthy rebuttals from both Spooner and Platt, the latter once growing so exasperated that he sarcastically suggested that perhaps Patterson might want the United States to assist Colombia in recapturing Panama. In another exchange, when Spooner and Platt described the United States as the trustee for the commercial nations of the world and the agent of civilization, Patterson, incensed, answered that "civilization means respect for law and obligation of duty, not coveting another country's territory."[65]

Noting that the president had boldly announced his intention to steal Panama or take it by sheer force, Patterson indicted those senators who had supported the administration's power play. In their hearts they knew that the United States had been both legally and morally wrong, he said, and he offered as proof a suggestion by Senator Hale that compensation be paid to Colombia for the loss of territory.[66] At home, the *Denver Post* editorialized that Patterson had reached his pinnacle by calling the president a cold-blooded, deliberate thief.[67] When Senator Platt accused him of impeaching the integrity of the president and Congress, Patterson responded that it was quite proper to question both the president and the Congress, especially in the latter's collective capacity.[68]

However able, the arguments by Patterson and Teller—just as in the case of the Philippines—stood no chance of changing the outcome of the vote ratifying the treaty with Panama. Supported during the debates primarily by Carmack, Tillman, and John T. Morgan of Alabama, the Coloradans argued well, but the opposition had the votes.

Patterson and Platt dominated the debate. Even granting that the United States somehow might be in the wrong, said Platt, the fact remained that Panama was ready to negotiate with the United States, the trustee of the world who accomplished the great work of building a canal in the interests of commerce, civilization, and peace.[69] Patterson's views, Platt maintained, did not represent the desires of the American people. In their fight against the final ratification of the treaty, Patterson, Teller, and their allies went down to a 66 to 14 defeat.[70]

Thus, during Roosevelt's first term, Patterson and his small group performed their role of dissent, questioning the actions of the majority but having no success in defeating foreign policy they viewed as unjust and unwise. Patterson later said that a senator with a minority view soon realized he was some sort of vermiform appendix with no particular function to perform, except to "irritate the body of which he is a part."[71] He did not believe that his positions in foreign affairs would ever be vindicated.

13
Maverick and Progressive

Senator Patterson is a curious man. . . . He is a man of very decided ability, but he is quite uncertain and you never know where he is coming from.

— William Howard Taft to Helen Taft
September 23, 1905

Senator Thomas Patterson spent his first years in office opposing the foreign policy of President Theodore Roosevelt. By 1904 he had also come to deplore the rise of conservative elements in the Democratic party. An ardent supporter of William Jennings Bryan since 1896, Patterson feared that reform elements in the Democratic party might be permanently displaced by those like the presidential nominee, Alton B. Parker, who were supported by the trusts and big money.[1] Uncomfortable with his own party's leadership, Patterson, at least for a time, believed that on domestic issues Roosevelt intended to move the country rapidly toward Bryanesque reforms,[2] a belief probably nurtured by his developing personal friendship with William Howard Taft.

In March of 1904 Taft wrote Patterson concerning a legislative proposal that would continue the American presence in the Philippine Islands. He sought Patterson's support for the measure. Failing that, he hoped that the Colorado senator would not try to prevent the matter from coming to a vote.[3] Patterson promised to discuss Taft's request with his former colleagues of the Committee on the Philippine Islands, and stated that it had been Taft's efforts to protect Filipinos from American exploitation in the areas of land-ownership and employment that had caused him to qualify his negative view of the occupation. Emphasizing that it was only a *feeling,* not a *conviction,* Patterson now inclined toward temporary control—as long as the Filipino might learn to be a proprietor and not a "peon of avaricious Americans." He went on to say that he still regarded Taft as committed to permanent retention and assumed that large American investors in the Islands would inevitably force the anti-imperialists from the field.[4]

Patterson spoke very little during the debates on measures affecting the Philippines. He showed none of his aggressive activity of 1902, stating simply that he regretted the retention of the Philippines and had no doubt they would be retained permanently.[5] During the following session, Patterson missed the final vote on the bill to extend the American presence in the Islands.

In 1905 Patterson accepted Taft's invitation to participate in an inspection tour of the Philippine Islands. The large traveling party included seven senators and twenty-four representatives of both political parties and their wives. It was apparently during this ten-week trip that the personal friendship between Taft and Patterson developed. On the return voyage, Taft wrote a thirty-three page letter to his wife in which he described all the passengers, including the Colorado senator:

> Senator Patterson is a curious man. . . . [H]e conducted the cross-examination of me when I came home from the Philippines the first time and abused me afterwards on the floor of the Senate for misrepresenting conditions in the Philippines though he afterwards apologized somewhat. . . . He is a man of very decided ability, but he is quite uncertain and you never know where he is coming from. Personally, and on such a trip as this, he is a pleasant member, and he it was I think who influenced the other Democrats into saying nothing that would interfere with the pleasant tenor of our ways through the Philippines.[6]

Following the trip to the Far East, Patterson sent clippings of editorials from the *Rocky Mountain News* to Taft, who responded with appreciation for Patterson's "kindly expressions" about a political opponent.[7] By 1906 Taft made a practice of forwarding Patterson's letters to Roosevelt in order to help enlighten the president on the political situation in Colorado.[8]

After Taft visited Denver in 1907, he expressed pleasure over his fair treatment by Patterson's newspapers and referred directly to the Philippine trip as the origin of their friendship.[9] According to Patterson's newspaper associate, Edward Keating, the two men maintained a warm and lasting friendship even though they agreed on virtually nothing.[10]

When Taft secured the Republican nomination in 1908, Patterson, although his political allegiance remained with William Jennings Bryan,

President Theodore Roosevelt. (Courtesy Colorado Historical Society.)

approved, saying: "If we must have a Republican in the White House for the next four years, I want to see you there above all others. I like you immensely and I honestly believe you will add luster to the office of Washington, Jefferson, Jackson, Lincoln, and Roosevelt."[11]

Shortly after becoming president, Taft again visited Denver. When the Republican-dominated chamber of commerce omitted Patterson from the reception committee, Taft made a special point of posing with him for photographers.[12] At least until 1908, Patterson seems to have viewed Taft (who was handpicked by Theodore Roosevelt to be his successor) as representing reform-minded elements in the Republican party. He greatly admired Taft for his humane and judicious direction of the American occupation of the Philippines.

By 1905 Roosevelt, by virtue of his actions in domestic politics, had also become more acceptable to Patterson. The president had intervened in the anthracite coal strike, revitalized the Sherman Antitrust Act with the Northern Securities case, and increased his pressure for regulation of the railroads.[13] It was during this time that the Dominican Republic, its finances in chaos, asked

Roosevelt to establish some kind of protectorate over the island to save it from its European creditors. The president responded by signing a protocol with the Caribbean country to supervise its revenues. Senator Teller immediately challenged the administration's right to take such action, with the result that the protocol came before the Senate for ratification. Because some members of the Republican majority resented Roosevelt's efforts to bypass the Senate, the verdict was very much in doubt. To pass, the protocol needed just four Democratic votes.[14]

On January 31, 1906, Patterson delivered a speech that astounded the Senate and left his Democratic colleagues in a rage.[15] While reserving the right to disagree with the president when he was wrong, Patterson praised him for earnestly maintaining the rights of the people against certain wealthy classes and for championing railroad legislation. He doubted that the Democratic candidate for president in 1904, had he been elected, would have shown such enthusiasm for the common people.[16]

Proclaiming faith in the president's patriotism and sincerity, the Colorado senator asserted that, while he had disagreed with previous administration foreign policy, this time Roosevelt was right and deserved support for the proposed protocol. Arguing that Santo Domingo had asked for help without having been coerced in any way, Patterson declared that the Monroe Doctrine should not become a party issue. To avoid the establishment of a foothold in the Western Hemisphere by European countries, it was imperative to help Santo Domingo meet its financial obligations.[17] He not only endorsed the Roosevelt Corollary but also praised the president's actions in domestic matters, comparing him favorably to the patron saint of the party, Andrew Jackson.[18]

No one rose either to challenge or support Patterson's remarks. According to the *Washington Post,* the Republicans were too "benumbed with joy to congratulate him" and the Democrats too "paralyzed with anger."[19] But his Democratic colleagues swiftly recovered and called a caucus to deal with his heresy. Republican John C. Spooner, in describing the purpose of the caucus, noted that the depth of the Democratic anger might lead to Tom Patterson's exclusion from "Democratic society." It was a "sinister and ugly" thing for any party to begin to caucus on foreign relations of this sort, he added, and he predicted that Patterson might possibly carry other Democrats with him.[20] So great was their concern that the Democrats specifically assigned Senators Joseph W. Bailey, Thomas S. Martin, and Asbury C. Latimer to prevent additional defectors.[21] The *New York Times* declared that Patterson's stand might save the proposed treaty with the Dominican Republic.[22]

The Democratic caucus reaffirmed its rule that if two-thirds of its number voted in favor of a specific stand on an issue, it was the duty of *every* Democratic senator to vote in accordance with the view of the majority.[23] Patterson left the caucus before the vote; all but four Democrats agreed with the rebuke against him. Thoroughly aroused, Patterson promptly presented an anti-caucus resolution to the full Senate on February 5, 1906. Arguing that the caucus violated the Constitution by coercing senators to disregard their oaths to faithfully discharge their duties, he declared that forcing him to vote against his convictions disenfranchised his state in the Senate.[24]

Referring to his earlier favorable comments about Roosevelt, Patterson further irritated his colleagues by adding that he only hoped the next Democratic convention might select a candidate who would win, by his character and good works, "the tremendous popular majority that was accorded to Theodore Roosevelt."[25] Senator Benjamin Tillman interrupted him "with a snarl," reported the *Washington Post*.[26] Patterson had thrown another bomb in the Senate. Private remarks by some Democrats concerning the Coloradan could not be reproduced in print.[27]

On February 7 the aisles of the Senate gallery bulged with visitors to witness a spectacular four-hour battle of words and ideas between Patterson and Democratic party leader Joseph Bailey of Texas.[28] The *Washington Post* judged Bailey the winner, with his "philippics" against all senators who defied party discipline.[29] Only when his old ally from the Committee on the Philippines, Charles A. Culberson, reminded him that two years earlier Patterson himself had voted for the binding rule did Patterson flush with anger. Later, the *Denver Republican* reminded him of his own caucus efforts to maintain Democratic solidarity in the Colorado legislature in order to get Teller re-elected to the Senate in 1903.[30]

During the debate Bailey described Patterson as an honest man, although an emotional one who persisted in error.[31] The Colorado senator, conceded the *Washington Post,* impressed the audience with his earnest argument that he was responsible to his own conscience and sense of duty.[32] Patterson refuted the charges of the Eastern press that he had been bought off by the administration with a promise of patronage control,[33] pointing out that his one patronage request in five years, a Philippine chaplaincy for a young Denver Episcopalian minister, had been denied.[34]

A more serious speculation centered on the possibility that Patterson planned to leave the Democratic party for the Republicans in order to secure re-election to the Senate with Roosevelt's support.[35] The *Washington Post* even published a front-page cartoon showing the GOP elephant pulling Patterson from his Democratic bed; he was labeled a "White House" Democrat. Back home, the *Denver Republican* implied that Patterson was receiving private encouragement from insurgent Republicans.[36]

Patterson's earlier bolt from the Democrats to the Populists seemed to give credence to this theory. But Tom declared that if his party chose to excommunicate him for his actions, he would bear it calmly and would remain a Democrat in the Senate, in Colorado, in national conventions, and in local councils. The *Denver Post* predicted that talk of reading Patterson out of the party would not alarm the senator, inasmuch as he had been "one of the fixed numbers on the programs at all political meetings in Colorado for the last quarter of a century."[37] The *Washington Evening Star* ridiculed the idea that Roosevelt could help re-elect Patterson in the "maze" of Colorado politics. Rather than accuse the Colorado senator of seeking political advantage, wrote the *Star,* an unbiased observer would applaud Patterson for his courage in submitting himself to such accusations in an age when nearly everyone was expected to place personal interests above those of either party or country.[38]

Years later, in retirement, Tom wrote to his nephew and former secretary, Arthur Johnson, that he was more convinced than ever that the caucus was a relic of the days when free talk and independent votes were crimes. He said that the two Colorado men who were serving in the Senate at the time—John Shafroth and his old friend and law partner, Charles Thomas—worried him. Shafroth permitted himself to be submerged in the caucus and Thomas had already sold out for social "blandishments" that accounted for his "ordinary" partisan virtue.[39]

Meanwhile, the Santo Domingo protocol failed when only one of Patterson's colleagues supported it.[40] But Roosevelt pursued its terms under executive prerogative, and a somewhat modified version was approved in the following session of Congress.[41] Patterson's anti-caucus resolution never reached the voting stage.

Throughout his career, Patterson showed a consistency in support of causes and philosophies he valued that outshone his apparent instability in regard to political party. His dedication to the cause of labor and the rights of the common man, and his intractable opposition to abuse of economic and political power by combinations of wealth, charted his course. These principles explain his bolt to the Populists, his efforts on behalf of fusion politics in Colorado, his return to the Democratic party upon Bryan's ascendancy, and his restlessness with the Democrats when the conservative elements nominated Parker in 1904.

Tom Patterson tended to use whatever political vehicle appeared to offer the best opportunity to advance his reform ideas, ideas that clearly had their roots in Populism and Bryanism. Even during the caucus fight, the *Washington Post* suggested that it was difficult to determine just how much of the opposition to Senator Patterson among his colleagues resulted from his admission that he was a Bryan-style Democrat.[42] It was the reform aspect of Roosevelt's presidency, not the Republican party or the president himself, that briefly attracted Patterson's support. And when the Bryanesque reforms of the administration remained unfulfilled and Bryan became a strong Democratic candidate for the presidency in the 1908 election, Patterson's enthusiasm for Roosevelt faded.

In his acceptance speech before the Colorado legislature as senator-elect in 1901, Patterson had devoted most of his time to a broad attack on the trusts.[43] While in the Senate he regularly challenged legislation that he regarded as adding to the power of large combinations of wealth, and he supported measures to expose their operations. In only his second vote in the Senate, Patterson had supported a measure requiring corporations to report their receipts, capital, wages, taxes, surpluses, and expenses each year. The measure lost by a vote of 31 to 17.[44]

During the Fifty-seventh Congress, Patterson criticized the practice of giving government subsidies to large shipping lines. He consistently supported amendments that would have brought government regulation to vessels operating with government money. When they failed, he voted against the Senate version of a ship subsidy bill, though it passed by a 42 to 31 vote.[45] The votes generally followed party lines, with Patterson voting in the company of such Democrats as Edward W. Carmack, Charles A. Culberson, Fred T. Dubois, Joseph W. Bailey, Augustus O. Bacon, and Patterson's colleague, Teller. The opposition included such leaders of the Republican majority as Nelson W. Aldrich, Albert J. Beveridge, Marcus A. Hanna, and Orville H. Platt.[46] The measure went to the House where, thanks to opposition from the South and the West, it was killed.[47]

But in 1906 the issue re-emerged, with Patterson arguing that the statute books unnecessarily "bristled with favors to the shipping trade" and complaining that the shipping industry constituted the most persistent and successful lobby ever gathered in Washington.[48] Despite Senator Robert M. LaFollette's leading a bolt by five Republicans and the unanimous opposition of the Democrats, the new bill calling for subsidies passed by a vote of 38 to 27.[49]

Patterson's activities in support of government regulation of railroads during his first years in the Senate were inconsequential.[50] But after Roosevelt's election in 1904, apparently convinced that he had misjudged the degree of the president's commitment to reform legislation, Patterson spent the next two years energetically supporting efforts to secure effective regulation. Roosevelt recognized him as an ally, and, on the occasion of a 1905 hunting party in Colorado, Roosevelt accepted a Denver Chamber of Commerce banquet invitation with the proviso that the chamber designate Patterson as host.[51] When the president returned to Washington and Patterson wrote him a note expressing discouragement, Roosevelt replied, "I can not help feeling, in spite of the apparent progress made (by the railroads) in the fight against governmental regulation of the rate-making power, that we shall win out all right."[52]

In 1906 the contest over railroad regulation emerged as a struggle between broad versus narrow court review of rate decisions by the Interstate Commerce Commission. Broad review advocates, generally the Old Guard Republicans, tried to prevent effective rate regulation by seeking legislation that would allow conservative federal courts to first suspend and later reverse the rates set by the ICC. If the ICC declared a rate extortionate, the court injunction could restore the extortionate rate until the case had been settled in court. Those Democrats and Republicans favoring narrow review, encouraged in the beginning by Roosevelt, worked for a law to permit as little interference with the ICC as was constitutionally possible.[53] Both Colorado senators argued for the narrow view. Teller defended the legality of forbidding the courts from issuing injunctions to suspend rates set by the ICC.[54]

Patterson not only supported Teller but went so far as to advocate making a test case for the Supreme Court by passing a law expressly forbidding temporary injunctions.[55] His most extreme suggestion urged turning the ICC itself into an interstate commerce *court,* since the ICC had mostly judicial powers and responsibilities anyway. Such a move, he argued, would prevent the delaying tactics used by corporations to evade ICC rulings.[56] As early as 1886 Patterson had argued that railroads were not purely private enterprises but were really public in nature and existed solely for public purposes. At that

FROM THE *TAFT* BERTH-EN ROUTE-: *"I DON'T SEE ANYTHING HERE SHOWIN' HOW HE DID IT!"*

Cartoon of President William Howard Taft, *Denver Post,* September 16, 1911.
(Courtesy Colorado Historical Society.)

time, he had called for legislation at the state level to attack rebates, pooling, and exorbitant rates. He suggested forfeiture of franchises and endorsed the concept of a railroad commission empowered to set limits on rates.[57]

As a senator, Patterson strongly feared the growing tendency of trusts to develop in the direction of vertical mergers. When Republican Senator

Robert M. LaFollette offered a proposal to prevent railroads from gaining control over coalfields, Patterson presented suggestions on how to close loopholes in the proposal. Denouncing centralization tendencies on the part of any industry, Patterson criticized "omissions" in proposals that failed to prohibit railroads from owning, mining, and selling coal in competition with other shippers.[58]

Along with several of his colleagues, including LaFollette, Tom condemned the complimentary railroad pass as a device designed to undermine the independence of politicians, and he suggested that until the "pernicious system" could be eliminated railroads submit a yearly list of recipients of passes to the ICC.[59]

After working for a time with the reform elements in Congress, Roosevelt eventually accepted a compromise policy that restored enough Republican harmony in the Senate to pass the Hepburn Act. That act proposed giving the ICC effective power for the first time since it was created in 1887. Although not everything the reformers had hoped for, the legislation still represented a substantial advance in railroad legislation. Missing from the final bill was LaFollette's idea of evaluating the physical properties of railroads for use in determining rates. But the act did authorize the ICC to prescribe maximum rates and to order conformity within thirty days; although the railroads could appeal, the burden of proof was on the carrier, not the ICC. Free passes were prohibited, and the railways would have to give up most of the steamship lines and coal mines they had purchased to stifle competition.[60]

Patterson missed the debates and several important votes during May of 1906. His enemies in Colorado seized upon his absence from the Senate as evidence that he lacked sincerity in his reform position.[61] In fact, he had returned to Denver at this time because of an extremely critical election involving corporate influence in Denver's municipal government, an issue he had fought against for years. He returned in time to join LaFollette in an effort to prevent changes in the wording of the conference report that would have weakened the act, and he participated in the voice vote that approved the final report. In another matter similarly strengthening government regulation, Patterson voted with an overwhelming majority to pass the Pure Food and Drug Act.[62]

Indicators had appeared earlier in Patterson's term that he might eventually favor far more than mere regulation of railroads. In 1905 he had spoken in favor of government ownership of the Panama railroad, and he had hinted at using the line as a "yardstick" by which to measure the honesty of other railroads.[63] In the following year, 1906, he predicted that because of the general corruption of private utility companies, municipal ownership of the utilities was the wave of the future. He cited a study of municipal ownership in England and discussed the benefits of such an arrangement. He also detailed the fight against the "insidious" political power of the utility companies and railroads in Denver, and he called for taxation of utilities and corporations based on property values.[64] He opposed the national government's giving franchises in general, since Congress thus would be taking away the property of the people. He objected to a charter being granted for completion of the Lake Erie and Ohio River canal as being in the interests of United States Steel; he said that while he was not advocating public ownership of the canal, the country would get to that point eventually all by itself.[65]

Yet Patterson refused to regard himself as a socialist. At no time did he call for the general abolition of private enterprise. He argued that the Republican policy itself provoked socialism by forcing those opposed to private monopoly to turn to government monopoly, a viewpoint given publicity by William Jennings Bryan in 1906.[66]

During the election campaign of 1906, the *Washington Post* accused the Colorado senator of disrupting the Democratic party by going "far ahead of even Mr. Bryan on the subject of government ownership of railroads."[67] On February 12, 1907, Tom Patterson introduced Senate Bill 8436, which provided for the acquisition, purchase, construction, and condemnation of all railroads engaged in interstate commerce, and for their subsequent operation by the government.[68]

To make certain that the Senate did not misinterpret his position, Patterson declared that he realized he would have no success with his proposal. Rather it was his hope to do what he could to speed up the mobilization of public opinion. He asserted that he had arrived at this position because, in spite of remedial legislation, the railroads had increased in power, aggressiveness, and indifference to public rights.

Constitutionally, according to Patterson, the railroads exercised a function of government in developing public highways. He proposed fair compensation for owners of transportation systems, with financing for this purpose to be achieved through the issuance of government bonds. He predicted benefits from nationalization in reduced freight and passenger rates, increased safety for passengers and workmen, fair women's compensation, insurance and pension systems for employees, orderly construction, more efficient service, and above all the eradication from public life of political pressure by the railroads.[69] No one rose to contend with such a radical proposal. By 1907 Patterson had concluded that, in the case of those great industrial enterprises directly affecting the public good, government regulation alone could not equal the potential for fairness possible through public ownership.

Patterson had long regarded high protective tariffs as one of the deplorable methods by which great combinations of wealth increased their power. And yet when sectional interests collided with his views on the tariff, he placed the needs of Colorado first. Speaking at the Transmississippi Congress in 1901, he called for protection for Colorado's "infant" beet sugar industry, causing Congressman Chester I. Long of Kansas to congratulate him on his switch to Republican tariff principles.[70]

In the Senate, Patterson opposed reciprocity proposals involving Cuba and the Philippine Islands, arguing in each case that the sugar trust intended to stifle domestic sugar growers. When the Philippine Revenue Bill proposed just such a reduction of duties, he predicted that the local sugar industries of the United States would be wiped out within ten years if the measure were adopted. Speaking against lowering the tariff on Cuban sugar, Patterson argued that cheap labor in Cuba would lead to cheap sugar and thereby destroy American beet and cane sugar growers in the West and South.[71]

Senator Albert Beveridge, claiming inconsistencies in Patterson's tariff views, challenged the Colorado senator to clarify his position. Patterson replied that as long as protection was the controlling economic philosophy of the country, he would stand for protection of products from his section, no matter what his beliefs were on tariffs in general.[72]

Patterson grew irritated whenever his opponents cloaked their profit motives in a professed desire to bring relief to the suffering workers in Cuba and the Philippines.[73] During an exchange with Senator Nelson Aldrich over the beet industry of Colorado, Patterson drew a distinction between a tariff protecting agricultural products, having a low profit margin and a high risk factor, and those tariffs that offered a refuge to every trust and monopoly.[74]

When he pinned the motive of greed on the sugar refiners and on the speculators in foreign plantations, he saw no conflict between that economic philosophy and his sectional interest. Considering the growing importance of the sugar beet industry in Colorado to workers and investors alike, Tom Patterson's stand was largely the result of responsibility to his constituents.

But even Roosevelt's insistence on a reduction of duties on Cuban and Philippine goods could not save the Philippine bill from defeat, though the

Cuban bill, which called for only a minor reduction, finally did pass in 1903. Patterson voted against the Philippine bill and was absent from the 1903 Cuban vote.[75]

Whatever goodwill Patterson held for Roosevelt eroded badly on another sectional issue. Under Roosevelt's direction, the administration sought to encourage a planned land system in the West. The issue had been a running battle for decades.

Historian G. Michael McCarthy has noted the irony and tragedy of the conflict. Anticonservationists failed to believe or understand the motives of the progressive conservationists. The Westerners feared that the leasing of public lands for grazing or timber rights would lead to increased control by combines and corporations, rather than helping local settlers, who had little money and even less influence. In the view of conservationists, opposition to their plans came only from "land sharks and timber thieves."[76]

The planners were more concerned with resource use than resource ownership, more interested in prevention of waste than prevention of monopoly. Big operations wanted to stabilize their investments with efficiency; not so the small farmers, miners, and stockmen. That pioneer class viewed conservation as only another instrument of big business. While Gifford Pinchot and Theodore Roosevelt talked of helping the little man, they proposed locking up the lands the little man needed to live on. In sum, the anticonservationists accused the planners of talking democracy while taking away pioneers' rights.[77]

Even before Patterson became a senator, his *Rocky Mountain News* had angrily attacked leasing proposals, arguing that the great corporations were doing their best "to drive small herd owners out of business" and demanding that "until the public lands are purchased by actual settlers, they must be kept free and open to all."[78]

Both Patterson and Teller reacted strongly to Roosevelt's expansion of forest reserves to include more than one-fifth of the total area of Colorado.[79] When Senator John Spooner accused Patterson of seeking to destroy forest reservations, the Colorado senator replied that no Westerner with any common sense wanted his forest land denuded, considering the damage it would do to flood control.

Patterson agreed that legitimate forest land should be preserved, but he accused the Forestry Service, under Gifford Pinchot's direction, of impinging on good agricultural land.[80] The net effect, he predicted, would be that as more and more of a state's undeveloped territory was removed from possible settlement, its population growth and economic development would be limited.

He also fought with Roosevelt over the administration's practice of granting licenses for grazing rights on government-owned timberlands. That, he said, had in practice closed those areas to homesteading because home seekers feared the hostility of sheepmen and cattlemen. He also protested against the practice of fencing government property because it helped cattle barons cut out smaller cattlemen.[81] In a letter to Patterson, the president argued that the money collected from grazing fees would serve conservation purposes by perpetually keeping forest and grazing reserves in good shape. But he also promised that serious efforts would be made to guard the interests of the small stockgrower and ranchman.[82]

A Colorado delegation sought an audience with the president to discuss the fees, and they selected Patterson, their most articulate spokesman, to present their case. But Roosevelt rejected their argument that such a grazing fee constituted an "intolerable usurpation of power."[83] When Teller fell ill in 1907, Patterson assumed leadership of the unsuccessful opposition to the Pinchot-Roosevelt conservation proposals. Perhaps in frustration over his failures, the Coloradan attempted to block an increase in Pinchot's salary, saying that the forestry chief was riding his "hobby" to a fall. Pinchot got his raise and Patterson had to be content with making his point about the evils of federal interference in the lives and affairs of Colorado's small ranchers and farmers.[84]

Teller and Patterson criticized the manner in which existing forest reserves were being administered, and Patterson attacked the "audacity" of the Forestry Service in its "invasion of the states,"[85] a charge that would become the chief weapon used by the *Rocky Mountain News* against the Republican administration during the election of 1908.[86]

In all phases of the conservation struggle, Patterson appears to have regarded himself as a modern-day Horatius at the bridge, steadfastly refusing to abandon his sectional interests. There is no reason to believe that he condoned the ravages and exploitation of the land, which occasionally did occur. His motive was clear. He fought not to gain power for greedy large operators but to preserve and protect the opportunities of the smaller members of his constituency.

Still another issue involving the West concerned efforts to elevate Oklahoma, New Mexico, and Arizona to statehood. Suspicious of the Democratic leanings of the territories, Republicans, led by Senators Beveridge and

Aldrich, feared that their admission might upset the balance of power in the Senate.[87] In 1903 a bitter fight to admit all three territories ended when Aldrich displaced the statehood bill just before the end of the session with his banking bill. In retaliation, Patterson joined Senators Teller, Bailey, and Carmack in a successful filibuster against the banking bill.[88]

When the issue rose again in 1905, Patterson opposed attempts to graft Arizona onto New Mexico. Attacking the idea that the size of Arizona's voting population was borderline, he suggested allowing women to vote for members of the territorial convention and for ratification of the constitution.[89] The next year, in a sharp debate with Beveridge, Patterson developed strong historical and geographical arguments for the admission of New Mexico and Arizona as separate states, and he pushed Beveridge into a position of denying the importance of local sentiment for statehood in the territories. Ultimately, Tom Patterson helped bring statehood to Oklahoma, but Arizona rejected joint entry with New Mexico.[90]

With the Indian problem no longer a threat to his constituents, Patterson's interest in that issue reflected some of the humanitarian concern of his views in the 1870s. He concentrated on the obligation of the federal government to make the full payments to the Indians called for under existing treaties. He condemned the practice of certain lawyers who bilked the Indians with unreasonably high fees, and he succeeded in having some fees reduced.[91] He also introduced an amendment for Teller, who was ill, that would grant citizenship to Native Americans.[92]

Patterson's strong commitment to labor explains the racism that appeared when he spoke on immigration policy. He clearly shared the American workers' horror of competition from cheap foreign labor, and he claimed to speak for organized labor in general—and specifically for the American Federation of Labor and the International Seaman's Union of America.[93]

Attacking corporations for attempts to bypass American labor, he pitched most of his complaints in racist terms. Perhaps his strongest language occurred when, in denouncing shipping interests for replacing American laborers with Chinese on board merchant vessels, he said: "If our flag is to be raised at the mast-heads of ships manned by a yellow-skinned, white-livered peon race, then it is better that our flag be taken down and cleansed."[94] His words should be measured in the tone of the general anti-oriental bias of an age in which the *New York Times* applauded restrictions placed on the "unwelcome Chinks."[95]

On the other hand, during debate on Roosevelt's action in dismissing three companies of black infantry after the Brownsville, Texas, uprising, Patterson criticized Senator Tillman for his prejudice, goading the South Carolina senator into a fiery speech on the race problem in the South. When Patterson noted that poll taxes and grandfather clauses in the South hurt the Democratic cause in the North, Tillman replied, "As long as the Negroes continue to ravish white women we will continue to lynch them."[96]

Patterson not only complained that the black was disenfranchised in the South but also took Northern senators to task for not appointing more blacks to office.[97] Representing a state with a small number of blacks, Patterson undoubtedly had little opportunity to appoint blacks to office, nor is there evidence that he ever did so. His seeming sensitivity to the rights of minority groups and oppressed foreign elements, however, was paternal in nature, with no indication that he ever faced up to the issue of accepting them as social equals.[98]

The year 1907 marked the end of Patterson's term. It is difficult to imagine a politician with Patterson's ambition abandoning efforts to achieve re-election to the Senate, especially inasmuch as the movement for progressive reform seemed to be gaining momentum just as his term expired. But with bimetallism no longer an issue, he realized that the fusion base that put him into office had eroded. As early as 1904, he had recognized the severity of an internal split in the Colorado Democratic party between progressives like himself and the Denver party machine fashioned by Mayor Robert Speer.

Even if the Democrats could control the Colorado legislature, Patterson seriously doubted that sufficient party unity could be maintained to defeat a Republican candidate.[99] Consequently, in a speech at Trinidad during the summer of 1906, he unequivocally removed himself as a candidate for re-election and implied his intention of quitting politics entirely.[100] One of his newspaper editors, Edward Keating, claimed that he again turned down a chance to run for the Senate in 1912.[101] Simon Guggenheim, a Republican whose mining interests caused reformers to view him as a "smelter trust senator," was elected in his place and generally voted with the Republican Old Guard.[102]

Within a month of the expiration of his term in the Senate, Patterson received a long, detailed letter from Roosevelt congratulating him on his "significant contributions" to reform efforts. Roosevelt expressed appreciation for articles in the *Rocky Mountain News* that had defended him against the venomous personal attacks in other newspapers. The problem with the men associated with corporate abuse, according to Roosevelt, was their frustration at being powerless to exert compelling influence on the administration. Roosevelt went on to congratulate Patterson on his efforts to make campaign contributions public, and offered a detailed explanation of the accusations by Averill Harriman that the president had exerted pressure on corporations for campaign contributions in 1904.[103] But the friendly tone of the letter, if it was meant to recruit Patterson's support in any way for the next election, failed.

Tom Patterson's basic allegiance to William Jennings Bryan never wavered in 1908—in spite of his friendship with Taft, who had been picked by Roosevelt to succeed him as president. In addition to unusually thorough coverage of Bryan's campaign and almost daily editorial support, the *News* ran regular appeals for campaign funds.[104] The newspaper centered its attack on Forestry Chief Gifford Pinchot's attempts to mute the development of the West. Noting that Taft was more at home in Manila than in Denver and that Roosevelt knew only "a little" about the West, the *News* identified Bryan as the only real Westerner of the three.[105]

Whatever good points Roosevelt had made came from Bryan, the *News* argued, noting the latter's concept of guaranteed bank deposits to prevent panics. The newspaper attacked Republican reluctance to publish the names of campaign contributors, and insisted that only Bryan could be relied upon to make an effective attack on the trust. Taft, said the *News*, was a "very good fellow, whose ideas are, in the main, wrong."[106]

In 1912 Woodrow Wilson was the Democratic presidential candidate, and Patterson vigorously campaigned on his behalf. As early as 1908 he had been impressed with Wilson, after hearing a speech in Denver to the American Bankers Association in which Wilson told the bankers that they must accept regulation.[107] The Republican candidate was his old friend William Howard Taft, whom Patterson's *News* now sorrowfully accused of having become the pliant tool of the trusts.[108] As for the third-party candidate, Theodore Roosevelt, Patterson's editor, George Creel, wrote that the New Yorker was a sham trustbuster and no real progressive when compared with Robert LaFollette.[109]

The Democratic win that swept Wilson into the White House was trumpeted by the *News* as a complete vindication for the principles of William Jennings Bryan. More than any other man, he deserved the credit for the rising tide of reform.[110]

After leaving the Senate, Tom Patterson occasionally looked back with the feeling that he could have done more to advance reform causes.[111] But considering the small coterie of allies with whom he worked, it is difficult to fault his efforts. Moralistic and stubbornly independent, he stood as a vocal and energetic advance agent of political change. Though highly individualistic in following his own conscience, he still condemned the kind of savage individualism that placed appetite for economic gain above justice.

The subjects that Patterson focused on were his passions: the welfare of the West and Colorado, corporate abuses, the rights of the common people, and the condition of labor. He sought to plug legislative loopholes through which corporations might escape. He chafed at compromise laws. And he was impatient with the slow growth of effective regulatory legislation.

When the Democratic party seemed to falter in regard to economic reform, he briefly supported Roosevelt. But ultimately Tom Patterson remained convinced that the party of Bryan offered the best hope of achieving desirable political and economic reforms. He was still the man who, during the heated debate with Senator Bailey over the caucus in 1906, had vehemently recalled that he had earlier bolted to the Populist party "so that the Democrats could ride on and catch up with me."[112]

14
Battling "the Beast"

Any party machine that is allowed unmolested control of a state or great city reaches the conclusion that their machine is the proprietor and the people the community of their serfs.

— Tom Patterson, *Rocky Mountain News,* May 5, 1904

Although Thomas Patterson fought what he regarded as abuses by corporate influence in politics at the national level, it was in Denver where Patterson led his greatest crusade. Convinced of the corporations' harmful influence on state and local governments, Patterson steadily directed special attacks on Denver's private utility companies, which he believed transparently opposed the rights of the common people. For more than twenty years he threw the full weight of his newspapers and political skills against those formidable adversaries, with varying degrees of success.

Colorado historians generally agree that abuse of corporate power and influence permeated the state capitol from 1890 to 1910.[1] Utility franchises, lucrative and ineffectively regulated, stimulated a system of alliances between the utility companies and officials in municipal and statehouse offices. Until 1903 the state legislature and the governor controlled the administrative boards of the city of Denver, which further complicated the general corruption and vote buying. As a result, warfare for control of city hall was continuous.[2]

The Colorado state government did possess revocation rights over charters "injurious to the state."[3] But under the pressures brought about by Denver's rapid growth, utility franchises had been granted without including regulations to limit unwarranted expansion, increases in rates, or to address the quality of services. Such practices as allowing the original gas franchise, issued in 1869, to remain in effect for fifty years without any provision for payment to the city were not unusual. By 1900 consolidation had replaced competition in all the vital public services, with the survivors enjoying enormous profits. Thanks to their control of Denver's city council and strong influence in the state administrative and legislative branches, their security was guaranteed.[4]

Scarcely a year passed that Patterson did not actively battle a privately owned utility, always arguing that the people of Denver were entitled to the benefits of cheap water, transportation, light, and gas. He called attention to the dangers of private control, and pointed to municipal ownership as the only way out of corporate abuse. Always fond of quoting statistical evidence, the *News* listed the lower cost of lighting in twelve cities as proof of how Denver's citizens were being exploited.[5]

As early as 1897, he suggested that the city should own and operate, for the benefit of all inhabitants, all city franchises involving natural monopolies.[6] Operating from this premise, Patterson filled the *News* with merciless caricatures of Denver's utility corporations.[7] Inevitably, he attracted the unqualified hostility of the city's power structure, and the hatred was reinforced by Patterson's steady defense of the rights of organized labor.

The leader of the "utilities crowd," William G. Evans, presided over the Denver Tramway Company. Evans, son of Colorado's second territorial governor, John Evans, was described by Patterson as the "most conscienceless boss that ever bestrode a suffering people."[8] Polly Pry, once a gossip columnist for the *Denver Post* who went on to publish her own weekly magazine, described Evans as a man with "an expressionless, impassive sort of face, with cold gray eyes and a firm hard mouth."[9]

A small coterie of other leaders included E. B. Field, director of the telephone company; Walter S. Cheesman, owner of the water company; Daniel Sullivan, comptroller of the Denver Gas and Electric Company; and David H. Moffat, founder of the First National Bank, a heavy investor in railroad and mining operations and a major stockholder in the streetcar franchise. The *News* called the system a "corporate snake."[10]

Of all Patterson's protracted struggles with these men and their operations, his most continuous battle involved the Denver Union Water Company, which owned the Denver water supply. For more than twenty years, the *News* bitterly protested the high rates charged by the company. A particularly vigorous attack was launched in 1897. One political cartoon, typical of the newspaper's caricatures, pictured Cheesman as a monkey trying to pull chestnuts from a fire; the chestnuts were labeled "franchises, tax exemptions, and high rates."[11]

In the spring election that followed, candidates of a nonpartisan Taxpayers Ticket, supported by the *News,* managed to take brief control of the city council, and the new officials set out to limit the excesses of the utility company.[12] Patterson claimed that their victory was the result of the presence of hundreds of voters who voluntarily attended the opening of the polls to prevent the introduction of "machine" substitute judges into strangely occurring vacancies and who had remained all day to watch the count.

After alleging that water rates were exorbitantly high, the council, again supported by the *News,* established a "reasonable" rate schedule. Pointing out that he had never denied the right to profit in a reasonable manner, Patterson asserted that the council's rates were based on the average of rates charged by companies in St. Louis, Chicago, and Cincinnati.[13] Water company officials refused to make any adjustments in their rates and warned that water users—including Patterson—who refused to comply with the company's rate schedule would have their water supply shut off.[14] When rival newspapers attacked the *News* for agitating on the water issue, Patterson responded by accusing the *Denver Times* and the *Denver Republican* of being under the corporation's control, soulless hirelings of an equally soulless corporation.[15]

After the *News* urged Denver residents to defy the water company, concerned citizens called a mass meeting and various civic groups organized to resist what the *News* had called the "thievish demands of the company."[16] The water company officials lashed out at their chief tormentor. Patterson, in a letter to Kate, appeared to be enjoying the battle, as usual, and reported that the water fight had broken out with new vigor. The company had shut off water to his Welton Street buildings in downtown Denver, but he had secured a temporary injunction to restore service. "Since then we have been bombarding the outfit with good effect. The episode has helped to banish the ennui which threatened us all."[17]

Because no one else in the area received the same treatment, Patterson had apparently been singled out. The property affected included five stores and thirty apartment dwellers. The fight held elements of comic opera, with Patterson setting a guard at the key water gate and the two sides alternately turning the water on and off.[18]

When the court refused to convert his temporary injunction into a permanent one, Patterson denounced the decision and encouraged the city council to pass an ordinance forbidding the exclusion of water service.[19] Subsequently, a protracted legal battle prevented the company from severing service but upheld the company's rates. Denver continued to pay what the company demanded.[20]

In challenging another public service corporation, the *Rocky Mountain News* quoted the city electrician as admitting that the production costs of the Denver Gas and Electric Company ran well below the rates charged; the paper encouraged the creation of a new electric company. Because Patterson had become a part owner of one of the companies bidding for the additional franchise he received criticism from opponents, who charged him with motives of self-interest rather than public interest.[21] He insisted privately, however, that his efforts were aimed at proving that cheaper and better service could be provided.[22] His company failed to get the franchise, and the successful bidder, the LaCombe Company, succumbed to the entrenched firm, the Denver Gas and Electric Company, after a rate war. The latter then declared bankruptcy in order to get a friendly court to invalidate the low rates agreed to during the rate war.[23]

At first, Patterson's criticism contained strongly partisan overtones. In the early 1890s, during almost continual attacks on municipal corruption, the *News* had hammered away at the "Republican gang." It had called for more effective police supervision of gambling houses and advocated monthly fines against law violators who were protected by their Republican friends in office. Having raised charges of forgery and fraud by officeholders, the *News* cheered the subsequent convictions of a deputy city auditor and deputy city treasurer.[24]

Patterson had backed up accusations of gross corruption and waste in the Republican administration of Mayor Wolfe Londoner when he exposed county clerks who made up to $1,000 a month in rake-offs on fees for filing abstracts by collecting five cents on each item. The procedure was "legalized" only by custom, since no law existed calling for such a fee. One clerk netted $3,796 over a six-month period with no accounting of the money to the county.[25] On numerous occasions, the Tramway Company and the Republican party had been assailed jointly for their "art of plundering," and a typical *News* headline had declared, "Denver Boldly Robbed and Intimidated by Their Political Servants."[26]

Patterson's early activities could be interpreted as those of a highly partisan Democrat-Populist seeking to undermine the Republican party. He supported any maverick Republican who challenged the machine. In 1897 Thomas S. McMurray, a longtime Republican who shared Patterson's desire for increased public regulation of the franchises, broke with the party and ran a successful campaign as an Independent with the support of the *News*.[27] Because of his experience as a leader of the silver fusionists during the 1890s,

Patterson was willing to support an occasional honest Republican. Yet he came to view the Democratic party as the most hopeful instrument for achieving the reforms he advocated. Reform, not party allegiance, drove his actions. When the occasion demanded, Patterson was quick to condemn any element of the Democratic party he believed had been subverted by business interests, calling them "new found Democratic allies" of the corporations.[28]

After the election of 1900, Patterson was the dominant figure in the fusion of Populists, Silver Democrats, and Silver Republicans, a fact that had won him the senatorship in 1901. But as bimetallism faded as an issue, the fragile alliance rapidly eroded. Patterson's decision to join the Democrats in the U.S. Senate failed to mute the hostility felt toward him by Democrats like his former law partner Charles Thomas, whom he had defeated for the Senate in 1901 and who had remained in the regular Democratic party during the years of silver agitation. Ironically, Patterson's claim to leadership within the Colorado Democratic party faced its most severe challenge at the same time that the rising power and machine tactics of the Denver Democratic organization most seriously distressed him.

When voting irregularities in the spring election of 1901 (such as the flagrant use of wholesale repeaters at the polls) appeared to have been engineered by Democratic officeholders, Patterson's *News* excoriated members of his own party. The opposition *Denver Times* happily noted that Patterson's outraged attacks were splitting the Democrats, since his primary target was Thomas Maloney, chairman of the Democratic Central Committee.[29] The *Denver Republican* reported that Patterson, as the leader of the Democrats, must have directed Maloney to engage in questionable tactics in order to preserve the Democrats in power. Patterson immediately countered by lodging a criminal libel suit against the newspaper, controlled by the family of Republican party leader Nathaniel P. Hill since the 1880s.[30]

The *Denver Times*, obviously enjoying itself, gave a running account of the confrontation between two of its chief competitors. The real issue, said the *Times*, was who the real boss of the Democrats was. The *Times* noted that the affair had severely strained Patterson's relationship with both Maloney and Denver's rising young Democrat, Robert Speer. Two months later the newspaper claimed that Patterson had dissolved the "partnership" with Speer.[31]

Defense attorneys for the *Republican* claimed that, as no Democrats had ever been officially charged with violations of the law, there had been no libel in associating Patterson with them.[32] In spite of the best efforts of Patterson's attorney and longtime political ally Thomas Jefferson O'Donnell, the jury, composed of ten Republicans and two Democrats, agreed with the defense argument and held *Republican* publisher Crawford Hill and editor William Stapleton not guilty of libeling Patterson. While the trial had not proved Patterson was responsible for the frauds, concluded the *Times,* it had exposed a distinct lack of solidarity in the Democratic party.[33]

Though the *Denver Post* as late as March of 1902 acknowledged that Patterson was "still leader" of the Democrats, the split between him and the Maloney-Speer forces of the Denver and Arapahoe County Democrats widened.[34] Members of the Democratic state central committee desperately tried to reunite the factions. But by the summer of 1902 the Republican press insinuated that Tom Patterson was losing his grip on Democratic politics.[35]

Apparently trying to rally rank-and-file Democrats and using his strength with non-Denver delegates, Patterson suggested that the Democratic state convention name the next candidate for the U.S. Senate and direct the next Democratic legislative caucus to follow the convention's instructions.[36] The move only succeeded in further alienating Charles Thomas, who sought to unseat incumbent Senator Henry M. Teller by a vote in the legislature. Patterson hoped to rally his strength with non-Denver delegates and held more hope of influencing the convention as a whole than the Democratic legislators. Already leaning toward direct democracy, he and Teller supported the concept of direct election of senators.[37]

By the time Denver and Arapahoe County Democrats gathered for their nominating convention in September, Patterson had publicly conceded that the political view of the *Rocky Mountain News* carried no influence with the Democratic machine, an organization whose power was increasingly identified as Mayor Robert Speer.[38]

Speer delegates controlled the Denver delegation to the Democratic state convention presided over by Charles S. Thomas. Still smarting from his loss of the senate seat to Patterson the year before, Thomas gained his revenge by repeatedly gaveling the senator into silence. The *Times* reported that Patterson was generally ignored, treated as if he didn't exist.[39] A combination of Thomas and Speer Democrats held a viselike grip of control over the sometimes tumultuous proceedings. Patterson-supported candidates, among them incumbent Governor Elias M. Ammons, were rejected. Only Teller was saved, by an appeal to the rank-and-file delegates who instructed the Democratic legislators to return him to office. Any party commitment to fusion was ended.[40]

As the November elections of 1902 approached, Tom Patterson's political fortunes as well as his reform crusades had reached a low ebb. The struggles against the utility companies had made little headway. He had suffered a trouncing in state politics from forces led by the man he had defeated for the Senate less than two years earlier. His fusion alliance lay permanently disabled. His political allies had been repudiated. Most significantly, the Democratic machine in Denver seemed to be firmly in the grip of Mayor Speer, a man who seemed completely at ease in his relationship with the corporations.

The Republicans swept nearly every important office in 1902. Patterson, in the *Rocky Mountain News,* analyzed the disaster with surprisingly little rancor. Pointing to the one bright spot, he accurately predicted that Teller, his colleague in the Senate, would be re-elected because of holdover legislators in the Colorado Senate.[41] Though the Democrats had waged a vigorous campaign, he wrote, they had erred in rejecting fusion with the Populists and in not repudiating dishonest Democratic county commissioners and denouncing Denver's administration, which had allowed corporations to escape fair taxation based on their stocks, bonds, and property.[42]

The defeat really came, Patterson argued, in an indirect reference to Speer, because the public believed that the Democrats in power had granted inordinate favors to corporations at public expense and that the party had ignored or condoned public and political misconduct.[43] That such misconduct was public knowledge months before the election is evident from several letters written to Patterson's close friend O'Donnell by several Democrats in outlying parts of the state. The Denver Democratic machine had acquired a reputation, said one writer, as a pack of "boodlers in office at their first opportunity." Another letter referred to "Republicanized Democratic County officials" whose "rascality" was defended by the Republican newspapers.[44]

Patterson clearly accused the Democratic party organization of following the Republican example when it succumbed to the temptation of using any means to perpetuate itself in office. Privately, he observed that the entire gang was a "tough proposition" and lamented, "We do not know men as well before they are elected as we do afterwards."[45] In spite of the setbacks, Patterson and the *News* picked up the cudgel again to fight the battle for reform on another front.

One of the key problems for Denver city government lay in the overlapping of city and state governmental functions. Some municipal officials were appointed by the governor and others were elected, a practice that led to frequent factionalism and inefficiency, as well as to susceptibility to corporate pressures.[46] Denver reform leaders such as Patterson, Judge Benjamin B. Lindsey, Edward Costigan, and John Rush believed that home rule was the answer. The *News,* a longtime advocate of full control by Denver citizens over their own affairs,[47] regularly published the ideas of many of the reformers.[48]

In 1902 reform pressure brought about the passage of the Rush Amendment, which allowed for a charter convention to be held in Denver for the purpose of determining what sort of home rule would be preferred. The convention proposed a unicameral city council, sought voter approval of all franchises, and included provisions for initiatives, referendums, and recall.

Supported by the clergy of Denver, whom the opposition press called "pulpit pounders,"[49] the charter seemed destined for victory. The Denver Tramway Company, alarmed over restrictions on its freight-carrying privileges under the proposed charter, led the utility companies to force selection of election managers instructed to defeat the charter by intimidating voters and stuffing ballot boxes.[50] When the proposal lost in a narrow election, the *News* charged that ten thousand illegal votes had been accepted by corporation-controlled officials.[51] *George's Weekly* declared that the Speer organization—known as the "Big Mitt"—had beaten Patterson.

A second convention that followed in March of 1904 drafted a plan more to the liking of the corporations. When ratified, it featured few significant reforms and left the city's power diffused.[52] Nevertheless, the first elections under the new charter became important for the utility corporations. John Springer, a Progressive Republican, opposed Democratic boss Robert Speer for the crucial office of mayor. The public utility companies, as part of an effort to give Colorado politics a myth of bipartisanship, generally supported Speer in municipal campaigns while reserving control of the state government to the Republicans. This situation led reform judge Ben Lindsey to observe, "The beast is bipartisan."

As the campaign developed, most reformers believed that Springer had been selected as a sacrificial goat while utilities-oriented Republicans planned to vote for Speer. When Republican Governor James H. Peabody refused Progressive Republican requests that he use the militia to ensure an honest election, one report claimed the governor had traded his decision for a pledge of support from Evans and Speer in the fall election.[53]

The situation outraged Patterson. After losing a struggle for control of the Democratic city convention and after being told to "go hire a hall" by the Speer Democrats, Patterson did just that. On May 4, 1904, speaking to an overflow crowd at the Denver Coliseum, Patterson delivered a lengthy speech that outlined the birth and growth of the Democratic machine headed by Speer and clearly described the reasoning behind his incessant warfare against Speer in the ensuing years.[54] He began by citing Democrat Samuel Tilden's opposition to the notorious Tweed Ring in New York City as a precedent for his own action in opposing Speer. He claimed to be speaking for 80 percent of the party, the "unorganized Democracy," as opposed to those organization Democrats who had sold out to the public utility corporation and gambling interests.[55]

Patterson next unleashed a scathing attack on Speer's performance as commissioner of the fire and police board. Ten years earlier Patterson had applauded Speer's record as a commissioner in limiting gambling, and his organizational and administrative skills. But now, perhaps more for rhetorical purposes than from conviction, Patterson maintained that within six months after Speer assumed office in 1900 the police department became completely demoralized; several members faced charges of bribery and extortion, and a violent reign of terror engulfed the city. No fewer than eight women had been assaulted on the capitol hill, gambling ran rampant, and ordinances were openly violated as Speer proved his incompetence.[56] But Speer's lack of executive ability, argued Patterson, paled before the more important issue of the purity of the ballot.

Patterson summarized the election events of the previous six years: A Republican city council, nominated by a Republican convention dominated by the city corporations, had collaborated closely with the Democratic machine to the point of asking the Democratic machine to nominate election judges who would ensure corporation victories. The water and tramway companies, according to Patterson, caused Republican and Democratic executive committees to work in close embrace, the one suggesting the scoundrels who should stuff the ballot boxes and forge the returns, the other appointing them as fast as they were suggested. The corporations received renewal of their franchises, the books were kept closed, and a mayor approved everything.[57]

Patterson proposed a solution. He called for the election of a reform city government that would take control of the tramway system, a move that would return $200,000 to $400,000 annually and also provide for three-cent fares. As for the water system, he advocated its outright purchase or the construction of an independent system that could terminate the "one million a year extortion" from the Denver consumers.[58]

While claiming that the Democratic party was closer to the fundamentals of free government than any party that ever existed, Patterson nevertheless warned that the future of the party in Denver depended upon the extermination, root and branch, of the Speer-Republican-utilities ring. To the roar of the crowd, he concluded his indictment:

> Any party machine that is allowed unmolested control of a state or great city, reaches the conclusion that their machine is the proprietor and the people of the community their serfs; that they own all taxable property, and have the right to extort in salaries and graft and overcharges, as much as they can get away with without being sent to the pen. I believe that the Democratic machine, represented by the Speer gang . . . is in that frame of mind.[59]

As he often had done before, Patterson stated beliefs that reflected his associations with the Populists, municipal reformers like Mayor Jones of Toledo, and William Jennings Bryan. He was convinced that goals of a democratic tradition, including the preservation of individualism, could be attained only through restraints placed on rapacious individualism. To Patterson, the practical agent of control was the government. With faith and trust in the popular majority, he believed it was vital that the people, not the bosses or the corporations, control the government. He further believed that bosses like Speer could control only when they were allowed to steal the political machinery. With implicit faith in his own motives and abilities, Patterson identified himself as the champion of the people.

Yet on election day—in spite of Patterson's efforts and the charge of election fraud leveled by the *News*—Speer defeated the Republican candidate, Springer. The defeated Springer made plans to contest the election results but gave the idea up under pressure from William G. Evans.[60] The defeat was a difficult one for Patterson. But the state elections lay ahead, and Patterson had no intention of giving up.

ETERNAL VIGILANCE IS THE PRICE OF A CHARTER.

WATCHING THAT CHICKEN COOP.

Cartoon from the *Rocky Mountain News,* 1903. (Courtesy Colorado Historical Society, *Colorado Magazine,* Winter 1977.) Reprinted with permission of the *Rocky Mountain News.*

15
Constructive Contempt

I consider the proceedings against me as a direct assault upon the freedom of the press, and I shall defend that ancient and important prerogative of a free people with all my power.

— Tom Patterson, *Rocky Mountain News,* June 30, 1905

The Denver utility companies, having engineered a Democratic machine municipal victory, turned to electing a Republican governor. Opposing them was Tom Patterson, with a long and colorful history of struggles against corporation influence. None, however, would match the sensational confrontation of the 1904 state elections.

The Republicans, after beating down a challenge from their progressive wing, renominated Governor James H. Peabody, whose chief claim to fame was his controversial effort to quell the Cripple Creek labor disturbance in 1903 and 1904. The Democrats countered with former governor Alva Adams, one of several compromise candidates chosen through Patterson's influence in the state convention. His campaign slogan was, "Citizens must vote if they are to win over the money interests."[1]

As Patterson stumped the state, he claimed that the large turnouts where he spoke were a sign of a Democratic victory. The campaign featured extensive demands for reform by both the Patterson newspapers and the *Denver Post.* With public hostility toward Peabody on the rise, Adams won by ten thousand votes.[2] The Denver newspaper most hostile to Patterson called the election "distinctly" his victory and grudgingly admitted that by long odds he was the ablest man in the state. Even *George's Weekly* recognized the campaign as the finest ever made in the state. To all appearances, the Democrats had gained a 19-to-15 margin in the state senate. Voters also approved an amendment that increased the size of the Colorado Supreme Court, which in turn opened the way for future Democratic appointments to the court. Across the state, Democrats expressed "exhilaration" over the end of Peabodyism.[3]

But the celebration was premature. The lame-duck Republicans, desperately trying to maintain themselves in power, turned to the still-friendly supreme court. The court promptly invalidated the votes in ten Denver precincts on the grounds that ballot-stuffing had occurred, converting two Republican senators and six Republican representatives from losers to winners and cutting Adams's majority to a thin margin.[4]

Adams's election still appeared secure until Governor Peabody, in a complicated deal with the utility corporations, agreed to appoint two business-oriented court judges in return for help in challenging Adams's election.[5] Eventually, the lame-duck legislature declared Adams's victory to be void on grounds of general voting irregularities. Peabody became governor on March 16, 1905, and resigned within twenty-four hours, allowing Republican Lieutenant Governor Jesse McDonald to become governor.[6]

This game of gubernatorial musical chairs infuriated reformers of all parties, including Tom Patterson. In a series of bitter editorials and articles, the *News* accused the legislature and the supreme court of being the tool of the utility corporations and the Republican state machine. It reported a meeting between attorneys for the utilities and railroads, for the purpose of selecting the two new court appointees to be named by the governor. In some detail, the stories described how the utilities selected one candidate and the railroads the other.[7] Patterson accused the supreme court justices of base and political motives, improper methods, and outright dishonesty. Referring to the court as a "great judicial slaughter-house," he published a cartoon depicting the chief justice as the "Lord High Executioner" in the act of beheading Democrats.[8]

Patterson knew that he was exposing himself to legal charges when he climaxed the assaults with a front-page story in which he declared his complete responsibility for everything written and predicted he would be summoned by the court:

> I know that . . . the tribunal to try me will be pretty much like a court-martial, only there will be no reviewing court or officer or other tribunal to interfere with whatever the court shall decide. I consider the proceedings against me as a direct assault upon the freedom of the press, and I shall defend that ancient and important prerogative of a free people with all my power.[9]

As expected, the supreme court cited Patterson for contempt and a lengthy trial followed. In spite of his impressive list of counselors, including Senator Henry Moore Teller, Charles S. Thomas, John Rush, Horace Hawkins, James Belford, and E. F. Richardson, a verdict of guilty was a foregone conclusion. But when the court permitted him a final statement, the tables turned.

Patterson said that as a lawyer he realized the importance of maintaining the image of an unsullied judiciary in order to keep the respect and confidence of the people. Nevertheless, the articles in the *News* represented his own deep convictions and he would not admit to being a libeler. Arguing the case for what he called "constructive contempt," he wondered if it had come to pass that because men were judges, the publisher of a newspaper could not tell the truth about them. Defiantly, he offered to prove every one of his accusations, challenged the court to call for an investigation of them, and declared that he would not be bound to any system that prevented an individual from telling the truth.[10] Though the audacity of Tom Patterson's declaration clearly invited a stringent penalty, the court probably feared that martyrdom would reinforce his cause. Because he was a U.S. senator at the time, any imprisonment would have drawn national attention to Colorado. In rendering the verdict, the court declined to comment or to allow an inquiry into the validity of Patterson's charges, omitted any jail sentence, and settled for a $1,000 fine.[11] But even the fine was too much for Justice Robert Steele. Generally taking a more liberal view than his fellow justices, he dissented from the majority decision with as bitter an arraignment of his colleagues' integrity as Patterson had delivered. Patterson's efforts to secure a reversal failed when the U.S. Supreme Court, with two dissenting opinions, refused to take jurisdiction.[12]

Reaction to the case overwhelmingly favored Patterson, although the *Denver Republican,* frequently labeled by the *News* as the primary corporation newspaper, complained that after admitting his guilt Patterson had arrogantly piled "insult upon insult in a most sinister manner." Though it condemned his "radicalism," the *Republican* conceded that his concluding speech had been "remarkedly adroit."[13]

Understandably, those who agreed with Patterson applauded his performance and courage. Judge Ben Lindsey approvingly called his speech one of the most scathing arraignments ever addressed to an American bench of justice,[14] and Edward Keating, editor of Patterson's recently purchased *Denver Times,* observed, "Senator, you know I have always admired you, but this is the greatest day of your life."[15]

The *Pueblo Chieftain* supported Patterson's contention that criticism of the courts constituted a legitimate function of the press, and support for Patterson's struggle against the advance of autocratic and "arbitrary power" also appeared in *Arena,* a national publication, in January of 1906. A decade later, the *Denver Express,* in evaluating Patterson's reform activities, judged his battle for freedom of speech the greatest moment of his career.[16] And many years after his death, other legal decisions sustained his position.[17]

For Tom Patterson, the trial was a significant victory. The court, in effect, had fled from a showdown on his charges. At least for a few days, he became the most popular man in the state.[18]

Tom's popularity did not extend to the Denver political machine. In June of 1905, he, Alva Adams, and Henry Teller were "deported" from a Democratic meeting. Speer—not Patterson—was in firm control of the Democratic state committee.[19]

Yet Patterson doggedly continued to publicize growing national sentiment for public ownership of utility companies and his papers reported any rebukes to local bosses. Typical of its support for national reform figures, the *News* gave impressive coverage to Democrat Joseph W. Folk, who had been elected governor of Missouri in spite of Theodore Roosevelt's landslide victory in 1904. Praising Folk's reform efforts, Patterson warned that in order to win elections the Democratic party must be truly democratic.[20]

At the local level, the new franchise proposals for the Denver Tramway Company and the Denver Gas and Electric Company sparked the next confrontation between Denver reformers and the Speer organization. Absenting himself from the U.S. Senate in order to oppose the proposed franchises, Patterson argued that payments to the city by the corporations under the proposals were far too low. *George's Weekly* sarcastically asserted that Patterson sought municipal ownership of everything except newspapers. In spite of Tom's efforts, the franchises were approved in a special spring election in 1906.[21]

Patterson claimed that all the franchises actually had been defeated, but that once again the corporations—through control of election machinery and lavish use of money—had succeeded in changing the election results. In order to vote, citizens had to show payment of property taxes. Reformers claimed, however, that many impostors who said they had "bought" lots for investment purposes were allowed to vote even though they could not identify their "property."[22]

When an overzealous judge, Frank T. Johnson, seized some of the ballot boxes and announced the possibility of a recount, the chief justice of the Colorado Supreme Court, William H. Gabbert, issued a writ of prohibition, denying his colleague's jurisdiction and stopping the proposed action. Throughout the legal sparring, the *News* printed the entire argument advanced by Republican reform attorney Edward P. Costigan.[23]

Some of the Denver reformers, enraged by the court's actions, organized the "Independents," a task force whose specific goal was to elect judges who were not corporation-controlled. The *News* thoroughly endorsed the group and applauded its leader, Costigan, for his "cold logic and impassioned oratory" before the Colorado Supreme Court.[24]

In 1906 the Denver reformers, who tended to fight among themselves, looked ineffective to Patterson. Impatient, Patterson announced the creation of another reform organization made up of "real" Democrats; its objective was to regain control of the party from the "Big Mitt."[25] He had spoken earlier in the year, on the Senate floor, of his belief that both parties in Colorado were tools of the utility corporations. And he wrote to William Howard Taft, advising his friend that the Republican party was seriously divided, with the corporation-dominated faction, an enemy to President Roosevelt, in control.[26]

Though Speer could control the Denver Democrats, Tom Patterson held strong influence with delegations from the rest of the state.[27] When the 1906 Democratic state convention assembled in the Denver Coliseum, the power struggle was renewed. A heated debate on party fidelity highlighted the conflict, with both sides claiming to be the only true Democrats.

The anti-Patterson forces defended machine politics as the best way to raise money, ensure solidarity, and win elections. After reminding Patterson that he, too, had received party favors, the Speer backers maintained that the only thing the senator had ever given his party was trouble.[28] But during the heat of the dispute, Speer personally admitted that every employee under his direction had given twenty-five percent of his monthly salary to help maintain party supremacy,[29] a claim proudly made but not calculated to please Patterson adherents. Ironically, when Patterson forces finally won control of the convention, it was the Speer supporters' turn to call themselves independent Democrats, not bound to support any ticket in the fall.[30]

The Denver newspapers were filled with "thrilling accounts" of the exclusion of the Speer machine from management of the Democratic state convention.[31] Patterson supported the candidacy of Alva Adams for governor. Still

Robert W. Speer, mayor of Denver, in 1906. (Courtesy Colorado Historical Society.)

smarting over Adams's having been "robbed" of his rightful election in 1904, both men hoped for victory in November, even without the support of Speer Democrats. But then, out of the blue, Judge Lindsey announced his own independent candidacy. The reform vote split, dealing Patterson's hopes a mortal blow. That such an occurrence could happen revealed the difficulty in forming a cohesive reform movement in Denver, where several determined factions were led by equally strong-willed men.[32]

Lindsey had long acknowledged important support from Patterson throughout his career, crediting the senator's personal and political influence for his successful bid for county court judge in 1901.[33] In *The Beast,* Lindsey often referred to the steady encouragement he received from the *Rocky Mountain News* and its reporters, and congratulated the Patterson newspapers for their reform activities. He specifically mentioned the articles that revealed unhappy jail conditions, publicity for his own exposé of graft involving city supplies, persistence in exposing crooked county commissioners, and rebates paid to the Tramway Company by the city. Among friendly reporters, he singled out Edward Keating, Harry Wilbur, and Ellis Meredith.[34]

Lindsey had expressed special appreciation for *News-Times* backing during his independent candidacy for judge in 1904, and in a letter to Patterson, he added: "I remember how you exposed corruption in our party when others, who were leaders, were weak or cowardly, and I know you would never advise me or permit me to do anything wrong."[35] In 1905 Lindsey wrote: "If I should undertake . . . to write you every time I have received a boost, a kindness, an encouraging word from you and the *News,* I fear I should consume your valuable time in reading letters, but I wish to assure you that it is appreciated more than you can possibly know."[36] Patterson, on his part, had congratulated Lindsey for his reform position, but admitted that they occasionally moved "along different lines."[37]

In 1904 Lindsey had rejoiced in Adams's apparent victory and endorsed his future candidacy for governor. But when Adams reappeared as a candidate in 1906, the judge believed Adams had reneged on a pledge not to run again.[38] Wanting to pursue his own ambitions to become governor, Lindsey attacked Adams and accused Patterson of being "deceived" by those who only professed to be reformers. He claimed that the utility companies had done well during Adams's previous term as governor, in the 1890s, and he identified Adams's campaign manager, Milton Smith, as an attorney for the corporations during his early career.[39] Patterson attacked Lindsey for splitting the reform vote and noted the many occasions on which the *News* had saved

Benjamin Barr Lindsey, Denver's first juvenile judge and an activist in Denver's municipal reform movement. (Courtesy Colorado Historical Society.)

the judge from "slaughter," complaining that he had the right to expect better from Lindsey.[40]

A general reading of Lindsey-Patterson correspondence supports the conclusion of the judge's biographer that Lindsey was guilty of poor judgment at best or peevishness at worst. Lindsey's attacks on Adams were supported only by hearsay and innuendo, and while understandable during the heat of the campaign were repeated "gratuitously" in *The Beast* three years later.[41]

During the ensuing election campaign the Democratic platform called for such reforms as the adoption of the initiative and referendum, direct election of senators, and the elimination of corruption and corporate rule in government. But Lindsey's candidacy had split the reform vote, and without Speer support they lost the election, the governorship going to Republican Henry Augustus Buchtel, chancellor of Denver University.[42]

Though the Speer machine continued to control Denver's government, in 1908 Patterson caused it some embarrassment by publishing excerpts from the "Freuauff Diary." Frank W. Freuauff, a prominent official of the Denver Gas and Electric Company, owned a memorandum book with listings of payments made by the company to public officials during the 1906 campaign. Speer's biographer, Charles Johnson, says flatly that Freuauff was unhappy with the organization and had handed the diary over to the *News.* George Creel, who worked for the *News,* believed that the diary had been lost or stolen.[43] How Patterson actually came into possession of the book remains a mystery.

During the campaign Patterson printed facsimiles of the most incriminating pages, showing company payments totaling $67,690 to individuals on the public payroll. Heading the list were two entries to Speer himself, which added up to $4,500.[44] Speer's campaign manager claimed that the money had gone into the party treasury. But the serious question of party ethics remained, and such disclosures almost certainly eroded the appeal of the Speer organization. Patterson also continued his attacks against Speer's gambling syndicate, ballot box stuffing, padded registrations, and cooperation with corporations. But on election day, in spite of Patterson's efforts, Speer's forces maintained themselves in office by a narrow margin.[45]

Although unable to dislodge Speer in the 1908 municipal elections, Patterson could regard the fall election results with a degree of satisfaction. During the campaign the *Rocky Mountain News* urged its readers to split the ticket by voting for Democrats William Jennings Bryan for president and John Shafroth for governor, and supporting progressive Republican candidates for district attorney, sheriff, and assessor. The paper also supported Colorado's "most famous citizen," Ben Lindsey, and four other reform candidates for the Colorado Supreme Court. The *News* attacked the four incumbent supreme court justices, participants in the Patterson contempt case. Behind the scenes, in efforts to achieve Democratic harmony, the only concession to the Speer organization was the endorsement of corporation lawyer Charles Hughes for the senate seat vacated by Teller, who had retired. Though Charles Thomas and Teller reluctantly supported Hughes in order to get a unified endorsement of Bryan and Shafroth, Tom Patterson stubbornly refused. Virtually all the candidates endorsed by the *News* won, and the Democrats achieved majorities in both houses of the state legislature.[46]

By the fall of 1909, reform attorney Edward Costigan, noting the increase in voter independence from party affiliations, saw a distinctly favorable trend in public opinion toward reform.[47] The constant preaching for independence from machine leadership and the encouragement of ticket-splitting by the *News* and the *Times* had certainly contributed significantly to this trend.

In 1910 elements of both major parties and independents, by finally cooperating, dealt the Speer organization its first significant defeat. The issue involved Tom Patterson's favorite target among the utility companies, the Denver Union Water Company, which was seeking a new franchise. The leading stockholder, David Moffat, argued that the water company had been founded in a spirit of altruism, for the welfare of the city, and had not been returning large profits.[48] The reformers, organized as a citizen's league, sought an amendment to the city charter allowing for municipal ownership of the waterworks.[49]

With the forces of Patterson, Lindsey, and Costigan cooperating with unaccustomed harmony, the Patterson newspapers helped spearhead success for the referendum. Although legal action brought by the corporations delayed actual municipal operation for several years, the machine had suffered a clear-cut defeat at the polls.[50]

Reform unity continued during the fall election campaign, with progressive Republicans and Democrats endorsing a unified county ticket of the Citizen's party. With Costigan working diligently to maintain harmony among the factions, with public sentiment growing increasingly favorable, and with Patterson furnishing the heart of the publicity in the *Rocky Mountain News,* the Citizen's party again ran well.[51] Although unable to dislodge

Edward P. Costigan, attorney and a leader in the municipal reform and Progressive movements. (Courtesy Colorado Historical Society.)

the Democratic machine, several reform candidates ran ahead of Republican opponents. At the state level, several reform Democrats won seats in the legislature and the reform-minded Governor John Shafroth was returned to office.[52]

A period of frustration for both reformers and machine politicians followed during the next session of the state legislature. In spite of a Democratic majority in the Colorado legislature, Governor Shafroth failed to make good on his party's pledge to complete reforms begun after the fall election of 1909. Shafroth had called a special session that summer, during which the legislature had passed laws allowing for the initiative and referendum. But he had failed to produce on other measures.[53] Democrat Charles Hughes died on January 12, 1911, after serving only two years of his Senate term. The reform Democrats flatly refused to caucus on the choice of a senator until reform legislation was enacted. The machine Democrats insisted on the selection of Speer as senator before they would allow consideration of such legislation.[54] An impasse loomed.

With the minority Republicans contributing to the tangle, a legislative deadlock dragged on for 120 days without resolution, effectively leading to a situation in which Colorado was represented by only one senator for nearly two years.[55] Patterson used his out-of-state support and persuaded ambitious legislators to combine their strength to stop Speer's Senate bid. One of Speer's associates, in a brief work favorable to the mayor, described Patterson's performance in holding the opposition together as a "miracle."[56] The *News* steadily supported anti-Speer legislators while calling on Speer's backers to give up the hopeless fight. From January to May the *News* published almost daily a list of "honor roll" legislators who were standing fast against Speer, eventually even publishing the photograph of each man.[57] Without doubt, Patterson played a major role in blocking Speer's nomination.

Meanwhile, encouraged by evidence of their increasing strength after the 1910 victory over the water company, the reform coalition launched a concerted effort to change Denver to a commission form of government. Once more the *Rocky Mountain News* served as the primary source of publicity for the reform effort, and it cheered when twenty thousand signatures were obtained supporting a petition seeking a special charter amendment.[58]

City officials, however, refused to honor the petitions calling for a referendum. But while the *News* fanned public indignation over Speer's defiance of the petitioners,[59] the mayor committed a tactical error in his own camp.

Henry J. Arnold, after his election in 1910 as the machine's candidate for assessor, had declared his independence of the Speer organization. He reduced assessments on home owners and raised the property valuation of wealthy individuals, utility companies, and banks.[60] When Arnold threatened to withhold his approval of the entire Speer-proposed tax levy for 1912, stating they violated the limits set by law, the mayor acted. On the night of December 14, 1911, Speer loyalists broke into Arnold's office and physically ejected the assessor in favor of a new appointee, claiming the mayor's right to replace an elected official when the position is vacated.[61]

George Creel, an editorial writer for the *News* at the time, called for a demonstration by all outraged citizens to be held at the capitol, a move Speer denounced as an invitation to mob violence.[62] During the noisy but orderly demonstrations, several thousand Denver citizens called for the restoration of Arnold and the resignation of Speer. Ben Lindsey enthusiastically described the whole affair as a "glorious blow-up."[63]

The reformers were suddenly armed with a martyred popular candidate, and they threw their support to Arnold for mayor on a platform committed to the introduction of commission government. A select nominating group of fifteen reform leaders representing all factions held closed meetings. Patterson felt compelled to defend the "anti-democratic" secrecy of the decision-making, arguing that those who had fought the machine through the years had earned the right to "gather in solemn counsel."[64] The voters agreed. Arnold and the Citizen's party scored a sweeping triumph over "boss" Speer's handpicked candidates, though Speer himself chose not to run. And Judge Lindsey acknowledged Patterson's leadership by praising the "twenty year fight" by Patterson and "others."[65]

In the midst of the election celebration, Patterson was cautioned by Edward Keating that Arnold's commitment to reform might not run very deep.[66] In part to keep an eye on the new mayor and in part as a reward for service to the reform effort, Patterson managed to have his editor, George Creel, named as police commissioner. Unfortunately, Keating's fears proved correct and Patterson's precautionary move failed. Arnold disappointed the reformers by failing to keep his reform pledges and by conducting an administration even more expensive than Speer's.[67]

Eventually, Creel challenged the mayor's failure to enforce many of the reform measures; Arnold fired him on the grounds of creating dissension and of making "offensive charges against fellow board members." In spite of an "eloquent" forty-minute speech by Patterson in which he contended that the charges against Creel were unjust and arbitrary, Creel's dismissal held.[68] When the new commission system went into effect in 1913, the reformers and the *News* worked against Arnold and he failed in his bid to be one of the six new commission members.[69]

The year 1912 proved to be productive and satisfying for Tom. Speer's organization had been ousted and Speer had been blocked from becoming a U.S. senator. Colorado had achieved the initiative and referendum, the direct primary, regulation of child labor, an eight-hour day for hazardous occupations, as well as acts dealing with campaign expenses, election registration, labor disputes, factory inspection, and coal mine inspection. In addition, the legislature had created a tax commission and a state conservation commission. Events at the state and national level promised hope that Populist-Progressive reforms neared fulfillment.[70]

Speaking to a pre-election rally of Denver Democrats, Tom Patterson said that it had been a long time since he could advise a Democratic gathering to vote the straight Democratic ticket, but he could do so with pleasure in 1912. He credited this turn of events to the first direct primary election, a technique of politics he said promised to replace the dominance of the bosses with the will of the people and forecasted a new era from the tyranny of special interests.[71] Aided by the Progressive Republican split from the conservative Republicans,[72] the Democrats sent reform governor John Shafroth to the Senate, replaced him as governor with Elias M. Ammons, and carried the state for Woodrow Wilson.

Among Colorado's leading reformers, Keating and Creel joined Patterson in support of Woodrow Wilson, while Costigan and Lindsey backed Theodore Roosevelt. Believing Wilson to be a true representative of democratic principles, Tom Patterson confidently predicted that the president would win his promised battle with big business, and he anticipated a major role for Bryan in the new national administration.[73]

An examination of Tom Patterson's career as a reformer reveals additional aspects of his complex character. He remained true to his Populist heritage and to the ideas advocated by William Jennings Bryan, the man who regarded Patterson as his "distinguished and beloved friend."[74] He placed great faith in the power of direct democracy and enthusiastically publicized in his newspapers many of the progressive political reforms sought from 1900 to World War I. Patterson maintained his faith despite repeated frustrations over election swindles by his machine-politics adversaries. He firmly believed that the victimized voters would ultimately rise up

Thomas M. Patterson, left center, and William Jennings Bryan, right center, at the Denver, Colorado, national Democratic convention in 1906. (Courtesy Archives, University of Colorado at Boulder Libraries, Patterson collection, Bx 8, Fd 1.)

in such overwhelming numbers that no amount of chicanery could save the bosses. He wanted a strong government, one more responsive to popular control, one that could restrict rampant individualism and conserve what he regarded as the chief value of democracy—the opportunity for every man to have his chance for upward mobility.

Viewed as an energetic self-made man, Tom Patterson resembles the Jacksonian-era Democrat, an aspiring entrepreneur, highly competitive, who keenly resented any actions by existing economic powers that might prevent the common man from entering the race for the spoils of commerce and public influence.[75] He preached the virtues of inherent popular rights. He thought of himself as a spokesman for those who believed that entrenched interests conspired to prevent the common man from getting ahead. He attacked capitalism, not in its essentials but in its operations. His collectivism stopped well short of socialism. He accused the socialist Lincoln Steffens of advocating anarchy and argued that the vital function of government was simply to make "bad men behave," and thus government would be needed until the millennium.[76]

Although he exhibited a strong sense of morality and easily identified himself with the forces of good, Patterson's sense of justice also stemmed from his workingman's background and his training and experience as a defense attorney.

Tom Patterson was eternally optimistic, and his stubborn ability to survive political defeats reflected a genuine exhilaration for combat and an egocentric desire to attract the spotlight. Defeat only caused his resiliency to surface, and his opponents must have wearied from his dogged persistence. His tenacity became legend in Denver; a close friend observed that persistence was his chief trait, adding that although he was not always right, he always believed he was.[77] Moreover, Patterson's considerable influence as the editor of the most influential newspaper in Colorado caused other politicians and leaders to seek his support and gave him an independence that escaped most other politicians.

His infighting with Mayor Speer demonstrated that reform was more important than partisan loyalty to Patterson. Yet he never swerved from his belief that democracy of the Bryan variety—faith in the common man, a belief in the efficacy of remedial legislation, a fundamental distrust of big business—held the greatest hope of achieving needed political and economic reforms in state and national government.[78] Tom Patterson operated at two levels, striving to construct a state Democratic organization supportive of

Populist-Bryan principles, but cooperating in nonpartisan efforts to break the power of the Speer machine.

Though he wrote in 1911 that city government had come to be recognized as city housekeeping rather than an arena for partisan conflict,[79] he overestimated the potential of the success. After the election of 1910 and the passage of a direct primary law, he proclaimed that the coming of direct democracy meant that "Colorado is free!" Like fellow reformer Lindsey, who in 1912 declared that "the Beast is strangled,"[80] Patterson miscalculated the effectiveness of the reform.

Municipal reform efforts in Denver, tardy in fulfillment, lacked staying power. Following an undistinguished performance by the commission government, Speer returned to power in 1916, when Patterson no longer owned the *News*.[81] The position of the Denver reformers suffered from internal weaknesses. In contrast to the strength of an entrenched opposition with their corporate allies, the reformers could not—or would not —restrain their own factional differences. Thus, although Patterson gave generous newspaper coverage to his allies and support to reform causes, he sought a position of leadership in whatever he undertook. One friend and admirer observed that, by virtue of Patterson's personality, he could be satisfied only by being at the head of some faction or party.[82] The wonder of the Denver reform movement lies in the degree of harmony achieved among men of strong wills and talent—men such as Ben Lindsey, Tom Patterson, Edward Costigan, John Rush, George Creel, and Ed Keating.

Even as Patterson expressed his belief that economic and political justice would prevail, he faced one final disappointment and repudiation by the citizens of Colorado. During 1913 and early 1914 Governor Ammons's handling of labor troubles in southern Colorado was rejected by a large number of voters. When he summoned the state militia to control violence connected with a strike, he reversed his stand of neutrality and supported the mine owners.[83] That, in turn, alienated traditional labor support for the Democrats. He also came under attack from "law and order" advocates who criticized him for not being positive enough in handling the situation.

Believing that Patterson stood the best chance of preserving the labor vote, Colorado Democrats nominated him for governor in 1914.[84] Republicans nominated the Reverend George Carlson, basing their campaign on the "law and order" issue and exploiting the growing sentiment for prohibition. The Progressives, who had run a strong second in the 1912 elections, nominated

Costigan for a second try for the governorship, thus pitting him against his fellow reformer, Patterson.[85]

Progressive leaders were keenly aware of Patterson's long record of pro-labor activities. The secretary of the Progressive party gloomily predicted that the "union people" would generally vote for Patterson and estimated that the Democratic position would cost the Progressives ten thousand votes.[86] Yet Costigan served as counsel for the United Mine Workers in litigation resulting from the strike and he figured to divide the prohibitionist vote with another teetotaler, Republican Carlson.

During the campaign, Patterson, who rarely drank, argued the case for local option, later qualifying his position by assuring the voters that if prohibition passed and he were elected, he would conscientiously endeavor to enforce the law. At home, when one of his grandsons in a letter from Exeter Preparatory School accused the older generation of hypocrisy on the issue, Patterson replied that there was a distinction between abstinence and prohibition, the latter cause "intended to abolish the evils of the public saloon." Although not favoring prohibition by state laws, he predicted that national prohibition was inevitable within a few years.[87]

He stood fast to his contention that the equitable resolution of industrial strife in the southern Colorado coalfields was the chief issue of the campaign. His confidence that he could settle the dispute pulled him from retirement in spite of questionable health. It was worth the effort, he said, even if it killed him.[88] Yet as the Democratic candidate, he bore the handicap of Ammons's record and was criticized by both labor and conservatives.

Patterson had sold the *Denver Times* in 1910 and the *Rocky Mountain News* in 1913. Now, as he ran for election, he sorely missed their support, so effective in previous campaigns. Charles Thomas described Patterson as mentally vigorous and as combative as ever during the campaign.[89] But at seventy-five Patterson did not travel the state as much as in previous election years; his close friend Keating thought he lacked some of the old fire.[90]

On election day, Carlson led the Republicans to victory in Colorado, attributing the win to the voters' view of "law and order" and prohibition. Patterson ran a strong second, with Costigan a distant third. Colorado voters overwhelmingly endorsed a statewide prohibition amendment.

One family member was convinced that Patterson's stand on prohibition was the issue that caused his defeat.[91] But contemporaries also pointed to the number of Patterson's vindictive enemies.[92] Personally, Patterson regretted he and Costigan had divided the reform forces. On the eve of the election he anticipated his own defeat, observing sadly that he seemed to be too radical for the conservatives and too conservative for the radicals.[93]

Tom Patterson's long and turbulent public career closed on a note of defeat, a condition with which he was not unfamiliar. Yet there were successes to be remembered. Shortly before his death in 1916, his long struggle for municipal ownership of water supplies stood on the verge of fulfillment. Legalistic delaying tactics by the Denver Union Water Company were coming to an end. Two years later, in 1918, municipal ownership would become a fact.[94] But in February of 1916, Patterson's daughter Margaret, writing of her hopes that the water business was finishing up in good shape, added, "If it does, I think the people of Denver should erect a monument to my revered father as the only true and *persevering* champion of popular rights."[95]

16
The Editor and the Man

Whether [as owner of the *Rocky Mountain News*] I have been faithful
to the trust, and earnest and honest in the defense of the people's rights
I will leave to its patrons to decide.

— Tom Patterson, *Rocky Mountain News,* October 23, 1913

For more than two decades, Thomas Patterson exercised journalistic power in
Colorado. He thoroughly enjoyed using that power. Throughout his ownership, the *Rocky Mountain News* loomed as an imposing vehicle for his ideas
and causes.[1] The *Denver Times,* which he owned from 1902 and 1910, was
put to the same use. Not only did the newspapers furnish continuity to Patterson's interests, but many facets of his temperament and training were displayed in its pages.

Reflecting the personality of its owner, the *News* furnished strong, impet-
uous, and emotional leadership in matters of concern to Colorado, occasionally balanced by reasonably argued editorials that revealed Patterson's legal
experience. Lively and controversial, the *News* became the best-known newspaper in the state and acquired a national reputation. The *Denver Times,* when
still owned by opposition forces, insisted Patterson was a hustler and always
ran the *News* by his motto "Let's have a fight."[2] The *Washington Post* referred to the *News* as one of the most influential newspapers between Kansas
City and San Francisco.[3]

Patterson committed the *News* to many causes he associated with the defense of civil liberties. In addition to defending freedom of speech, the right
of labor to organize, and the right of Denver citizens to control their public
utility companies, Patterson also stubbornly attacked religious bigotry.

When the American Protective Association (APA), a forerunner of the
second Ku Klux Klan, began to exert influence over Colorado politics during the 1890s, it pursued a course of rabid anti-Catholicism and warned of

a papal takeover of politics in the United States. The APA briefly assumed virtual control of the Republican party in Colorado. Catholics could not handle the situation effectively, and ultimately Protestant leaders brought the episode to an end.[4]

Patterson, a rather undedicated Episcopalian who did not place much value on his association with the church, once criticized his daughter Margaret for spending too much of her energy in church activity.[5] But the dangers he saw in the tenets of the APA went against all his moral and ethical precepts. When some members came to ask for his support, Patterson pounded his desk and replied that he would see the *News* in the lowest pit of bankruptcy before he would consent to abuse men because they belonged to a particular church.[6] He began a tenacious assault against the APA, becoming its most feared adversary.

The *News* deplored APA warnings against Catholics holding public office and belittled false alarms of a "Catholic takeover."[7] During an exposé of the APA's philosophy and activities, he ridiculed the rumor that Catholics were shipping rifles packed in coffins and storing them in church cellars. He discredited the APA's contention that the Catholic Church sought to destroy the public schools as a long-range means of dominating the civil government.[8] Labeling members of the organization as self-seeking politicians and deluded bigots, the *News* argued that American institutions could survive without their "protection."[9]

Eventually, *News* contacts inside the organization brought about a full exposure of APA secret passwords and rituals, and Patterson published an extensive list of members' names. *News* informants even quoted the city coroner's speech at an APA gathering in which he identified Patterson as "the man most dangerous to us."[10] When the Republican mayor in 1894 renounced the APA and appointed a Catholic as a commissioner of inspection, the *News,* which had opposed the mayor on other issues, rallied to his defense.[11] By 1897 general revulsion over the highly publicized APA activities undoubtedly contributed to the defeat of many Republican candidates and the election of Patterson-supported reformers, who temporarily gained control of the city government. The hysteria faded as abruptly as it had begun.

Consistent with his views on equality of opportunity, Patterson committed the *News* to support women's suffrage. Certainly, the three strong-willed women in his family, described at the time as "ardent and effective" suffragettes, were an influence.[12] Kate became involved as early as 1877, serving as corresponding secretary and home leader of the Women's Suffrage Association. That same year, Kate's sister, Mary Grafton Campbell, wrote a column in the *News* (then owned by William Byers) on women's suffrage. In 1890 Kate headed a substantial subscription drive on behalf of the Women's Suffrage Association, and Mary and Margaret helped organize a Young Women's League auxiliary.

One of the women reporters Patterson hired credited him with converting his early partner, John Arkin, to the cause of women's suffrage. And the newspaper soon opened its pages to many women contributors and assigned Ellis Meredith to political stories, instead of limiting her to society articles.[13] In 1893 Colorado men approved women's suffrage by over six thousand votes.[14] When the *News*-backed candidate, Republican Thomas S. McMurray, and several other reform candidates won in the 1897 city elections, Patterson credited their success to the female vote and called it a powerful new weapon for good government.[15]

Although Tom Patterson concentrated on support for reform movements, he never lost track of journalistic techniques for cultivating a broad readership. The *News* presented its patrons with a wide variety of features. A typical Sunday edition in 1897 included a science column describing the latest experiments in x-rays, round-by-round drawings of the Bob Fitzsimmons–Jim Corbett prizefight, recipes and ladies' fashion, maps and sketches, political cartoons, short stories, brief reports from cities and towns around the state, a column by Mark Twain and one by humorist Finley Peter Dunne (creator of Mr. Dooley), mining and stock columns, theater reviews, and a weather forecast from Foster's Forecast in St. Joseph, Missouri.[16] The newspaper also had a special Wyoming department and published serialized novels.

As the newspaper prospered, Patterson periodically relocated his plant. He took pride in keeping the *News* abreast of changing techniques, experimenting with new formats and ordering innovative machinery. He made a practice of visiting large Eastern newspapers to pick up ideas and sent an agent on a tour in search of time- and labor-saving devices.[17] As late as 1911 the *News* published a timetable showing how it was beating the arrival of its competitor's papers to Boulder, Greeley, Loveland, and Ft. Collins.[18]

A systematic reading of Denver newspapers from 1890 to 1913 reveals that the reporting style of the *News,* although more lively than that of most of its competitors, reflected the bias common among newspapers of the day. Objective stories dealing with controversial issues were scarce, and facts were construed to reflect the editorial position of the paper. The *Denver Post* for a time did not even bother to run an editorial page, tacitly conceding that the entire coverage reflected the views of its owners. To judge by remarks he occasionally made to his family, Tom Patterson agreed that the editorial certainly was not the only tool in presenting the case to readers.

In times of unusual tension, such as election campaigns, "news" stories and editorials contained appeals to passion and prejudice, euphemistically described by one Colorado historian as "undue manifestations of vigor."[19] Though Patterson operated during a time of highly personal journalism and was not above slanting the interpretation of the facts, he never condoned "false reporting."[20] Yet because his reporters reflected his viewpoints, the *News* was a thoroughly biased journal.

Patterson supported his reporters and editors in times of crises and received their loyalty in return. Among his employees were Edward Keating, who served as a member of the House of Representatives and became the editor of *Labor* magazine; George Creel, who became prominent during the Woodrow Wilson administration as chairman of the Committee on Public Information; Alfred Damon Runyon, famous for his stories about New York City; Lowell Thomas, who became a leading radio journalist; and William MacLeod Raine, later known as the dean of Western novelists.

Patterson normally assumed that he stood on the side of the angels, and the *News* particularly irritated its competition with its extremely moralistic tone. The *Denver Post* complained about Patterson's "holier-than-thou" attitude, declaring that the *News* had "no monopoly on the morality of this community."[21] Tom's moral position was occasionally Victorian. During a drive by the *News* to force a cleanup of prostitution, George Creel had difficulty convincing Patterson to allow mention of syphilis and gonorrhea in the paper; and even after Creel succeeded, Patterson refused to read the articles.[22]

In describing his editorial philosophy, Patterson wrote: "It is the editor's duty to stand sentinel over the public welfare—to advocate, to praise, and confirm measures and official conduct with such impartiality as the editor's intelligence and disinterested loyalty to the public's interest can command."[23] Though he qualified his interpretation of "impartiality," he went on to challenge "the world" to deny he had lived by this rule of conduct.

He also declared that, although he had not written every editorial in the *News,* he accepted full responsibility for all of them. Even during his years in Washington as senator he personally supervised the editorial page. Not until 1910 did he turn the responsibility over to George Creel.[24]

Patterson's law partner, Horace Hawkins, insisted that Patterson adhered to a strict code of ethics in separating his law practice from the *News,* refusing any case that might interfere with the policy of the newspaper. Hawkins said that Patterson refused the business of large corporations while he contended with them on matters of public affairs. Once, when the *News* was advocating a protective tariff on sugar, the paper's business manager accepted a full-page advertisement by the Great Western Sugar Company. Patterson discovered the advertisement after thousands of copies had been printed and ordered it taken out. The early papers were destroyed and the company's money refunded. Charles Thomas, frequently at odds with Patterson politically, claimed that the editor's opponents were never denied a hearing and had access to the public through the *News.*[25]

Tom Patterson's chief adversaries during the 1890s were the *Denver Republican* and the *Denver Times,* both of which favored the conservative Republican point of view on most issues. Financier Nathaniel P. Hill owned the *Republican* during those years and carried on a lively feud with the *News.* When Margaret Patterson complained that one of her father's attacks on Hill was "undignified," Patterson replied that, even if so, it had been effective.[26] The *News* continued to wage an all-out battle in the circulation struggle; by 1899 the *Republican* was forced to resort to cut rates as it fell so far behind the other newspapers that "no one knew it existed."[27] Perhaps in an effort to have the last say, the *Republican* succeeded in labeling Patterson "Old Perplexity," referring to Patterson's owlish and quizzical appearance behind spectacles that accentuated his large grey eyes—a mocking phrase that annoyed him for the rest of his career.

The *News* more than held its own with the *Denver Times* during the 1890s. In 1899 Patterson wrote his nephew, Arthur Johnson, who was serving as a war correspondent in the Philippines, that the *News* was prospering and "keeping ahead of its sleepy contemporaries."[28] With his son-in-law, Richard Campbell, as his partner, Tom Patterson bought the *Denver Times,* an afternoon daily, in 1902. The paper's format instantly changed with the use of banner headlines and greater emphasis on sensational stories. Only the fading *Republican* and the highly successful afternoon *Denver Post* remained as competitors.

Among the newspapers engaged in the journalistic wars, the *Denver Post* was Patterson's nemesis. It had been virtually dead at the time it was purchased in 1897 by two flamboyant operators, Frederick G. Bonfils and Harry H. Tammen. Neither man knew much about newspapers. Tammen, the successful operator of a museum curio shop, always conceded he was three-quarters con man. Bonfils, lofty and regal, furnished the business sense that proved vital to the newspaper's success. Under their leadership, the paper became a journalistic three-ring circus, exhibiting the most extreme features of "yellow" journalism. Scandals flourished on its pages and systematic attacks scathed public officials, nonadvertising businessmen, and anyone else who got in its way. To build their audience, Bonfils and Tammen sponsored every sort of event, including a forty-one-mile roller skating derby to Greeley. Denver's reading public was fascinated, and, though it expressed distaste for many *Post* policies, it subscribed in ever-increasing numbers. Tammen replied to critics, "Sure we're yellow, but we're read, and we're true blue." [29]

The *Rocky Mountain News,* itself sensational when compared with papers other than the *Post,* tried to ignore the *Post*'s theatrics by concentrating on issues of municipal reform, an arena where the *Post*'s record was inconsistent, offering its allegiance where the price was right. [30]

Patterson watched in dismay as the *Post*'s circulation caught and overtook his paper's. Though neither of the *Post*'s owners claimed to bear Patterson any ill will, Bonfils ordered his editors to "keep hammering at Patterson," and he attacked him in his own column. [31] Temperamentally unable to ignore the attacks, Patterson replied in kind. The bitter exchanges reached a climax in December of 1907, when he editorially charged the *Post* with blackmailing advertisers and depicted Bonfils in a political cartoon as Captain Kidd. Bonfils promptly ambushed Patterson in a vacant lot as he was on his way to the *News,* raining blows on the fallen sixty-seven-year-old editor and threatening further harm if the *News* ever again printed his name. Through bloodied lips Patterson replied that he would do his duty whatever the cost, and charged the *Post* owner with malicious assault. [32]

On the witness stand during the ensuing trial, Patterson tried to avoid naming *Post* victims in order to protect them from reprisals, but an inept performance by Bonfils's attorney, John T. Bottom, virtually forced the editor of the *News* to recite examples of the *Post*'s blackmailing and strong-arm tactics. Typical of such actions, said Patterson, was when the owner of a small department store called The Fair switched his advertising from the *Post* to the *News.* The *Post* immediately started a series of articles on alleged cruelties by the owner toward his employees. When the owner, Edward Monash, switched back to the *Post,* the articles abruptly ended. Still other advertisers were brought into line when the *Post* accused them of cheating the city and of maltreatment of women.

Challenging Bonfils to sue for civil damages, Tom Patterson promised to prove everything he had ever written about Bonfils. The *Post* publisher quietly paid his fifty-dollar fine.

Patterson remained baffled over how best to cope with the *Post*'s tactics. As his subscription list lagged behind his competitor's, he ineffectively adopted such ploys as offering special deals on vacuum cleaners to loyal subscribers. But such efforts failed to stem the tide of defections and, some advertisers indeed had been intimidated by the *Post,* the harsh economic reality indicated that advertisers could reach more readers by placing their advertisements in the *Post.*

At the time Patterson sold the *News* to John Shaffer, in 1913, it remained the strongest morning paper in Denver and was still readable and combative.[33] But it no longer could lay claim to the dominance it had once enjoyed. And following Patterson's departure, political observers of the day declared that the *News* was "absolutely dead."[34]

Yet even as Patterson lost the circulation battle with the *Post,* he continued to receive increasing admiration and respect. Those who once had feared some of his ideas as "radical" welcomed him into their homes, a fact duly noted by Bonfils and one that considerably irritated him.[35] Upon the sale of the *News,* Patterson was given an ovation by members of the Denver Real Estate Exchange. He reflected on his years at the *News*: "Whether I have been faithful to the trust, and earnest and honest in the defense of the people's rights I will leave to its patrons to decide."[36]

Though he lost the governorship in 1914, Patterson maintained his interest in various community projects. As he had done since first coming to Colorado, he continued to walk to and from his office, now at 17th and Tremont. He devoted most of his time to working for more equitable freight rates for Colorado businessmen and farmers.

One day in late spring of 1916, as he worked at his office, he suffered a stroke, paralyzing his right side. Telling no one, he left the office, boarded a streetcar, and arrived home, his dignity intact. During the weeks that followed, he lost his hearing, making conversation difficult. Irritated over his loss of faculties, he feared he would soon become a burden to his family. On July 23, 1916, after a brief conversation with his daughter Margaret, Tom Patterson died in his sleep at his Pennsylvania Street home.

The next day, Governor George Carlson ordered all state offices closed for a day, in Patterson's honor.[37]

Thomas M. Patterson left a legacy of more than forty years of significant involvement in the public affairs of the state of Colorado, and a reputation as one of its most influential citizens. His philosophy found roots in the democratic principles of Thomas Jefferson and Andrew Jackson, and was reinforced by his Irish heritage and family code of conduct.

Though the frontier contributed to shaping his attitudes, he functioned in a city that faced the growing problems of urban society. His public career spanned both the Populist and Progressive eras, making Tom Patterson a transitional figure. He was as much at home sharing a platform with a prairie Populist like "Sockless" Jerry Simpson of Kansas as he was when editorially praising the municipal reform efforts of Samuel "Golden Rule" Jones of Toledo, Ohio.

During the 1890s he simultaneously fought for agrarian and Populist-inspired reforms, while campaigning for uniquely urban changes like public ownership of Denver's water supply. Even as he tried to cope with municipal machine politics, his beliefs remained strongly grounded in his rural Midwestern background and heritage.

Idealism and ambition guided Patterson's entire career, and he rarely separated them in his mind. He identified himself with the common people. Underlying his attitudes on sectionalism, imperialism, and labor organizations was his opposition to the exploitation of the underdog. He struggled to bring about changes in society that he believed would enable those who aspired to both prove and improve themselves. His considerable ambition brought him success and influence in Colorado as lawyer, journalist, and politician. Contemporary attitudes toward him were never neutral. People either admired and loved him or feared and despised him.

Those who knew Patterson well frequently referred to traits they associated with his Irish background and relatively humble origins. He maintained a strong sense of his heritage, participating in an Irish-American League and raising money for the freeing of Irish patriots from English prisons. He never lost his anti-English bias, attributable to the long history of Irish subjugation and English absentee-landlordism. He spoke with emotion on the subject of a free Ireland. These sentiments certainly contributed to his sympathy toward the victims of any type of exploitation, and

Margaret Patterson Campbell with her father, Thomas M. Patterson, circa 1915. (Courtesy Archives, University of Colorado at Boulder Libraries, Patterson collection, Bx 8, Fd 1.)

they help to explain his hostility toward those in American society who abused their strength and power.

Contemporary observers stressed that Patterson never forgot his close relationship with the common people, even after he acquired considerable wealth. This feeling of kinship stemmed partly from his family, especially his father, James, a tradesman, who greatly admired Andrew Jackson and Thomas Jefferson. Patterson frequently recalled his days as a journeyman printer and the many courtesies extended to him by the inhabitants of rural Indiana during his years as a struggling lawyer. He was particularly proud of the fact that he had supported himself from the time he was fourteen, working his way through college and as he "read the law" in preparation for passing the bar examination. He considered himself a common man who had accomplished a great deal in life. His stories through the years reinforced his humble beginnings, though his sister indignantly rejected as false his tale that the family had been so poor they were forced to come to America in steerage.

Much of his success resulted from his deep commitment to a work ethic derived from his parents, who stressed high standards of honesty and morality. Honest toil and strong self-discipline were family maxims, and Patterson admired anyone who adhered to them. His natural talents as an orator and his effective work habits combined to ensure his success as a lawyer. His skills in the advocacy technique became legendary, and courtroom observers marveled at the impressive manner in which he combined the traits of the "emotional" Irish and the calculating, "cold" Irish. Meticulously prepared, coldly logical and composed under courtroom pressures, he could sway juries with theatrical performances and passionate appeals. Not surprisingly, his greatest legal fame resulted from his frequent role as a criminal defense attorney, capable of terrifying witnesses during cross-examination.

While Patterson's heritage and training partly explain his later accomplishments, his immersion into a frontier environment probably accentuated certain aspects of his personality. Although occasionally exhausted by his arduous journeys, Patterson generally responded enthusiastically to the venturesome side of life in Colorado. He traveled the high country on horseback in unpredictable weather. He crawled through mine tunnels. He defended accused murderers in the volatile atmosphere of mining camps. Most significantly, he regarded self-improvement as the greatest adventure.

From the first days of his arrival in the town of Denver in 1872 he saw opportunity everywhere. The land was cheap and his small capital would go far. The population and the economy were booming. Here his plans for a political career could be realized more easily and more quickly than in older communities in the East.

Patterson was a man of action. He was blessed with prodigious energy and good health. Thanks to his disciplined mind, capable of superb organization of time and details, he could handle several projects simultaneously. He exercised self-denial, maintained a rigid schedule, scorned laziness, and regarded time-wasting as immoral. Unlike the usual story of men who attained wealth in the West by a lucky mining strike or a windfall, Patterson succeeded by dint of sheer hard work.

Patterson always expected he would succeed. The expansion of Colorado was a fact. If he applied his time and talents with diligence, the improvement of his position would follow. He believed in, and demanded equality of, opportunity as he set out to prove what he was worth. His rebellious spirit flared when he encountered what he regarded as restraints on his freedom to advance himself, and as a result he became known as a "scrapper."

Frequently described as "aggressive" and "belligerent," Patterson engaged in at least three recorded fistfights, and he reveled in intellectual combat. Throughout his careers as lawyer, editor, and politician, he thrived on the encounters that demanded the most of him or were particularly competitive. No one ever faulted him for lack of courage. He continued to defend the Cripple Creek miners in the hostile environment of Colorado Springs amid threats that he would be tarred and feathered. He defied the boycott of his newspapers by the Citizens Alliance. He challenged the supreme court of Colorado in defense of his right to freedom of the press, despite the risk of severe financial loss and possible imprisonment. He was certainly aware that his constant attacks against corporation-dominated public officials could result in the sort of retaliation that befell his colleague in the senate, Edward Carmack, who was killed in the streets of Nashville by a victim of Carmack's journalistic abuse.

Patterson suffered many setbacks but rarely admitted defeat. He displayed a remarkable ability to recover from a lost battle because he knew he would inevitably win the war. Friends and foes alike were impressed with his resiliency and referred to him as "tenacious." Highly competitive, he did not like to lose at anything. Whether defending a client, attacking corporate power or corrupt public officials, debating in the Senate, challenging the supreme court, striving to dominate newspaper circulation, or simply playing cards, he strove desperately to win.

In his legal practice he won so consistently in a large number of difficult cases that he became conditioned to winning, and his successes gave him the stamina and optimism to face reversals. He always retained a basic belief that, whatever the detours, ultimate success would be his.

Patterson's confidence in himself and his abilities led him into occasional displays of vanity, which he recognized in himself during moments of reflection. In his letters, he frequently reported with obvious pleasure the impact he had made in some speaking engagement or editorial argument. And the evidence suggests he could be satisfied only when at the head of some party or faction.

Ironically, his early success and fame as a criminal defense lawyer, coupled with his exploitation of a technicality to reach the U.S. House of Representatives, burdened him with a reputation for using devious methods to attain his goals. Unquestionably, he could and did maneuver to take advantage of every weakness and error of the opposition. But although he would fight fire with fire, he refused to take any action he considered dishonest. Exuding a spirited and sometimes stuffy honesty, he sincerely tried to follow moral standards he thought should guide the behavior of all men. Lawyers regarded him as "incorruptible" in legal matters. As a newspaper publisher, he could never be bought. And his belief in the worthiness and basic honesty of his causes made him an even more effective crusader.

Yet Patterson's moralism frequently caused him to assume the sanctimonious position as champion of good versus evil. He often sat in judgment of men in the same vindictive and autocratic manner that he criticized in others. He could be inflexible and self-righteous, though he rarely recognized that in himself. When he once wondered why no one had ever mentioned him for a position as judge, his friend and law partner, Horace Hawkins, humorously pointed out his constant and total identification with one side of every issue; he suggested that even then he remained oblivious to his violent and frequently self-righteous partisanship.[38]

Ultimately it was his private life where the consequences of his principles and dogged determination were most evident. Patterson liked women with intelligence. His wife, Kate, was such a person. He depended on her for moral support, and he valued her insights on politics. He saw her as a partner, a mother of their children. The deaths of five of their six children both bound them together and split them apart. Though he may have had casual liaisons through the years, it was Kate he loved. Kate tried to believe it, yet she always was unsure. Further, her fragile health and her hearing loss did not fit with

Tom's energy and love of the outdoors. She tended to whine, and Tom had no patience with whiners.

Ironically, Kate was both the beneficiary and the victim of his driving ambition. His wealth and influence enabled her to live well and be among Denver's society leaders. Yet it also was at the root of long separations that at times literally tested the limits of her sanity. Midway in their marriage they struck a truce, limiting their relationship to that of friends. In the end, their shared view of life and its purpose proved enough to see them through.

Patterson held great hopes for all his children. He imbued them with the Victorian ethic of hard work and high moral standards. His son James concerned him the most, and he worried about the boy's unfortunate tendency toward lazy habits and association with the wrong people. They had lived together, in Washington, father and child—proud of each other—during Tom's year as a territorial delegate and then as a congressman. When James was taken to Germany by his mother, to live away from his father's influence, Tom Patterson could not help worrying—and for good reason. By the time of his return, to enroll in Johns Hopkins University and later in the University of Virginia Law School, James was already trapped in his addiction to codeine. Still, his father clung to the hope of better days. His dreams that James might someday become his law partner remained. Even up to the final day of his son's suicide by an overdose, Patterson held firm to his belief that somehow his son would persevere and emerge the individual he had hoped he would be.

Stoical in public about his loss, Patterson privately told his former law partner, Charley Thomas, that, as life had become a torment, his easiest course lay in plunging straight ahead without regard to personal consequences. In his grief he implied he had nothing more to lose, not knowing that two years later his favorite daughter, Mary, would die. Mary was devoted, intelligent, adoring—she was the child of his dreams. Yet, like her mother, Mary was always in delicate health, and at twenty-seven she died. Following on the heels of James's death, the loss was almost too great for her father to bear. It came at a particularly turbulent period of his career, a time when he bolted the national Democratic party and was forced out of both the Democratic and Populist state conventions. His lifelong friend J. K. Mullen, who described Patterson as a gentle man, concluded that the loss of James and Mary caused him to turn inward and made him insensitive toward others.

Ironically, only Margaret, his least favorite child, remained. Yet it was she who brought her father the comfort of a happy family, a well-regulated household, and three grandchildren he adored. He was particularly close to

Richard Campbell family, 1906, in Grand Lake, Colorado. *Left to right* Tom, young
Richard, Richard, Margaret, and baby Katherine.

his oldest grandson, Tom. When young Tom and his brother, Richard, went
back East to prep school, Patterson spent hours in the evenings and on Sun-
days playing double solitaire and spinning tales with his granddaughter,
Katharine.

Margaret, more than her sister and brother, seemed to understand her father's compulsion to succeed and to lead. Her husband, Richard, became
Patterson's business manager at the *News* and his partner in various business
ventures. The family lived with Patterson in his house on Pennsylvania Street.
When Tom died, Margaret was by his side.

Politically, Tom was known as an opportunist, a man who was apt to bolt
his party whenever it would benefit his material and political fortunes.
Yet in fact he never wavered in his ideological position. Specific candidates
and issues changed with time, but Patterson's fundamental defense of the
people against the moneyed powers, against corporation exploitation,
and against corruption in government remained steadfast. Charges of inconsistency levied against him came primarily from his history of switching his

allegiance from various parties and factions. Yet the record reveals that Patterson, who believed that party lines should give way to principle, never saw any problem with his actions.

After fifteen years as "Mr. Democrat" in Colorado, Patterson joined the Populists primarily because of the Democratic position on bimetallism. Grover Cleveland and other "goldbugs" not only threatened Colorado's sectional interests, but also denied Patterson's solution to the economic plight of the common people. Tom's subsequent challenge to Davis Waite within the Populist cause reflected his conviction that Waite was endangering the viability of the party through inept leadership, and that the only way to eventually achieve other Populist reforms was to concentrate on the single issue of free silver.

When William Jennings Bryan became the Democratic presidential nominee in 1896, Patterson saw it as an opportune time to fuse the elements of the various parties on the silver issue. As a result of his efforts, traditional voting lines were broken and Colorado became a true two-party state, instead of the exclusive domain of the Republican party.

At the time Patterson received the senatorship as a reward for his fusion efforts and announced his intention to join the Democratic caucus in the Senate, die-hard Populists charged him with opportunism and regular Colorado Democrats questioned his claim to party membership. Yet it should be noted that in 1901 Bryan still headed the Democratic party. As he always had, Patterson believed that Bryan's leadership offered the best chance to bring about reforms. His subsequent disagreement with Senate Democrats over caucus discipline, after he had praised Theodore Roosevelt's attempts to curb big business, came at a time when Democratic party leadership had fallen temporarily under the control of conservative forces less amenable to Patterson's desired reforms.

When Roosevelt failed to move toward reform rapidly or effectively, Patterson enthusiastically supported the return of Bryan to Democratic leadership in 1908 and Woodrow Wilson's New Freedom in 1912. He consistently selected the alternative that seemed to offer the best opportunity to limit the power of men and organizations that stood in the way of success for those at the bottom.

His defense of the little man operated simultaneously at the national, state, and local levels. Patterson's most prolonged and significant impact on Colorado politics was his relentless warfare against established power, regardless of which political party he judged to be "guilty of corruption." He climaxed a municipal drive against the Republicans with a citizen's reform victory in 1897 and helped achieve "home rule" for Denver, a phrase that rested well with his Irish sensibilities.

Later, as the "Big Mitt" organization of Mayor Robert Speer spread its control over the city, Patterson conducted a running battle against those who were not "real" Democrats—especially when they caved in, as the Republicans had, to the blandishments of the corporations. The eventual victories achieved by the Denver reformers were a result of yet another fusion effort, after Patterson and his newspapers successfully argued that municipal government was essentially a housekeeping operation and above partisanship.

Patterson, the "bolter," consistently aimed to increase the political power of the common people and to curtail what he regarded as the abuse of power and exploitation of Colorado's citizens by those who controlled the means of production. His steady adherence to the cause of expanding direct democracy and limiting corporate power explains those moves for which he was criticized as an opportunist.

Yet Patterson was by instinct a traditionalist. He called for a modification, not a disruption, of the social order, condemning labor violence and arguing for the inviolability of contracts. His true labor heroes were Samuel Gompers and John Mitchell, not William "Big Bill" Haywood. Although he accepted the need for investments of capital in such entities as corporations, he refused to acquiesce to combinations of wealth that strangled competition. Basically, he embraced the ideas of classical economics, supporting the concept that if everyone were allowed to make his proper contribution productivity would be maximized; self-interest would lead to benefit for all of society.

He reconciled his own personal ambition with his idealism, and saw his materialistic drive compatible with the country's open, mobile society. That belief also reinforced his criticism of forces that might disrupt the market system by restricting an individual from making the most effective contribution to society. The way should be open for those as talented as himself.

Patterson's brand of individualism did not preclude the spirit of cooperation represented by labor unions, and when the passing of the frontier altered conditions, he accepted and supported a widening of governmental power as a check to industrial monopoly—a controlled capitalism. He believed that in some areas the public interest could be served best by public ownership, as in the case of natural or technical monopolies like utility companies and railroads, and he fought for this goal with more consistency and endurance than any other figure in Colorado.

Contrary to accusations from his opponents that he advocated radical and anarchistic political and economic changes, Patterson denied the promises of socialism as unreal and unworkable. Those who sincerely worried over what they regarded as his tendency toward collectivism underestimated his dedication to the proposition that every man should be self-dependent. In one of his most revealing statements, Patterson said, "Socialism, proper, is paternalism as against individualism."[39]

His consistent agitation for the principle of arbitration demonstrated his ideas regarding the role of government in a free society: to provide a means to mediate differences, modify rules or the meaning of rules, and to enforce compliance by those who would not otherwise play the game or would play it unfairly. Patterson earnestly desired to play the capitalistic game, but insisted on an umpire.

Thomas Patterson, though an extraordinary man, was a product of his time. He held to his personal philosophical persuasion with tenacity and conviction. He made the mistakes all strong men make, but his purposes and thoughts most often aimed for the common good. And he never lost faith in himself.

Notes

Preface

1. *Denver Times,* July 24, 1916.

1: The Young Man From Indiana

1. Mary Bell Johnson Pease, unpublished account of the Patterson family history. Arthur C. Johnson papers, Western Historical Collection, University of Colorado, Boulder.

2. *Denver Times,* July 25, 1916.

3. Pease, Patterson family history.

4. Ibid.

5. Ibid.

6. Dwight W. Hoover, *A Pictorial History of Indiana* (Bloomington: Indiana University Press, 1980), 71.

7. Robert L. Chase, "Thomas Patterson," *Rocky Mountain News,* February 10, 1929.

8. Emma Lou Thornbrough, *Indiana in the Civil War Era* (Indiana Historical Bureau and Historical Society, 1965), 537.

9. Ibid., 77.

10. Claim for pension by Thomas M. Patterson, U.S. Dept. of the Interior, Washington, D.C., August 7, 1914.

11. Hoover, *Pictorial History of Indiana,* 90.

12. Family stories were related to author Sybil Downing by various members of the Patterson family.

13. A *Compendium of the War of the Rebellion,* ed. Frederick H. Dyer. National Historical Society (Dayton, Ohio: Morningside, 1979), 1122.

14. *Denver Times,* July 25, 1916.

15. Robert Chase, *Rocky Mountain News,* July 10, 1929.

16. *Denver Post,* July 17, 1902.

17. Thomas Campbell III, great–great–grandson of Thomas M. Patterson and professor of Wabash College, in "Thomas McDonald Patterson, Wabash 1868: One of Our Wayward Sons Comes Home," (an unpublished speech given to the Ouiatenon Club, Wabash College, Crawfordsville, Indiana, November 10, 1992.)

18. Claim for pension, Thomas M. Patterson.

19. *Rocky Mountain News,* July 24, 1916.

20. Thornbrough, *Indiana in the Civil War Era,* 538.

21. T. M. Patterson, Crawfordsville, Indiana, to K. M. Patterson, Watertown, New York, September 24, 1866. Patterson papers, Western Historical Collection, University of Colorado, Boulder [hereafter referred to as Patterson papers].

22. Ibid.

23. T. M. Patterson to K. M. Patterson, September 23, 1866. Patterson papers.

24. Campbell, "Thomas McDonald Patterson, Wabash 1868."

25. *Denver Times,* July 25, 1916; *Rocky Mountain News,* February 10, 1929.

26. T. M. Patterson, Crawfordsville, Indiana, to K. M. Patterson at Wapella, Illinois, July 13, 1868. Patterson papers.

27. Campbell, "Thomas McDonald Patterson, Wabash 1868."

28. T. M. Patterson, Crawfordsville, Indiana, to K. M. Patterson, Wapella, Illinois, July 13, 1868. Patterson papers.

29. T. M. Patterson, Crawfordsville, Indiana, to K. M. Patterson, Watertown, Illinois, September 23, 1868. Patterson papers.

30. K. M. Patterson to T. M. Patterson, July 26, 1869. Patterson papers.

31. Sewell Thomas, *Silhouettes of Charles S. Thomas* (Caldwell, Idaho: Caxton, 1959), 13.

32. *Denver Post,* July 24, 1916.

33. T. M. Patterson to K. M. Patterson, July 10, 1872.

34. Charles S. Thomas, "Honorable T. M. Patterson," (unpublished, undated). Charles S. Thomas Collection, Colorado Historical Society.

35. T. M. Patterson to K. M. Patterson, May 11, 1873. Patterson papers.

36. T. M. Patterson to K. M. Patterson, May 25, 1873. Patterson papers.

37. Frank Hall, *History of Colorado* (Chicago: Blakeley, 1891), 3:64.

38. *Rocky Mountain News,* June 25, 1873.

39. Ibid.

40. *Rocky Mountain News,* September 3, 1873.

41. Edward Keating, *The Gentleman From Colorado* (Denver: Sage, 1964), 86, 87.

42. *Denver Times,* September 17, 1902.

43. Howard Lamar, *The Far Southwest, 1846–1912* (New Haven: Yale University Press, 1966), 273.

44. Hall, *History of Colorado* 2:359.

45. Elmer Ellis, *Henry Moore Teller: Defender of the West* (Caldwell, Idaho: Caxton printers, 1941), 89.

46. Ibid.

47. Thomas F. Dawson, "Major Thompson, Chief Ouray and the Utes," *Colorado Magazine* 7 (May 1930): 113–22; Carl Ubbelohde, Maxine Benson, and Duane A. Smith, *A Colorado History,* 6th ed. (Boulder, Colo.: Pruett, 1988), 149.

48. Mary Fonda Adams, "Thomas M. Patterson: Some Aspects of His Political Career" (Master's thesis, University of Colorado, 1933), 11.

49. Thomas, *Silhouettes,* 20.

2: Hurrah for Colorado!

1. R. G. Dill, *The Political Campaigns of Colorado* (Denver, Colo.: Arapahoe, 1895), 6, 7.

2. Elmer Ellis, *Henry Moore Teller: Defender of the West* (Caldwell, Idaho: Caxton, 1941), 62–94.

3. Mary Fonda Adams, "Thomas M. Patterson: Some Aspects of His Political Career" (Master's thesis, University of Colorado, 1933), 11.

4. *Rocky Mountain News,* March 4, 1874.

5. *Rocky Mountain News,* April 8, 1874.

6. Dill, *Political Campaigns of Colorado,* 5.

7. Adams, "Thomas M. Patterson," 12.

8. Frank Hall, *History of the State of Colorado* (Chicago: Blakeley, 1891), 2:249, 250.

9. *Rocky Mountain News,* July 29, 1874.

10. *Rocky Mountain News,* August 5, 1874.

11. *Pueblo Chieftain,* August 3, 1874.

12. *Rocky Mountain News,* August 19, 1874.

13. *Rocky Mountain News,* August 26, 1874.

14. Ibid.

15. *Rocky Mountain News,* September 2, 1874.

16. K. M. Patterson to T. M. Patterson, June 2, 1874. Patterson papers, Western Historical Collection, University of Colorado, Boulder [hereafter referred to as Patterson papers].

17. T. M. Patterson to K. M. Patterson, August 8, 1874. Patterson papers.

18. T. M. Patterson to K. M. Patterson, September 21, 1874. Patterson papers.

19. Dill, *Political Campaigns,* 6, 7; Ellis, *Henry Moore Teller,* 89–91.

20. K. M. Patterson, Denver, Colorado, to T. M. Patterson, Washington, D.C., February 15, 1875. Patterson papers.

21. T. M. Patterson, Washington, D.C., to K. M. Patterson, Denver, Colorado, February 16, 1875. Patterson papers.

22. Ibid.

23. Howard Lamar, *The Far Southwest, 1846–1912* (New Haven: Yale University Press, 1966), 264.

24. Ellis, *Henry Moore Teller,* 62–94.

25. T. M. Patterson to K. M. Patterson, February 16, 1875. Patterson papers.

26. Wilbur Fisk Stone, *History of Colorado* (Chicago: S. J. Clarke, 1918), 1:425.

27. Hall, *History of Colorado,* 2:237.

28. T. M. Patterson, Washington, D.C., to K. M. Patterson, Denver, Colorado, February 21, 1875. Patterson papers. James Belford held no bitterness over the election. He was enough of a friend to join Patterson's defense team in his trial before the Colorado Supreme Court in 1905.

29. Hall, *History of Colorado,* 2:271.

30. T. M. Patterson, Boston, Massachusetts, to K. M. Patterson, Denver, Colorado, March 10, 1875. Patterson papers.

31. Ibid.

32. *Congressional Record,* 44th Cong., 1st Sess., 4:3, 2425.

33. Ibid., 4:5, 4701.

34. Ibid., 4702.

35. *Congressional Record,* 44th Cong., 1st Sess., 4:3, 2754.

36. Ibid.

37. Ibid., 2051.

38. Ibid.

39. *Congressional Record,* 44th Cong., 1st Sess., 4:4, 4100–4109.

40. Ibid., 4:1, 619.

41. Ibid.

42. Ibid., 4:3, 2635, 2655.

43. Ibid., 2861.

44. Adams, "Thomas M. Patterson," 30.

45. T. M. Patterson, Washington, D.C., to K. M. Patterson, Denver, Colorado, April 28, 1876. Patterson papers.

46 *Rocky Mountain News,* July 15, 1896.

47. *Congressional Record,* 44th Cong., 1st Sess., 4:3, 2635.

48. Ibid.

49. *Congressional Record,* 44th Cong., 1st Sess., 4:4, 4982–85.

50. T. M. Patterson, Washington, D.C., to K. M. Patterson, Denver Colorado, March 3, 1876. Patterson papers.

51. Dill, *Political Campaigns,* 6, 7.

52. Sewell Thomas, *Silhouettes of Charles S. Thomas* (Caldwell, Idaho: Caxton, 1959), 21.

53. Hall, *History of Colorado,* 2:356.

54. Wilfred E. Binkley, *American Political Parties: Their Natural History* (New York: Knopf, 1943), 305–8.

55. Edward Keating, *Gentleman from Colorado,* (Denver, Colo.: Sage, 1964), 90.

3: Meeting the Challenge

1. T. M. Patterson, Washington, D.C., to K. M. Patterson, Denver, Colorado, June 10, 1876. Patterson papers, Western History Collection, University of Colorado, Boulder [hereafter referred to as Patterson papers].

2. T. M. Patterson, Washington, D.C., to K. M. Patterson, Denver, Colorado. June 22, 1876. Patterson papers.

3. Ibid. Patterson papers.

4. T. M. Patterson, Washington, D.C., to K. M. Patterson, Denver, Colorado. July 16, 1876. Patterson papers.

5. T. M. Patterson, Washington, D.C., to K. M. Patterson, Denver, Colorado. July 23, 1876. Patterson papers.

6. T. M. Patterson, Washington, D.C., to K. M. Patterson, Denver, Colorado. August 5, 1876. Patterson papers.

7. T. M. Patterson, Washington, D.C., to K. M. Patterson, Denver, Colorado. August 11, 1876. Patterson papers.

8. K. M. Patterson, Denver, Colorado, to T. M. Patterson, Washington, D.C., January 26, 1876. Patterson papers.

9. T. M. Patterson, Washington, D.C., to K. M. Patterson, Denver, Colorado, February 2, 1876. Patterson papers.

10. T. M. Patterson, Washington, D.C., to K. M. Patterson, Denver, Colorado. June 8, 1876. Patterson papers.

11. T. M. Patterson, Washington, D.C., to K. M. Patterson, Denver, Colorado. June 15, 1876. Patterson papers.

12. T. M. Patterson, Washington, D.C., to K. M. Patterson, Denver, Colorado. June 19, 1876. Patterson papers.

13. T. M. Patterson, Washington, D.C., to K. M. Patterson, Denver, Colorado. August 5, 1876. Patterson papers.

14. Frank Hall, *History of the State of Colorado* (Chicago: Blakeley, 1891), 3:66.

15. R. G. Dill, *The Political Campaigns of Colorado* (Denver, Colo.: Arapahoe, 1895), 13, 14.

16. Ibid., 17–20.

17. Ibid.

18. Hall, *History of Colorado,* 2:343.

19. Mary Fonda Adams, "Thomas M. Patterson: Some Aspects of His Political Career" (Master's thesis, University of Colorado, 1933), 37.

20. Dill, *Political Campaigns,* 18.

21. Ibid., 16.

22. Adams, "Thomas M. Patterson," 39.

23. Dill, *Political Campaigns,* 17.

24. Adams, "Thomas M. Patterson," 40.

25. Dill, *Political Campaigns,* 20.

26. Adams, "Thomas M. Patterson," 43.

27. Dill, *Political Campaigns,* 20.

28. Adams, "Thomas M. Patterson," 43.

29. Ibid., 42.

30. *Congressional Record,* 45th Cong., 2nd Sess., 7:1, 193.

31. Ibid., 196.

32. Ibid., 199.

33. Ibid.

34. T. M. Patterson, Washington, D.C., to K. M. Patterson, Denver, Colorado, December 14, 1877. Patterson papers.

4: Supreme Sectionalist

1. James Patterson, Washington, D.C., to K. M. Patterson, Denver, Colorado, 1877. Patterson papers, Western Historical Collection, University of Colorado [hereafter referred to as Patterson papers].

2. K. M. Patterson, Denver, Colorado, to T. M. Patterson, Washington, D.C., January 11, 1878. Patterson papers.

3. T. M. Patterson, Washington, D.C., to K. M. Patterson, Denver, Colorado, January 20, 1878. Patterson papers.

4. K. M. Patterson, Denver, Colorado, to T. M. Patterson, Washington, D.C., February 9, 1878. Patterson papers.

5. *Congressional Record,* 45th Cong., 2nd Sess., 7:3, 2424–27.

6. *Congressional Record,* 45th Cong., 2nd Sess., 7:4, 3680.

7. *Congressional Record,* 45th Cong., 2nd Sess., 7:3, 2031.

8. *Congressional Record,* 45th Cong., 2nd Sess., 7:4, 3809.

9. Ibid., 3840, 38–41.

10. 20 U.S. Stat. at L., 145.

11. *Congressional Record,* 45th Cong., 2nd Sess., 7:1, 318.

12. *Congressional Record,* 45th Cong., 2nd Sess., 7:4, 3951.

13. *Congressional Record,* 45th Cong., 2nd Sess., 7:3, 2974.

14. Ibid.

15. Ibid.

16. Ibid.

17. T. M. Patterson, Washington, D.C., to K. M. Patterson, Denver, Colorado, May 12, 1878. Patterson papers.

18. Ibid.

19. *Congressional Record,* 45th Cong., 2nd Sess., 7:2, 1532–34.

20. Ibid.
21. Mary Fonda Adams, "Thomas M. Patterson: Some Aspects of His Political Career" (Master's thesis, University of Colorado, 1933), 60.
22. *Congressional Record,* 45th Cong., 2nd Sess., 7:4, 3327, 3328.
23. T. M. Patterson, Washington, D.C., to K. M. Patterson, Denver, Colorado, May 12, 1878. Patterson papers.
24. T. M. Patterson, Washington, D.C., to K. M. Patterson, Denver, Colorado, June 14, 1878. Patterson papers.
25. T. M. Patterson, Washington, D.C., to K. M. Patterson, Denver, Colorado, April 23, 1878. Patterson papers.
26. T. M. Patterson, Washington, D.C., to K. M. Patterson, Denver, Colorado, May 29, 1878. Patterson papers.
27. Don and Jean Griswold (authors of *The Carbonate Camp Called Leadville*) to author Robert Smith.
28. T. M. Patterson, Alma, Colorado, to K. M. Patterson, Denver, Colorado, September 26, 1878. Patterson papers.
29. Ibid.
30. R. G. Dill, *The Political Campaigns of Colorado* (Denver, Colo.: Arapahoe, 1895), 45.

5: The Self-Made Man

1. Certificate admitting T. M. Patterson to practice before the U.S. Supreme Court, 1877, Patterson papers, Western Historical Collection, University of Colorado at Boulder [hereafter referred to as Patterson papers].
2. Jerome W. Johnson, "Murder on the Uncompahgre," *Colorado Magazine* 43 (summer 1966), 219.
3. Sewell Thomas, *Silhouettes of Charles S. Thomas* (Caldwell, Idaho: Caxton, 1959), 31.
4. T. M. Patterson, Wagon Wheel Gap, Colorado, to K. M. Patterson, Denver, Colorado, December 8, 1879, Patterson papers.
5. T. M. Patterson, Saguache, Colorado, to K. M. Patterson, Denver, Colorado, December 2, 1879. Patterson papers.
6. K. M. Patterson, New York City, to T. M. Patterson, Denver, Colorado, March 3, 1881. Patterson papers.

7. In the absence of any evidence, it can be speculated that Mary Campbell, Kate Patterson's sister, fabricated Mrs. Morgan and her letters in hopes of placing her husband and herself in a better light with Kate.

8. T. M. Patterson, Denver, Colorado, to K. M. Patterson, Arnheim, Germany, April 3, 1881. Patterson papers.

9. Ibid.

10. Ibid.

11. T. M. Patterson, Leadville, Colorado, to K. M. Patterson, Denver, Colorado, January 23, 1888. Patterson papers.

12. T. M. Patterson, Denver, Colorado, to K. M. Patterson, Heidelberg, Germany, October 8, 1881. Patterson papers.

13. T. M. Patterson, Denver, Colorado, to K. M. Patterson, Arnstadt, Germany, September 23, 1883. Patterson papers.

14. T. M. Patterson, Denver, Colorado, to Margaret Patterson, location unknown, November 21, 1886. Patterson papers.

15. *Iron Silver Mining Company v. Cheesman* (1885), 116 U.S. 529 6 S. Ct. 481 (29 L. ed. 712). Walter Scott Cheesman was Denver's premier real estate and water tycoon.

16. Paul Rodman, *Mining Frontiers of the Far West, 1848–1880* (New York: Holt, Rinehart, and Winston, 1963), 173–75; William H. Robinson, "Charles S. Thomas: The Tall Sycamore of Cherry Creek," *Rocky Mountain Law Review,* 3 (April 1931): 160.

17. Thomas Rickard, *A History of American Mining* (New York: McGraw-Hill, 1932), 363.

18. *Denver Post,* July 24, 1916.

19. T. M. Patterson, Leadville, Colorado, to K. M. Patterson, Heidelberg, Germany, January 27, 1882. Patterson papers.

20. T. M. Patterson, Gunnison, Colorado, to K. M. Patterson at Heidelberg, Germany, July 29, 1882. Patterson papers.

21. T. M. Patterson, Montrose, Colorado, to K. M. Patterson, Denver, Colorado, June 26, 1885. Patterson papers.

22. *J. J. Richey v. the People* (1896), 23 Colo., 314–32; also *47 Pac.,* 272–74.

23. *Denver Post,* July 24, 1916.

24. Charles S. Thomas, "Thomas M. Patterson," (unpublished manuscript, Thomas papers, Colorado State Historical Society, Denver, Colorado.)

25. Edward Keating, *The Gentleman From Colorado* (Denver: Sage, 1964), chapters 8 and 9.

26. T. M. Patterson, from an undated written account of this episode, Patterson papers.

27. T. M. Patterson, Denver, Colorado, to K. M. Patterson, Arnstadt, Germany, September 23, 1883. Patterson papers.

28. F. Edward Little, "Thomas M. Patterson: Gamecock of the Colorado Courts," *Rocky Mountain Law Review* XI (April, 1939), 156.

29. *Denver Post,* July 24, 1916.

30. Little, "Thomas M. Patterson," 157.

31. T. M. Patterson, New York City, to K. M. Patterson, Denver, Colorado, February 8 and 11, 1898. Patterson papers.

32. Thomas, "Thomas M. Patterson," 7.

33. Mr. and Mrs. J. Wilbur, Cheyenne, Wyoming, to T. M. Patterson, Denver, Colorado, August 3, 1888. Patterson papers.

34. Frank Hall, *History of the State of Colorado* (Chicago: Blakeley, 1891), 2:70.

35. Ibid.

36. *Denver Post,* July 24, 1916.

37. Ibid.

38. Fitzjames McCarthy, "Thomas M. Patterson," in *Political Portraits* (Colorado Springs, Colo.: Gazette, 1888), 25.

39. *Denver Post,* July 24, 1916.

40. George F. Dunklee, "Tributes to the Memory of Hon. Thomas M. Patterson" (speech given at a memorial service held by the Denver Bar Association, Denver, Colorado, March 26, 1917), Arthur C. Johnson papers, Western Historical Collection, University of Colorado at Boulder.

41. Marshall Sprague, *Money Mountain* (Boston: Little, Brown, 1953), 230.

42. Thomas F. Dawson, *The Life and Character of Edward C. Wolcott* (New York: Knickerbocker, 1911).

43. *Denver Post,* July 24, 1916.

44. Thomas, "Thomas M. Patterson," 9.

45. T. M. Patterson, Leadville, Colorado, to K. M. Patterson, Heidelberg, Germany, July 28 and September 23, 1881. Patterson papers.

46. T. M. Patterson, Denver, Colorado, to K. M. Patterson, Heidelberg, Germany, September 24, 1881. Patterson papers.

47. *Denver Post,* July 24, 1916.

48. Ibid.

49. Ibid.

50. Thomas, "Thomas M. Patterson," 8.

51. *Rocky Mountain News,* July 24, 1916.

52. *Denver Times,* January 8, 1917.

53. Major properties held at the time of Tom Patterson's death included four lots at 19th and Curtis Streets in east Denver; four lots at 18th and Champa, opposite the post office; four lots on Glenarm, between 17th and 18th Streets in downtown Denver; four lots at 17th and Welton Streets adjoining his newspaper; four lots at 15th and Cheyenne Place; the Albany and Markham Hotels; the old *Denver Republican* building's additional property in Pueblo and Jefferson Counties. *Denver Post,* July 24, 1916.

54. Hall, *History of Colorado,* 2:66.

55. Ibid.

6: Field Marshal Patterson

1. *Denver Tribune,* September 4, 1875.

2. T. M. Patterson, Saguache, Colorado, to K. M. Patterson, Denver, Colorado, December 2, 1879. Patterson papers, Western Historical Collection, University of Colorado at Boulder [hereafter referred to as Patterson papers].

3. Carl Ubbelohde, Maxine Benson, and Duane A. Smith, *A Colorado History,* 6th ed. (Boulder, Colo.: Pruett, 1988), 218.

4. R. G. Dill, *The Political Campaigns of Colorado* (Denver, Colo.: Arapahoe, 1895), 48.

5. Ibid., 49.

6. Ibid., 52.

7. Robert L. Perkin, *The First Hundred Years* (Garden City, N.Y.: Doubleday, 1959), 344.

8. Dill, *Political Campaigns,* 54.

9. Paul T. Bechtol, Jr., "The 1880 Labor Dispute in Leadville," *Colorado Magazine* 47 (fall 1970): 312–25.

10. Dill, *Political Campaigns,* 54; Percy Stanley Fritz, *Colorado: The Centennial State* (New York: Prentice-Hall, 1941), 368.

11. Dill, *Political Campaigns*, 54.

12. Don Griswold and Jean Griswold, "Leadville: A City of Contrast," *Leadville Herald Democrat*, July 2, 1965.

13. Ibid., July 9, 1965.

14. Ibid.

15. Dill, *Political Campaigns*, 55.

16. *Denver Times*, June 29, 1880.

17. *Denver Times*, July 1 and August 25, 1880.

18. *Denver Tribune*, September 4 and 28, 1880.

19. *Rocky Mountain News*, November 2, 1880.

20. *Denver Times*, July 29 and September 27, 1880.

21. *Denver Republican*, November 2, 1880; *Rocky Mountains News*, November 1, 1880; and Jerome C. Smiley, *The History of Denver* (Denver, Colo.: Times-Sun Publishing, 1901), 471–73.

22. *Denver Times*, November 1, 1880.

23. *Denver Tribune*, November 2, 1880.

24. Dill, *Political Campaigns*, 55.

25. *Denver Tribune*, November 2, 1880.

26. *Denver Times*, November 3, 1880.

27. *Denver Times*, October 2, 1882.

28. Ibid.

29. *Central City Post*, September 23, 1882.

30. Frank Hall, *History of the State of Colorado* (Chicago: Blakeley, 1895), 2:36, 37; Dill, *Political Campaigns*, 76.

31. *Central City Post*, October 21, 1882.

32. *Denver Times*, October 20, 1882.

33. K. M. Patterson, Denver, Colorado, to Mary Patterson, Paris, France, October 27, 1882. Patterson papers.

34. *Denver Times*, October 16 and 31, and November 3, 1882.

35. Ibid.

36. Dill, *Political Campaigns*, 76.

37. *Central City Post*, October 14, 1882.

38. *Silver Cliff Weekly Herald*, October 19, 1882.

39. *Denver Times,* November 10, 1882.

40. *Denver Republican,* January 15 and 16, 1883.

41. *Denver Times,* January 18, 1883.

42. *Denver Republican,* January 26, 1883; Dill, *Political Campaigns,* 80.

43. K. M. Patterson, Denver, Colorado, to Mary Patterson, Paris, France, November 13, 1882. Patterson papers.

44. T. M. Patterson, Denver, Colorado, to K. M. Patterson, location unknown. April 20, 1883. Patterson papers.

45. *Rocky Mountain News,* September 26, 1884.

46. *Denver Times,* September 18, 1884.

47. *Rocky Mountain News,* October 3, 9, and 11, 1884.

48. T. M. Patterson, Crested Butte, Colorado, to K. M. Patterson, Denver, Colorado, October 11, 1884. Patterson papers.

49. *Colorado Springs Gazette,* October 31, 1884.

50. T. M. Patterson, New York City, to K. M. Patterson, Denver, Colorado, July 13, 1884. Patterson papers.

51. *Denver Times,* October 23 and 24, 1884.

52. *Pueblo Chieftain,* October 23, 1884.

53. *Georgetown Miner,* as quoted in the *Rocky Mountain News,* September 3, 1884; *Denver Times,* November 6, 1884.

54. Dill, *Political Campaigns,* 102, 103.

55. *Denver Times,* October 4–7, 1886.

56. *Denver Republican,* October 31, 1886; *Denver Times,* October 19, 1886.

57. *Denver Times,* October 7 and 25, 1886.

58. *Denver Republican,* October 31 and November 1 and 2, 1886.

59. *Pueblo Chieftain,* October 14 and 23, 1886; *Denver Times,* October 6, 1886.

60. *Grand Junction News,* as quoted in the *Pueblo Chieftain,* October 14, 1886.

61. T. M. Patterson, Denver, Colorado, to Mary Patterson, Bryn Mawr College, Pennsylvania, November 7, 1886. Patterson papers.

62. Dill, *Political Campaigns,* 109, 112, 113.

63. *Denver Republican,* November 4, 1886.

64. *Pueblo Chieftain,* November 7, 1886.

65. T. M. Patterson, Denver, Colorado, to K. M. Patterson, Halle, Germany, June 23, 1883. Patterson papers.

66. T. M. Patterson, Denver, Colorado, to K. M. Patterson, Halle, Germany, April 4, 1883. Patterson papers.

67. Family history based on reading of correspondence, Patterson papers.

68. *Grand Junction News,* June 4 and 16, 1888.

69. *Colorado Springs Gazette,* September 13, 1888.

70. Mary Campbell, Denver, Colorado, to K. M. Patterson, New Cumberland, West Virginia, September 14, 1888. Patterson papers.

71. Ibid.

72. Fitzjames McCarthy, "Thomas M. Patterson," in *Political Portraits* (Colorado Springs, Colo., 1888), 25.

73. *Grand Junction News,* July 21, 1888; Dill, *Political Campaigns,* 125.

74. Perkin, *First Hundred Years,* 352.

75. *Colorado Springs Gazette,* October 7, 1888.

76. *Colorado Springs Gazette,* October 25, 1888.

77. Ibid.

78. Ibid.

79. *Pueblo Chieftain,* August 10 and 20, 1888.

80. *Grand Junction News,* October 6, 1888.

81. *Silver Cliff Rustler,* October 25, 1888.

82. *Pueblo Chieftain,* September 13, 1888.

83. Dill, *Political Campaigns,* 132, 133.

84. T. M. Patterson, Denver, Colorado, to Margaret Patterson, Bryn Mawr, Pennsylvania, November 8, 1888. Patterson papers.

7: The Fusionist

1. James Patterson, Hot Springs, Arkansas, to K. M. Patterson, Boston, Massachusetts, March 27, 1890. Patterson papers, Western Historical Collection, University of Colorado at Boulder [hereafter referred to as Patterson papers].

2. Sally Davis and Betty Baldwin, *Denver's Dwellings and Descendants* (Denver, Colo.: Sage, 1963), 171–72.

3. *Rocky Mountain News,* August 19, 1894; Robert L. Perkin, *The First Hundred Years* (Garden City, N.Y.: Doubleday, 1959), 383; author Robert Smith's personal interview with T. Campbell, Tom Patterson's grandson, Denver, Colorado, August 28, 1969.

4. Professor John D. Hicks described the farm problem in his book *The Populist Revolt* (Minneapolis: University of Minnesota Press, 1931). See also Walter T. K. Nugent, *The Tolerant Populists* (Chicago: University of Chicago Press, 1963) and Norman Pollack, *The Populist Response to Industrial America* (Cambridge: Harvard University Press, 1962).

5. A thorough summary of Senator Henry M. Teller's scholarly analysis of the case for bimetallism can be found in Elmer Ellis, *Henry Moore Teller: Defender of the West* (Caldwell, Idaho: Caxton, 1941), 184–87. While both Teller and Patterson primarily wanted a recovery of the price of silver, they also displayed concern over the appreciating dollar as a cause of human misery.

6. *Congressional Record,* 44th Cong., 1st Sess., 4:4, 4982–4985.

7. James Patterson, Pasadena, California, to T. M. Patterson, Denver, Colorado, February 24, 1892. Patterson papers.

8. T. M. Patterson, Denver, Colorado, to James Patterson, Pasadena, California, March 7, 1892. Patterson papers.

9. *Rocky Mountain News,* March 10, 1892.

10. *Rocky Mountain News,* March 8, 1892; Leon W. Fuller, "Governor Waite and His Silver Panacea," *Colorado Magazine* 10 (March 1933): 41.

11. *Rocky Mountain News,* March 8, 1892. Shortly thereafter the *Denver Sun* abandoned its hostile attitude toward the silverites, and the *News* in its March 12, 1892, issue gleefully claimed that the reversal came as a result of the *Sun's* loss of circulation and business.

12. *Rocky Mountain News,* April 7 and 8, 1892.

13. T. M. Patterson, Denver, Colorado, to K. M. Patterson, Boston, Massachusetts, April 24, 1892. Patterson papers.

14. *Rocky Mountain News,* April 24, 1892.

15. *Denver Republican,* April 26, 1892.

16. *Rocky Mountain News,* April 26 and 28, 1892.

17. T. M. Patterson, Denver, Colorado, to K. M. Patterson, Boston, Massachusetts, May 8, 1892. Patterson papers.

18. *Rocky Mountain News,* May 26, 1892.

19. T. M. Patterson, Washington, D.C., to K. M. Patterson, Boston, Massachusetts, May 27, 1892. Patterson papers.

20. *Rocky Mountain News,* June 10, 11, and 17, 1892.

21. *Rocky Mountain News,* June 21, 1892.

22. *Denver Republican,* June 21, 1892.

23. Ibid.

24. *Rocky Mountain News,* June 21–23, 1892.

25. *Denver Republican,* June 23, 1892.

26. Ellis Meredith, "Three Distinguished Figures of the *Early Rocky Mountain News,*" *Colorado Magazine* 27 (January 1950): 45, 46.

27. Ibid.

28. *Denver Republican,* June 25, 1892.

29. T. M. Patterson, Denver, Colorado, to K. M. Patterson, Boston, Massachusetts, June 28, 1892. Patterson papers.

30. *Rocky Mountain News,* July 5, 1892.

31. *Rocky Mountain News,* June 28 and July 6, 1892.

32. *Denver Times,* July 4, 1892; R. C. Dill, *The Political Campaigns of Colorado* (Denver, Colo.: Arapahoe, 1895), 167.

33. *Denver Republican,* June 25, 1892.

34. Dill, *Political Campaigns,* 170.

35. *Denver Republican,* July 28–30, 1892.

36. Perkin, *First Hundred Years,* 401.

37. *Denver Post,* August 10, 1892.

38. T. J. O'Donnell and Patterson worked closely on many political issues for twenty years, and the former was especially prominent in the efforts for municipal reform.

39. *Denver Republican,* September 12 and 13, 1892; *Pueblo Chieftain,* September 12 and 13, 1892; Dill, *Political Campaigns,* 180–85.

40. *Rocky Mountain News,* August 15, 1892.

41. Dill, *Political Campaigns,* 177.

42. Leon W. Fuller, "A Populist Newspaper of the Nineties," *Colorado Magazine* 9 (May 1932): 81–87. For a thorough summary of Waite's views, see John Robert Morris, "Davis Hanson Waite: The Ideology of a Western Populist" (Ph.D. dissertation, University of Colorado, Boulder, Colorado, 1965).

43. Morris, "Davis Hanson Waite," 286–98.

44. John D. Hicks, *The Populist Revolt* (Minneapolis: University of Minnesota Press, 1931), 406.

45. Fuller, "A Populist Newspaper," 84.

46. Ibid., 82.

47. *Rocky Mountain News,* July 30 and August 4 and 5, 1892.

48. Morris, "Davis Hanson Waite," 293.

49. *Aspen Union Era,* July 7 and August 4, 1892.

50. Dill, *Political Campaigns,* 195.

51. According to contemporary observer R. C. Dill, Davis Waite, under pressure from his own Populist committee, promised to allow the Silver Democrats to name a few gubernatorial appointments but later evaded the loose terms of the agreement. *Political Campaigns,* 191, 192.

52. *Denver Times,* October 5, 7, and 19, 1892.

53. Fuller, "A Populist Newspaper," 82–84.

54. *Rocky Mountain News,* October 23, 1892.

55. Dill, *Political Campaigns,* 184, 185; *Denver Times,* October 27–29, 1892.

56. *Rocky Mountains News,* August 21 and October 28, 1892.

57. Dill, *Political Campaigns,* 183, 194; *Denver Times,* November 4, 1892; Thomas F. Dawson, *The Life and Character of Edward O. Wolcott* (New York: Knickerbocker, 1911), 207.

58. *Loveland Leader,* October 21, 1892.

59. T. M. Patterson, Denver, Colorado, to K. M. Patterson, Boston, Massachusetts, July 22, 1892. Patterson papers.

60. *Rocky Mountain News,* October 24 and November 3, 1892.

61. Dill, *Political Campaigns,* 204.

62. Charles S. Thomas, "Recollection of Thomas M. Patterson" (Unpublished article in the Charles S. Thomas papers, Colorado State Historical Society), 43.

63. Percy Stanley Fritz, *Colorado: The Centennial State* (New York: Prentice-Hall, 1941), 353; Dill, *Political Campaigns,* 182, 202; Dawson, *The Life and Character of Edward O. Wolcott,* 205; Wilbur Fisk Stone, ed., *History of Colorado* (Chicago: Clarke, 1918), 1:437.

64. Jane Werner, "The Press and the Populists," *Colorado Magazine* 47 (winter 1970): 60, 61.

65. Official totals gave Waite 44,242, Republican Joseph C. Helm 38,806, and Democrat James Maupin 8,944. *House Journal, Ninth Legislative Session, State of Colorado* (Denver, Colo., 1893), 36.

66. *Denver Times,* November 26, 1892.

67. K. M. Patterson, Boston, Massachusetts, to T. M. Patterson, Denver, Colorado, November 14, 1892; Mary Patterson, Boston, Massachusetts, to T. M. Patterson, Denver, Colorado, November 14, 1892. Patterson papers.

68. T. M. Patterson, Denver, Colorado, to K. M. Patterson, Boston, Massachusetts, November 15, 1892. Patterson papers.

69. *Denver Times,* November 26, 1892.

70. T.M. Patterson, Denver, Colorado, to K.M. Patterson, Boston, Massachusetts, November 15, 1892. Patterson papers.

71. *Rocky Mountain News,* September 14, 1893.

72. *Denver Times,* November 26 and 28, 1892.

8: *Bloody Bridles*

1. *Rocky Mountain News,* January 5, 1893.

2. *Denver Republican,* April 5, 1893.

3. T. M. Patterson, Denver, Colorado, to K. M. Patterson, Grand Lake, Colorado, August 12, 1894. Patterson papers, Western Historical Collection, University of Colorado at Boulder [hereafter referred to as Patterson papers].

4. Percy Stanley Fritz, *Colorado: The Centennial State* (New York: Prentice-Hall, 1941), 354.

5. Stephen J. Leonard and Thomas J. Noel, *Denver, Mining Camp to Metropolis* (Niwot: University Press of Colorado, 1991), 103.

6. Ibid., 104.

7. Biennial Report, *Colorado Bureau of Labor Statistics, 1893–1894,* 24.

8. *New York Times,* July 12, 1893.

9. John R. Morris, "Davis Hanson Waite: The Ideology of a Western Populist," (Ph.D. dissertation, University of Colorado, 1965), 108.

10. Fritz, *Colorado: The Centennial State,* 355.

11. Morris, "Davis Hanson Waite," 110–22 and 298.

12. *Rocky Mountain News,* January 6, 1894.

13. *Rocky Mountain News,* January 11, 1894.

14. Carl Ubbelohde, Maxine Benson, and Duane A. Smith, *A Colorado History,* 6th ed. (Boulder, Colo.: Pruett, 1988), 231.

15. *Rocky Mountain News,* January 6 and 11, 1894.

16. *Rocky Mountain News,* January 2 and 7, 1894.

17. *Rocky Mountain News,* January 3 and 4, 1894.

18. *Rocky Mountain News,* January 6 and 8, 1894.

19. Ellis Meredith, "Three Distinguished Figures of the *Early Rocky Mountain News,*" *Colorado Magazine* 27 (January 1950): 48.

20. Ibid, 43.

21. Ibid, 48.

22. Joseph G. Brown, *The History of Equal Suffrage in Colorado, 1868–1898* (Denver: Denver News Job Printing, 1898), 10, 13, and 16. For a guide to Colorado and national women's suffrage sources, see Marcia T. Goldstein and Rebecca A. Hunt, "From Suffrage to Centennial," *Colorado Heritage* (spring 1993): 40–48.

23. Meredith, "Three Distinguished Figures," 48.

24. Edward Keating, *The Gentleman From Colorado* (Denver: Sage, 1964), 74.

25. *Rocky Mountain News,* January 11 and 15, 1894.

26. *Rocky Mountain News,* March 15 and May 30, 1894.

27. Robert L. Perkin, *The First Hundred Years* (Garden City, N.Y.: Doubleday, 1959), 388; Ubbelohde, *A Colorado History,* 232.

28. Davis Waite was concerned that the court, dominated by Republicans, would let the matter drift until after the fall elections and perhaps even until his term of office had expired. Morris, "Davis Hanson Waite," 299.

29. *Rocky Mountain News,* March 15 and 22, 1894.

30. Morris, "Davis Hanson Waite," 299.

31. Perkin, *First Hundred Years,* 387.

32. *Rocky Mountain News,* May 18 and 19, 1894.

33. *Rocky Mountain News,* March 22, May 18, July 30, and September 2 and 3, 1894.

34. Keating, *Gentleman From Colorado,* 75; *Rocky Mountain News,* September 6, 1894.

35. *Rocky Mountain News,* September 7 and 8, October 18, and November 1 and 4, 1894.

36. *Rocky Mountain News,* October 18 and November 4, 1894.

37. *Rocky Mountain News,* May 10 and 19, August 8, and June 16, 1894.

38. R. C. Dill, *The Political Campaigns of Colorado* (Denver: Arapahoe, 1895), 280–83.

39. Keating, *Gentleman From Colorado,* 73.

40. *Rocky Mountain News,* November 8 and 17, 1894.

41. *Rocky Mountain News,* March 12, 1894.

42. *Rocky Mountain News,* January 24, 1896.

43. *Rocky Mountain News,* May 26 and 27, 1896.

44. Elmer Ellis, *Henry Moore Teller: Defender of the West* (Caldwell, Idaho: Caxton, 1941), 260.

45. *Rocky Mountain News,* June 19, 1896.

46. *Rocky Mountain News,* May 31, 1896.

47. Louis W. Koenig, *Bryan: A Political Biography of William Jennings Bryan* (New York: Putnam, 1971), 191.

48. Sewell Thomas, *Silhouettes of Charles S. Thomas* (Caldwell, Idaho: Caxton, 1959), 66.

49. *Rocky Mountain News,* June 13 and July 11, 1896.

50. *Denver Times,* July 4, 1896.

51. *Rocky Mountain News,* July 22–25, 1896.

52. William Jennings Bryan, *The First Battle* (Chicago: W. B. Conkey, 1896), 271.

53. *Rocky Mountain News,* July 24, 1896.

54. T. M. Patterson, Terre Haute, Indiana, to K. M. Patterson, Denver, Colorado, October 2, 1896. Patterson papers; Perkin, *First Hundred Years,* 388; *Jackson Morning Patriot* (Michigan), October 10, 1896.

55. Susan M. Hall, Denver, Colorado, to K. M. Patterson, Denver, Colorado, November 14, 1896.

56. *Denver Times,* July 20, 1896.

57. *Rocky Mountain News,* September 28, 1898.

58. Wilbur Fisk Stone, ed., *History of Colorado* (Chicago: Clarke, 1918), 1:441.

59. *Rocky Mountain News,* May 8, 1900.

60. Koenig, *Bryan: A Political Biography,* 257.

61. *Denver Republican,* May 9, 1900.

62. *Denver Times,* May 10 and 11, 1900; *Rocky Mountain News,* May 11, 1900.

63. *Denver Times,* May 9 and 11, 1900.

64. T. M. Patterson, Grand Lake, Colorado, to K. M. Patterson, Denver, Colorado, August 11 and 26, 1900. Patterson papers.

65. Statement to author Robert Smith by T. Campbell, Patterson's grandson, Denver, Colorado, August 28, 1969.

66. T. M. Patterson, Grand Lake, Colorado, to K. M. Patterson, Denver, Colorado, July 22, 1900. Patterson papers.

67. Perkin, *First Hundred Years,* 388. The friendship with Bryan endured until Tom Patterson's death in 1916. *Rocky Mountain News,* February 10, 1929.

68. *Denver Times,* January 16, 1901.

9: The Violence of Good Men

1. Edward Keating, *The Gentleman From Colorado* (Denver: Sage, 1964), 245.

2. *Rocky Mountain News,* July 8, 1892.

3. Ibid.

4. *Rocky Mountain News,* August 19 and 23, 1892, January 21, 1893, and October 9 and 13, 1898.

5. *Rocky Mountain News,* August 6, 1892.

6. *Denver Times,* October 16, 1902.

7. *Denver Times,* June 7, 1902.

8. *Denver Times,* October 2, 7, and 16, 1902.

9. Ibid.

10. *Rocky Mountain News,* October 17, 1902.

11. *Rocky Mountain News,* July 5, 1904; T. M. Patterson, Denver, Colorado, to his grandson Thomas Patterson Campbell, Hanover, New Hampshire, March 15, 1916. Patterson papers, Western Historical Collection, University of Colorado at Boulder [hereafter referred to as Patterson papers].

12. For an account of Gladstone's views, see Michael R.D. Foot and J. L. LeBreton Hammon, *Gladstone and Liberalism* (London: English University Press, 1952) or Philip M. Magnus, *Gladstone, a Biography* (New York: Dutton, 1954).

13. *Rocky Mountain News,* January 27, 1894.

14. *Rocky Mountain News,* August 6, 9, and 23, and November 27, 1892, and March 3, 1893.

15. *Rocky Mountain News,* July 8 and 9, 1892.

16. *Rocky Mountain News,* March 6, 1892.

17. *Rocky Mountain News,* May 3, 1894.

18. *Rocky Mountain News,* May 9–13, 1894; *Denver Republican,* May 9–12, 1894.

19. *Rocky Mountain News,* July 4 and 8, 1894.

20. *Rocky Mountain News,* June 1, 1902.

21. *Rocky Mountain News,* August 14, 1892, September 10, 1893, and September 2, 1894.

22. Vernon Jensen, *Heritage of Conflict: Labor Relations in the Nonferrous Metals Industry up to 1930* (Ithaca: Cornell University Press, 1950), 38–52; Stuart Holbrook, *The Rocky Mountain Revolution* (New York: Holt, 1956), 73; Benjamin M. Rastall, *The Labor History of the Cripple Creek District: A Study in Industrial Relations* (Madison: University of Wisconsin, 1908), 15–21.

23. *Rocky Mountain News,* January 3, 1894.

24. Patterson later asserted that "as mighty as capital is, public sentiment, enlisted on the side of humanity, is far mightier." *Rocky Mountain News,* October 13, 1898.

25. Ibid.

26. Marshall Sprague, *Money Mountain* (Boston: Little, Brown, 1953), 138.

27. Jensen, *Heritage of Conflict,* 42, 43; Rastall, *Labor History,* 30.

28. In 1880, Tom Patterson had supported the Leadville miners when martial law had been used to break a miners' strike.

29. *Rocky Mountain News,* March 18, 1894.

30. Holbrook, *Rocky Mountain Revolution,* 76.

31. John Robert Morris, "Davis Hanson Waite: The Ideology of a Western Populist," (Ph.D. dissertation, University of Colorado, 1965), 289, 290.

32. Jensen, *Heritage of Conflict,* 46–49.

33. *Rocky Mountain News,* May 28–30, 1894.

34. Rastall, *Labor History,* 53–60.

35. *Rocky Mountain News,* June 5 and 8, 1894.

36. *Denver Times,* June 6, 1894.

37. *Colorado Springs Gazette,* May 31, 1894.

38. Jensen, *Heritage of Conflict,* 53.

39. *Colorado Springs Gazette,* June 28 and July 19, 1894; *Denver Republican,* June 28, 1894.

40. Horace Hawkins, "Tribute to the Memory of Thomas M. Patterson" (speech on the occasion of a memorial service held by the Denver Bar Association, March 26, 1917).

41. *Colorado Springs Gazette,* November 15, 1894; *Cripple Creek Morning Journal,* October 30 and 31, 1894.

42. T. M. Patterson, Denver, Colorado, to K. M. Patterson, Belmar, New Jersey, June 30, 1895. Patterson papers.

43. *Colorado Springs Gazette,* February 27 and March 7, 1895.

44. *Colorado Springs Gazette,* from a general reading of the newspaper from February 28 to April 26, 1895. See especially February 28 and March 9 and 20, 1895.

45. Hawkins, "Tribute," 9; F. Edward Little, "Thomas M. Patterson: Gamecock of the Colorado Courts," *Rocky Mountain Law Review* 11 (April 1939): 156.

46. Jensen, *Heritage of Conflict,* 52.

47. Percy Stanley Fritz, *Colorado: the Centennial State* (New York: Prentice-Hall, 1941), 370.

48. Newman, described as sympathetic to the miners, later was removed from office on charges of having taken bribes from Leadville gamblers. Following a change of venue, he was tried and convicted in Fairplay on July 31, 1896. Patterson won Newman a stay, then a *superdeas,* and it required six more months before Newman was deposed from office. Don Griswold and Jean Griswold, "Leadville, a City of Contrast," *Leadville Herald-Democrat,* March 6 and 20, 1970.

49. Jensen, *Heritage of Conflict,* 58, 59.

50. Griswold, "Leadville," *Leadville Herald-Democrat,* April 10, 1970.

51. Griswold, "Leadville," *Leadville Herald-Democrat,* May 1, 1970; Fritz, *Colorado,* 370, 371.

52. *Rocky Mountain News,* November 8, 1896.

53. *Denver Republican,* February 19 and March 11, 1897.

54. *Rocky Mountain News,* February 12, 1897.

55. *Rocky Mountain News,* February 12, 1897.

56. The arbitration committee consisted of two union men and two representatives of the owners plus a fifth man chosen by the first four. Griswold, "Leadville," *Leadville Herald-Democrat,* April 4, 1970.

57. Jensen, *Heritage of Conflict,* 59; *Rocky Mountain News,* February 27 and March 10, 1897.

58. Jensen, *Heritage of Conflict,* 42, 55; *Miners Magazine,* April 1903, 13.

59. Tom Patterson reflected his consistent support for the principle of arbitration by applauding it for having solved a meat-packers' strike in Chicago. He had called for enactment of national arbitration laws as early as 1898. *Rocky Mountain News,* July 21, 1904, and October 9, 1898.

60. Griswold, "Leadville," *Leadville Herald-Democrat,* April 17, 1970.

61. *Miners Magazine,* January 1903, 9.

62. *Rocky Mountain News,* March 10, 1897.

10: Mile-High Armageddon

1. Vernon Jensen, *Heritage of Conflict: Labor Relations in the Nonferrous Metals Industry up to 1930* (Ithaca: Cornell University Press, 1950), 119.

2. *Miners Magazine,* October 1903, 5; Elmer Ellis, *Henry Moore Teller, Defender of the West* (Caldwell, Idaho: Caxton, 1941), 360. For a complete picture of the pressures polarizing militants on both sides, see Jensen, *Heritage of Conflict,* 119–158.

3. Jensen, *Heritage of Conflict,* 128, 129.

4. George G. Suggs, *Colorado's War on Militant Unionism* (Detroit, Wayne University Press, 1972), 102; *Rocky Mountain News,* October 4, 1903.

5. Suggs, *Colorado's War on Militant Unionism,* 136–38.

6. Ibid., 146.

7. Ibid., 158; Percy Stanley Fritz, *Colorado: The Centennial State* (New York: Prentice-Hall, 1941), 376; Suggs, *Colorado's War on Militant Unionism,* 108–10.

8. Edward Berman, *Labor Disputes and the President of the United States* (New York: Columbia University, 1924), 61, 62.

9. Jensen, *Heritage of Conflict,* 158.

10. *Congressional Record,* 58th Cong., 2nd Sess., 38:1, 113, 693, 694; *Congressional Record,* 58th Cong., 2nd Sess., 38:3, 2108.

11. *Congressional Record,* 58th Cong., 2nd Sess., 38:1, 693.

12. Ibid., 694.

13. *Miners Magazine,* April 1903, 14, 15, 19, and 28; *Western Federation of Miners: Official Proceedings, 1904* (Denver, 1904), 65, 81, and 89.

14. *Miners Magazine,* January and August, 1903.

15. *Rocky Mountain News,* June 19 and July 1 and 2, 1904.

16. *George's Weekly,* October 15, 1904, and April 22, 1905; *Western Federation of Miners: Official Proceedings, 1904,* 69, 71, 79, 99, and 107.

17. *George's Weekly,* May 4, 1901, and March 1, 1902.

18. *Denver Post,* June 8, 1904.

19. *George's Weekly,* August 8, 1903.

20. *George's Weekly,* April 18 and June 13, 1903.

21. *Rocky Mountain News,* June 18, 1904.

22. Mary Fonda Adams, "Thomas M. Patterson: Some Aspects of his Political Career," (Master's thesis, University of Colorado, 1933), 96.

23. Edward Keating, *The Gentleman From Colorado* (Denver: Sage, 1964), 93.

24. *Rocky Mountain News,* June 20–29 and July 2–8, 1904.

25. *Rocky Mountain News,* June 20–29, 1904. See especially June 23, 1904.

26. *Rocky Mountain News,* June 20 and 23, 1904.

27. *George's Weekly,* September 25, 1903.

28. 34 Stat, 1415; *Congressional Record,* 59th Cong., 2nd Sess., 41:1, 824, 879.

29. *Congressional Record,* 59th Cong., 2nd Sess., 41:1, 891.

30. *Congressional Record,* 59th Cong., 2nd Sess., 41:5, 4636.

31. *Congressional Record,* 59th Cong., 1st Sess., 40:3, 2336–43.

32. *Congressional Record,* 57th Cong., 1st Sess., 35:3, 3117.

33. *Congressional Record,* 57th Cong., 2nd Sess., 36:3, 2612, 2613.

34. Berman, *Labor Disputes,* 77; Fritz, *Colorado: The Centennial State,* 377–79; Samuel Yellen, *American Labor Struggles* (New York: Harcourt Brace, 1936), 205–50. For an anti–union account, see E. M. Ammons, "Colorado Strike," *North American Review* 200 (July 1914): 35–44. For a pro–union account, see Barron B. Beshoar, *Out of the Depths* (Denver: Colorado Labor Historical Committee of the Denver Trade and Labor Assembly, 1942).

35. *Rocky Mountain News,* (Denver), June 6, 1914.

36. *Congressional Record,* 63rd Cong., 2nd Sess., 51:10, 10345, 10346. Tom Patterson also appeared as a pro–labor witness before the Federal Industrial Relations Commission. *Denver Times,* July 24, 1916.

37. *Denver Times,* July 23, 1916.

38. *Cripple Creek Morning Journal,* October 19, 1894.

39. Horace Hawkins, "Tribute to Thomas M. Patterson" (speech on the occasion of a memorial service held by the Denver Bar Association, March 26, 1917), 9.

40. *Denver Express,* July 24, 1916.

41. Woodrow Wilson, Trenton, New Jersey, to Margaret (Patterson) Campbell, Denver, Colorado, April 14, 1911. Patterson papers, Western Historical Collection, University of Colorado at Boulder.

11: Showdown for the Senate

1. Elmer Ellis, *Henry Moore Teller: Defender of the West* (Caldwell, Idaho: Caxton, 1941.), 279.

2. Ibid., 331, 332.

3. K. M. Patterson, Denver, Colorado, to Mary Patterson, Paris, France, November 13, 1882. Patterson papers, Western Historical Collection, University of Colorado at Boulder [hereafter referred to as Patterson papers].

4. R. C. Dill, *The Political Campaigns of Colorado* (Denver: Arapaho, 1895), 80.

5. Ellis, *Henry Moore Teller,* 333.

6. Sewell Thomas, *Silhouettes of Charles S. Thomas* (Caldwell: Idaho: Caxton, 1959), 77.

7. Dill, *Political Campaigns,* 184, 185.

8. *Rocky Mountain News,* September 28, 1898.

9. Thomas, *Silhouettes of Charles S. Thomas,* 66.

10. Edward Keating, *The Gentleman From Colorado* (Denver: Sage, 1964), 140.

11. Thomas, *Silhouettes of Charles S. Thomas,* 77.

12. *Rocky Mountain News,* January 10, 1901.

13. *Rocky Mountain News,* January 11, 1901.

14. Alva Adams, Denver, Colorado, to C. S. Thomas, Denver, Colorado, January 1, 1901. Thomas papers, Colorado State Historical Society, Denver.

15. Thomas, *Silhouettes of Charles S. Thomas,* 73.

16. *Denver Times,* January 15, 1901; *Cincinnati Enquirer,* January 12, 1901.

17. *Denver Times,* January 16, 1901.

18. William Jennings Bryan, location unknown, to Henry Moore Teller, Washington, D.C., February 1, 1901. Henry M. Teller papers, Colorado State Historical Society, Denver.

19. *Denver Times,* January 16, 1901.

20. Among the newspapers taking a favorable view of Patterson's election were the *Victor Times, Loveland Reporter, Glenwood Avalanche, Boulder County-Herald, Rocky Ford Tribune, Grand Junction Daily Sentinel, Salida Record,* and the *Colorado Springs Gazette.*

21. T. J. O'Donnell, Denver, Colorado, to T. M. Patterson, Washington, D.C., March 29, 1901. T. J. O'Donnell papers, Western Historical Collection, University of Colorado.

22. *George's Weekly,* January 12, 1901. Additional evidence found in undated clippings from: *Victor Daily Record, Cripple Creek Star, Durango Daily Herald,* and *Gillette Forum.* Undated clippings in the Thomas Dawson papers, Colorado State Historical Society, Denver.

23. Ibid.

24. *Congressional Record,* 58th Cong., 2nd Sess., 38:2, 1653–1655.

25. A. C. Johnson, Washington, D.C. to C. Johnson, Denver, Colorado, December 12, 1901, and January 11 and April 17, 1902. Arthur C. Johnson papers, Western Historical Collection, University of Colorado at Boulder.

26. *Rocky Mountain News,* July 17, 1902.

12: The Anti-Imperialist

1. A. C. Johnson, Washington, D.C., to C. Johnson, Denver, Colorado, November 15, 1901, and November 23, 1905. Arthur C. Johnson papers, Western Historical Collection, University of Colorado at Boulder.

2. Patterson was assigned to two particularly prominent committees: the Committee on the Philippines and the Committee on Interstate Commerce. Other assignments included: Irrigation and Reclamation of Arid Lands, Pension, Territories, and Contingent Expenses of the Senate. *Congressional Record,* 57th Cong., 1st Sess., 35:1, 387, 388.

3. T. M. Patterson, Washington, D.C., to K. M. Patterson, Denver, Colorado, March 9, 1902. Patterson papers, Western Historical Collection, University of Colorado at Boulder [hereafter referred to as Patterson papers].

4. T. M. Patterson, Washington, D.C., to K. M. Patterson, Bethany, West Virginia, May 9, 1902. Patterson papers.

5. George E. Mowry, *Era of Theodore Roosevelt 1900–1912* (New York: Harper Brothers, 1958), 117.

6. Elmer Ellis, *Henry Moore Teller: Defender of the West* (Caldwell, Idaho: Caxton, 1941), 336.

7. Mowry, *Era of Theodore Roosevelt,* 117.

8. *Denver Times,* July 5, 1902.

9. Mowry, *Era of Theodore Roosevelt,* 130.

10. Since 1890 Teller and Patterson had agreed on nearly all public questions. Ellis, *Henry Moore Teller,* 336, 337; as publisher and editor of the *Nashville Democrat* and the *Memphis Commercial,* Senator Carmack possessed a background somewhat similar to Patterson's. *Congressional Directory,* 58th Cong., 3rd Sess., 1904, 113.

11. A. C. Johnson, Washington, D.C., to C. Johnson, Denver, Colorado, January 21, 1902, Johnson papers.

12. *Washington Post,* February 21, 1902.

13. A. C. Johnson, Washington, D.C., to C. Johnson, Denver, Colorado, February 10 and 23, 1902. Johnson papers.

14. A.C. Johnson, Washington, D.C., to C. Johnson, Denver, Colorado, March 6, April 2, and May 23, 1902, Johnson papers.

15. *Indianapolis Journal,* as quoted in the *Denver Times,* February 21, 1902.

16. *New York Sun,* as quoted in the *Denver Republican,* May 22 and 23, 1902.

17. Ibid.

18. *Congressional Record,* 58th Cong., 2nd Sess., 38:3, 2310.

19. *Congressional Record,* 57th Cong., 2nd Sess., 36:3, 2984; *Congressional Record,* 59th Cong., 1st Sess., 40:4, 3529; *Washington Post,* April 23, 1902.

20. *Congressional Record,* 57th Cong., 1st Sess., 35:3, 2087-90; A. C. Johnson, Washington, D.C., to C. Johnson, Denver, Colorado, February 23, 1902, Johnson papers.

21. A. C. Johnson, Washington, D.C., to C. Johnson, Denver, Colorado, March 6 and May 23, 1902, Johnson papers.

22. *Denver Times,* July 3, 1902.

23. The *Washington Post,* as cited in the *Denver Republican,* January 16, 1906.

24. Claude G. Bowers, *Beveridge and the Progressive Era* (Boston: Houghton, Mifflin, 1932), 179. Complete testimony before the Committee on the Philippines is contained in Sen. Doc., 57th Cong., 1st Sess., No. 331, *Hearings on*

Affairs in Philippine Island, 3 vols. Witnesses before the committee included Secretary of War William Howard Taft, Admiral George Dewey, General Arthur MacArthur, and several other high-ranking military officers.

25. *Congressional Record,* 57th Cong., 1st Sess., 35:2, 1576–83, 1640–52, 2023–25.

26. Ibid., 1657, 1658. Tom Patterson also likened the position of the United States to France's relationship to the United States during the Revolutionary era: The two countries were allies. As such, the United States should not be considered sovereign over the Philippines. Ibid., 1398, 1399.

27. The Federal party, according to the Roosevelt Administration, was a mainstay in securing peace in the Philippines — although the party frequently criticized American policies. *Congressional Record,* 57th Cong., 1st Sess., 35:2, 1657, 1965.

28. *Congressional Record,* 57th Cong., 1st Sess., 35:2, 1965–74.

29. Ibid., 1979–80.

30. *Congressional Record,* 57th Cong., 1st Sess., 35:5, 5072–5075.

31. *Congressional Record,* 57th Cong., 1st Sess., 35:6, 5968.

32. *Washington Post,* April 12, 1902.

33. *Congressional Record,* 57th Cong., 1st Sess., 35:4, 3326–29; *Congressional Record,* 57th Cong., 1st Sess., 35:5, 4862–68 and 4920–23; *Congressional Record,* 57th Cong., 1st Sess., 35:6, 6226–28.

34. *Denver Republican,* May 14–17, 1902.

35. *Denver Post,* March 12, 1902.

36. *Denver Post,* April 12, 1902.

37. *Washington Post,* July 3, 1902.

38. *Congressional Record,* 57th Cong., 1st Sess., 35:2, 2021.

39. Henry F. Pringle, *The Life and Times of William Howard Taft* (New York: Farrar and Rinehart, 1939), 219.

40. *Denver Republican,* May 22, 1902; T. M. Patterson, Washington, D.C., to Margaret Patterson Campbell, Denver, Colorado, May 25, 1902. Patterson papers.

41. A. C. Johnson, Washington, D.C., to C. Johnson, Denver, Colorado, March 6, 1902. Johnson papers.

42. Teller had also changed his views about imperialism, and he was reminded of speeches he had made in the campaign of 1898. *Congressional Record,* 56th Cong., 2nd Sess., 34:1, 535–37.

43. A. C. Johnson, Washington, D.C., to C. Johnson, Denver, Colorado, February 23, 1902. Johnson papers.

44. *Congressional Record,* 57th Cong., 1st Sess., 35:65, 5909–21.

45. *Congressional Record,* 57th Cong., 1st Sess., 35:2, 2025.

46. Ibid.

47. *Congressional Record,* 57th Cong., 1st Sess., 35:8, 7735–37.

48. Tom Patterson viewed the president's Philippine Commission in the islands as an oligarchy. *Congressional Record,* 57th Cong., 1st Sess., 35:2, 2055; *Congressional Record,* 57th Cong., 1st Sess., 35:8, 7736.

49. *Congressional Record,* 57th Cong., 1st Sess., 35:6, 5968.

50. Virtually the only senator, imperialist or anti-imperialist, who did not share this view was Senator Hoar. Robert L. Beisner, *Twelve Against Empire* (New York: McGraw Hill, 1968), 152, 153. It should be noted that Tom Patterson was not among Beisner's twelve anti-imperialists; Beisner wrote primarily about events that preceded Patterson's arrival in the Senate, and most of the people he wrote about were in fields other than politics.

51. *Congressional Record,* 57th Cong., 1st Sess., 35:3, 2125, 2131–2133.

52. *Denver Post,* July 9, 1902.

53. Beisner, *Twelve Against Empire,* 238, 239; Ellis, *Henry Moore Teller,* 341.

54. *Congressional Record,* 57th Cong., 1st Sess., 35:5, 5072.

55. *Denver Post,* March 5, 1902.

56. Albert J. Beveridge, Torrington, Colorado, to Edward W. Carmack, Memphis, Tennessee, August 8, 1902. Contained in the papers of A. J. Beveridge, located in the Library of Congress.

57. *Congressional Record,* 58th Cong., 1st Sess., 37:1, 478.

58. *Washington Post,* January 15–22, 1904; *Denver Republican,* January 20–24, 1904.

59. *Denver Post,* January 2 and 23, 1904.

60. *Congressional Record,* 58th Cong., 2nd Sess., 38:1, 796–805, 918.

61. *Washington Post,* January 28, 1904.

62. *Congressional Record,* 58th Cong., 2nd Sess., 38:1, 916.

63. Ibid.

64. *Congressional Record,* 58th Cong., 2nd Sess., 38:2, 1016.

65. *Congressional Record,* 58th Cong., 2nd Sess., 38:1, 913.

66. *Congressional Record,* 58th Cong., 2nd Sess., 38:1, 630, 916.

67. *Denver Post,* January 22, 1904.

68. *Congressional Record,* 58th Cong., 2nd Sess., 38:1, 919.

69. Ibid.

70. *Congressional Record,* 58th Cong., 2nd Sess., 38:3, 2261.

71. *Congressional Record,* 59th Cong., 1st Sess., 40:9, 8395.

13: Maverick and Progressive

1. J. Rogers Hollingsworth, *The Whirligig of Politics: The Democracy of Cleveland and Bryan* (Chicago: University of Chicago, 1963), 217–22.

2. *Rocky Mountain News,* September 24–26 and November 5–7, 1904; *Denver Times,* November 4–8, 1904.

3. William Howard Taft, locations unknown, to T. M. Patterson,Washington, D.C., March 30, 1904. William Howard Taft papers, in Library of Congress.

4. T. M. Patterson, location unknown, to W. H. Taft, location unknown, April 4, 1904. Taft papers.

5. *Congressional Record,* 58th Cong., 2nd Sess., 38:3, 2912–14.

6. W. H. Taft, *S.S. Korea,* to Helen Taft, Oxford, England, September 23, 1905. Taft papers.

7. T. M. Patterson, location unknown, to W. H. Taft, location unknown, October 2, 1905; W. H. Taft, location unknown, to T. M. Patterson, location unknown, October 5, 1905. Taft papers.

8. W. H. Taft, location unknown, to T. M. Patterson, location unknown, June 28, 1906. Taft papers.

9. W. H. Taft, Yellowstone Park, to T. M. Patterson, Denver, Colorado, August 31, 1907. Taft papers.

10. Edward Keating, *The Gentleman From Colorado* (Denver: Sage, 1964), 99, 100.

11. T. M. Patterson, location unknown, to W. H. Taft, location unknown, June 19, 1908. Taft papers.

12. Keating, *Gentleman From Colorado,* 100.

13. George E. Mowry refers to the increase in anti-trust activity in *The Era of Theodore Roosevelt, 1900–1912* (New York: Harper Brothers, 1958), 133, 152; see also G. Wallace Chessman, *Theodore Roosevelt and the Politics of Power* (Boston: Little, Brown, 1969), 84, 85, 89–92.

14. *Washington Post,* February 1, 1906.

15. *Congressional Record,* 59th Cong., 1st Sess., 40:2, 1802–6; *Washington Post,* February 1, 1906; *New York Times,* February 1, 1906; *Denver Republican,* February 1, 1906.

16. *Congressional Record,* 59th Cong., 1st Sess., 40:2, 1802; *New York Times,* February 1, 1906.

17. *Congressional Record,* 59th Cong., 1st Sess., 40:2, 1802–6. Patterson also endorsed Roosevelt's involvement in the Algeciras Conference.

18. Ibid., 1802; *Washington Post,* February 1, 1906. Assuming that the *Rocky Mountain News* accurately reflected the views of its owner, it would appear that Patterson considered the Santo Domingo situation a political problem, although he saw the Philippines as a case of economic exploitation. *Rocky Mountain News,* February 1–4, 1906; *Denver Republican,* February 2, 1906.

19. *Washington Post,* February 1, 1906.

20. John C. Spooner, Washington, D.C. to S. M. Cullom, St. Augustine, Florida, February 5, 1906. John C. Spooner papers, Library of Congress.

21. *Denver Republican,* February 1, 1906.

22. *New York Times,* February 1, 1906.

23. *Congressional Record,* 59th Cong., 1st Sess., 40:3, 2053. *Washington Post,* February 2, 1906.

24. *Congressional Record,* 59th Cong., 1st Sess., 40:3, 2053, 2207.

25. Ibid., 2212.

26. *Washington Post,* February 6, 1906.

27. *Washington Post,* February 7 and 8, 1906.

28. *Congressional Record,* 59th Cong., 1st Sess., 40:3, 2207–19. There is little evidence to support the *Washington Post*'s speculation of February 8, 1906, that Tom Patterson might have received assistance from Spooner in preparing arguments for the debate. The two men were seen talking briefly in the cloakroom prior to the debate. *New York Times,* February 8, 1906.

29. *Washington Post,* February 8, 1906. The *Post*'s position was clearly revealed when it said that the Democratic party had become a discordant mob after it deserted Grover Cleveland and enlisted under the banner of Populism. February 18, 1906.

30. *Denver Republican,* February 7, 1906. For an account of the struggle, see Elmer Ellis, *Henry Moore Teller: Defender of the West* (Caldwell, Idaho: Caxton, 1941), 348–51.

31. *Congressional Record,* 59th Cong., 1st Sess., 40:3, 2212.

32. *Washington Post,* February 8, and 9, 1906.

33. *Washington Post,* March 10, 1906; *New York Times,* February 1, 1906.

34. *Congressional Record,* 59th Cong., 1st Sess., 40:3, 2053.

35. *Washington Post,* February 1, 1906; *New York Evening Post,* as quoted in the *Denver Post,* February 8, 1906.

36. *Denver Republican,* February 9, 1906.

37. *Denver Post,* February 2, 1906.

38. *Washington Star,* February 3 and 8, 1906.

39. T. M. Patterson, Denver, Colorado, to A. C. Johnson, Washington, D.C., June 25, 1913. Arthur C. Johnson papers, Western Historical Collection, University of Colorado at Boulder.

40. Senator Samuel D. McEnery of Louisiana had been for the treaty from the outset and had boycotted the caucus. *New York Times,* February 3, 1906.

41. *Congressional Record,* 59th Cong., 1st Sess., 40:1, 793.

42. *Washington Post,* February 11, 1906.

43. *Denver Times,* January 15, 1901.

44. Among those on the losing side with Patterson were Senators Carmack, Dubois, Teller, and Tillman. *Congressional Record,* 57th Cong., 1st Sess., 35:2, 1804.

45. *Congressional Record,* 57th Cong., 1st Sess., 35:3, 2901, 2903, 2904, 2906, 2907.

46. Some Western Republicans, including William B. Allison of Iowa and John C. Spooner, did vote against it. *Congressional Record,* 57th Cong., 1st Sess., 35:3, 2907.

47. Mowry, *Theodore Roosevelt,* 130.

48. *Congressional Record,* 57th Cong., 1st Sess., 40:2, 1944–52; *Washington Post,* February 3, 1906.

49. *Washington Post,* February 15, 1906; *Congressional Record,* 59th Cong., 1st Sess., 40:3, 2608.

50. In 1902 Patterson opposed efforts to amend a railroad safety law, claiming that vague phrases in the proposal would create a loophole through which railroads could avoid responsibility. Receiving no support and pressured by Senator Joseph B. Foraker, Patterson withdrew his objection, saying that he did not want to delay the bill, even with its imperfections. *Congressional Record,* 57th Cong., 1st Sess., 35:7, 7300, 7301.

51. Theodore Roosevelt, Washington, D.C., to T. M. Patterson, Denver, Colorado, April 14, 1905. Theodore Roosevelt papers, Library of Congress.

52. Theodore Roosevelt, Washington, D.C., to T.M. Patterson, Denver, Colorado, May 24, 1905. Theodore Roosevelt papers.

53. Ellis, *Henry Moore Teller*, 370; Mowry, *Theodore Roosevelt*, 133.

54. *Congressional Record*, 59th Cong., 1st Sess., 40:5, 4283; *Congressional Record*, 59th Cong., 1st Sess., 40:7, b355.

55. *Congressional Record*, 59th Cong., 1st Sess., 40:5, 4438.

56. Ibid.

57. Address of T. M. Patterson to the Manufacturers' Exposition at Denver, Colorado, October 7, 1886, 14. Patterson papers.

58. *Congressional Record*, 59th Cong., 1st Sess., 40:4, 3258; *Congressional Record*, 59th Cong., 1st Sess., 40:8, 7335, 7336.

59. *Congressional Record*, 59th Cong., 1st Sess., 40:8, 7991.

60. 334 Stat. 584.

61. *Denver Republican*, June 29, 1906.

62. Specifically, they prevented the word *knowingly* being inserted into the following clause: "Every person or portion, whether carrier or shipper, who shall (knowingly) offer, grant, or give or solicit, accept, or receive any such rebates, concessions, or discriminations . . ." Patterson and LaFollette argued that any lawyer would realize the difficulty for the prosecution in proving actual knowledge on the part of the accused. *Congressional Record*, 59th Cong., 1st Sess., 40:10, 9655; *Congressional Record*, 59th Cong., 1st Sess., 40:8, 7990–92.

63. *Congressional Record*, 58th Cong., 3rd Sess., 39:3, 3024, 3025; *Washington Post*, February 22, 1905.

64. Patterson cited statistics from United States government investigation in Great Britain involving Glasgow, Scotland, and Sydney, Australia. *Congressional Record*, 59th Cong., 1st Sess., 40:8, 7334–37.

65. *Congressional Record*, 57th Cong., 1st Sess., 35:5, 4519, 4520; *Congressional Record*, 57th Cong., 1st Sess., 40:9, 8615–30.

66. *Congressional Record*, 57th Cong., 1st Sess., 35:5, 1653–56. In 1906 Bryan had called for government ownership of all railroad trunk lines and the extermination of trusts. *New York Times*, August 31, 1906.

67. *Washington Post*, October 29, 1906.

68. *Congressional Record*, 59th Cong., 2nd Sess., 41:5, 4076–80.

69. Patterson's presentation contained the documentation associated with those issues on which he had strong feelings and ample time to prepare. He quoted from a table of sixty-three countries in comparing the existing degree of private versus public ownership of railroads, including a breakdown by type of government involved. He cited several court decisions in asserting that the government had legal power to engage anywhere in construction of railroads and canals, and in condemnation proceedings. He explored the results of investigations by both the ICC and the Census Bureau as a basis for valuation of the railroads, as well as computations based on the selling price of stocks, bonds, and other debentures. He further submitted tables dealing with assessments by individual states, average value per mile of track, and ratio of assessments to commercial value. In assessing the probable benefits of nationalization, he numerated the advantages officially claimed by Germany, Belgium, and Australia. *Congressional Record,* 59th Cong., 2nd Sess., 41:5, 4076–80.

70. *Denver Republican,* July 17, 1901.

71. *Congressional Record,* 57th Cong., 2nd Sess., 36:3, 2186, 2187.

72. Ibid., 3002–5.

73. Ibid., 2979–2984, 3005; *Congressional Record,* 58th Cong., 2nd Sess., 38:1, 247–55.

74. Results of a Teller-sponsored Senate investigation proved that the American Sugar Refining Company had acquired vast cane lands in Cuba by 1902, that the sugar industry was largely in the hands of American and European capitalists, and that the sugar trust had supported propaganda agencies for reciprocity proposals. Sen. Docs., 57th Cong., 1st Sess., 434.

75. Mowry, *Theodore Roosevelt,* 129; *Congressional Record,* 57th Cong., 1st Sess., 35:3, 2133; *Congressional Record,* 58th Cong., 2nd Sess., 38:1, 286.

76. G. Michael McCarthy, *Hour of Trial: The Conservation Conflict in Colorado and the West, 1891–1907* (Norman: University of Oklahoma Press, 1977), 91, 92.

77. Ibid.

78. *Rocky Mountain News,* January 16 and April 8, 1900.

79. Chessman, *Theodore Roosevelt,* 162, 163; Mowry, *Theodore Roosevelt,* 214; Ellis, *Henry Moore Teller,* 373.

80. *Congressional Record,* 59th Cong., 2nd Sess., 41:4, 3723.

81. *Congressional Record,* 59th Cong., 2nd Sess., 41:4, 3532–40, 3721.

82. Theodore Roosevelt, White House, to T. M. Patterson, U.S. Senate, December 21, 1905. Roosevelt papers.

83. McCarthy, *Hour of Trial,* 161.
84. Ibid., 205.
85. *Congressional Record,* 59th Cong., 2nd Sess., 41:4, 3192–95, 3869.
86. *Rocky Mountain News,* September 1 to November 5, 1908. See especially October 1 and 15.
87. For a concise coverage of this issue, see John Braeman, *Albert J. Beveridge: American Nationalist* (Chicago: University of Chicago Press, 1971), 81–97.
88. *Congressional Record,* 57th Cong., 2nd Sess., 36:3, 2907–10, 2970–75.
89. *Congressional Record,* 58th Cong., 3rd Sess., 39:2, 1876–80, 2002, 2003; *Washington Post,* February 7, 1905.
90. *Congressional Record,* 59th Cong., 1st Sess., 40:4, 3508–13, 3597; *Washington Post,* March 9, 1906.
91. *Congressional Record,* 58th Cong., 2nd Sess., 38:4, 3556; *Congressional Record,* 59th Cong., 1st Sess., 40:9, 8168–71.
92. *Congressional Record,* 59th Cong., 1st Sess., 40:3, 2505–10; *Congressional Record,* 57th Cong., 1st Sess., 40:9, 8799, 8800.
93. *Congressional Record,* 57th Cong., 1st Sess., 35:4, 3823, 3829; *Congressional Record,* 57th Cong., 1st Sess., 35:5, 4239; *Congressional Record,* 58th Cong., 2nd Sess., 38:3, 2413, 2414, 2463–68; *Congressional Record,* 58th Cong., 2nd Sess., 38:5, 4083, 4472–78, 4560; *Congressional Record,* 59th Cong., 1st Sess., 40:3, 2535–40; *Congressional Record,* 57th Cong., 1st Sess., 35:3, 2888, 2889; *Washington Post,* February 15, 1906.
94. *Congressional Record,* 57th Cong., 1st Sess., 35:4, 4213, 4214.
95. *New York Times,* August 29, 1906. The racism prevailing among both imperialists and anti–imperialists is a central theme in Howard K. Beale, *Theodore Roosevelt and the Rise of America to World Power* (Baltimore: Johns Hopkins Press, 1956).
96. *Congressional Record,* 59th Cong., 2nd Sess., 41:2, 1046.
97. Ibid., 1045.
98. In his personal correspondence Patterson never indulged in the use of derogatory names when referring to blacks, although his nephew, Arthur Johnson, used the word "coon." Arthur C. Johnson papers.
99. Author Robert Smith's personal interview with Patterson's grandson, Thomas Patterson Campbell, Denver, Colorado, August 18, 1969.
100. *Denver Republican,* July 26, 1906.
101. Keating, *Gentleman From Colorado,* 330.

102. Ellis, *Henry Moore Teller,* 381.

103. Theodore Roosevelt, Washington, D.C., to T. M. Patterson, Denver, April 8, 1907. Roosevelt papers. Patterson's bill, which did not clear the Judiciary Committee, had called for all contributions for electing national officials to be reported to Congress prior to election day. *Congressional Record,* 59th Cong., 1st Sess., 40:2, 1067, 1068.

104. *Rocky Mountain News,* September 15 and November 2, 1906.

105. *Rocky Mountain News,* October 1, 16, and 25, 1908.

106. *Rocky Mountain News,* October 1–3, 16, 1908, and November 1 and 4, 1908.

107. *Rocky Mountain News,* October 1, 1908.

108. *Rocky Mountain News,* November 3 and 6, 1912.

109. *Rocky Mountain News,* November 3, 1912.

110. *Rocky Mountain News,* November 6, 1912.

111. Keating, *Gentleman From Colorado,* 97.

112. *New York Times,* February 8, 1906.

14: Battling "the Beast"

1.   Carl Ubbelohde, Maxine Benson, and Duane A. Smith, *A Colorado History,* 6th ed. (Boulder, Colo.: Pruett, 1988), 274; Roland L. DeLorme, "Turn-of-the-Century Denver: An Invitation to Reform," *Colorado Magazine* 45 (winter 1968): 1–15; Clyde L. King, *The History of the Government of Denver with Special Reference to Its Relations with Public Service Corporations* (Denver: Fisher Book, 1911); Robert L. Perkin, *The First Hundred Years* (Garden City, N.Y.: Doubleday, 1959), 407–8. Other sources in which municipal and state corruption are a continuing theme include William H. Tolman, *Municipal Reform Movements in the United States* (New York: F. L. Revell, 1895); Benjamin B. Lindsey and Rube Borough, *The Dangerous Life* (New York: Horace Liveright, 1931); Benjamin B. Lindsey and Harvey J. O'Higgins, *The Beast* (New York: Doubleday, Page, 1910); George Creel, *Rebel at Large: Recollections of Fifty Crowded Years* (New York: G. Putnam, 1947); Edward Keating, *Gentleman From Colorado* (Denver, Colo.: Sage, 1964); Frances A. Huber, "The Progressive Career of Ben B. Lindsey, 1900–1920," (Ph.D. dissertation, University of Michigan, 1963); Roland L. DeLorme, "The Shaping of a Progressive: Edward Costigan and Urban Reform in Denver, 1910–1911," (Ph.D. dissertation, University of Colorado, 1965).

2.   Ubbelohde, *A Colorado History,* 262.

3. Leroy R. Hafen, ed., *Colorado and Its People: A Narrative and Topical History of the Centennial State* (New York: Davis Historical Publishing, 1948), 1:349.

4. King, *History of Denver,* 79, 80, 131–57.

5. *Rocky Mountain News,* August 6, 1897.

6. The *Rocky Mountain News* endorsed the view expressed by Samuel M. "Golden Rule" Jones, mayor of Toledo, Ohio, that the city should own everything that could be conducted to greater advantage to the people by public rather than private ownership. October 16, 1898. Quoting from Richard T. Ely's *Monopolies and Trust* (New York: Macmillan, 1900), Patterson supported Ely's contention that there must be either effective public control of private utilities or direct public management. Ely preferred the latter, and so did the *News,* said Patterson. *Rocky Mountain News,* May 8, 1900.

7. *Rocky Mountain News,* March 14–17, 1897.

8. *Rocky Mountain News,* June 24, 1905.

9. Polly Pry, *Denver Post,* September 1903, quoted in Allen D. Breck's, *William Gray Evans, 1855–1924* (Denver: Alan Swallow, 1964), 101.

10. Charles A. Johnson, *Denver's Mayor Speer* (Denver: Green Mountain, 1969), 61–71; King, *History of Denver,* 99, 159, 210; Lindsey and Borough, *Dangerous Life*; Breck, *William Gray Evans.* See also the *Rocky Mountain News,* April 4, 1897, for a description of the "corporate snake." An unsigned manuscript-chart, "The System," claimed to diagram the system through which the corporations controlled Colorado. Richard L. DeLorme wrote that the handwriting on the chart, located in the Edward Costigan papers at the University of Colorado, points to authorship by George Winters, an attorney for the reform State Voters League. DeLorme, "Turn of the Century Denver," 14.

11. *Rocky Mountain News,* February 20 and March 7, 1897.

12. The *Denver Post* claimed that the *News* dominated the reform convention. September, 27, 1897; *Rocky Mountain News,* April 7, 1897.

13. *Rocky Mountain News,* June 19, 1897.

14. *Rocky Mountain News,* June 20, 1897.

15. *Rocky Mountain News,* July 28, 1897.

16. *Rocky Mountain News,* June 20, 1897.

17. T. M. Patterson, Denver, to K. M. Patterson, Block Island, Rhode Island, July 30, 1897, Patterson papers, Western Historical Collection, University of Colorado at Boulder [hereafter referred to as Patterson papers].

18. *Denver Post,* July 27, 1897; *Rocky Mountain News,* July 28, 1897.

19. *Denver Post,* July 29, 1897.

20. *Denver Republican,* December 6, 1897; Mary Fonda Adams, "Thomas M. Patterson: Some Aspects of His Political Career," (Master's thesis, University of Colorado, 1933), 91, 92.

21. *Rocky Mountain News,* February 24, 1899, January 1 through February 10, 1900. See especially January 16 and 27 and February 3–5 and 7–9, 1900.

22. Author Robert Smith's personal interview with Patterson's grandson, Thomas Campbell, Denver, Colorado, August 28, 1969.

23. Delos F. Wilcox, *Municipal Franchises* (Rochester, New York: Gervaise, 1910), 186–88.

24. *Rocky Mountain News,* March 4 and 5, 1892.

25. *Rocky Mountain News,* July 18, 1892.

26. *Rocky Mountain News,* March 30, 1893. See also November 6 and 9 and December 18 and 25, 1892, and March 26, April 5 and 7, and July 26, 1893. *Denver Republican,* January 25, 1893.

27. *Rocky Mountain News,* April 7, 1897; *Denver Post,* April 7 and 8, 1897; *Denver Times,* September 23, 1897; Keating, *Gentleman From Colorado,* 128.

28. Johnson, *Mayor Speer,* 73–90; *Rocky Mountain News,* February 23, 1897; Lindsey, *The Beast,* 126.

29. *Rocky Mountain News,* April 3–6, 1901.

30. *Denver Times,* April 8, 1901; *Denver Republican,* April 8, 9, and 14, 1901.

31. *Denver Times,* April 8, 10, and 13, and June 13, 1901.

32. *Denver Times,* April 15, 1901.

33. *Denver Times,* June 13, 1901.

34. *Denver Post,* March 18, 1902.

35. *Denver Republican,* July 5 and 15, 1902; *Denver Times,* September 4 and 7, 1902.

36. *Denver Post,* March 15, 1902.

37. *Denver Post,* March 15, 1902.

38. *Rocky Mountain News,* September 3, 4, 6, and 7, 1902; *Denver Times,* September 5 and 8, 1902.

39. *Denver Times,* September 10 and 11, 1902.

40. *Denver Post,* September 11, 1902.

41. Even in this struggle it proved to be difficult to maintain enough solidarity for victory. T. J. O'Donnell, Denver, Colorado, to T. M. Patterson, Washington, D.C., December 18, 1902. O'Donnell papers, Western Historical Collection, University of Colorado at Boulder.

42. Tom Patterson claimed that most Populists defected to the Socialists. *Rocky Mountain News,* November 6, 1902. Another thorough analysis of corporate avoidance of taxes appears in the *Denver Post,* February 23, 1902.

43. *Rocky Mountain News,* November 6, 1902.

44. J. S. Swan, Debeque, Colorado, to T. J. O'Donnell, Denver, Colorado, December 9, 1902. O'Donnell papers.

45. T. M. Patterson, Washington, D.C., to T. J. O'Donnell, Denver, Colorado, December 9, 1902. O'Donnell papers.

46. Perkin, *First Hundred Years,* 409.

47. *Rocky Mountain News,* October 1, 1898, and March 2–5, 1899; *Denver Times,* March 7, 1899.

48. *Denver Times,* October 1, 1902. Lindsey gained national fame for his pioneering work with juvenile courts. His story is told in *The Beast.* For additional information on his work see Charles Larsen, *The Good Fight* (Chicago: Quadrangle, 1972); Lincoln Steffens, "Ben B. Lindsey: The Just Judge," *McClure's Magazine* 27 (October 1906): 563–82. For studies of Costigan, see DeLorme, "Shaping of a Progressive" and Fred Greenbaum, *Edward Costigan: Fighting Progressive* (Washington, D.C.: Public Affairs Press, 1971). For an example of reformers' articles in the *Rocky Mountain News,* see John Rush's article on taxation under Speer's administration, *Rocky Mountain News,* May 17, 1908.

49. *George's Weekly,* September 5, 1903.

50. Breck, *William Gray Evans,* 129; J. Richard Snyder, "The Election of 1904: An Attempt at Reform," *Colorado Magazine* 45 (winter 1968): 18; Benjamin B. Lindsey, "The Rule of Plutocracy in Colorado," (pamphlet in papers of B. B. Lindsey), 15, 16. Colorado State Historical Society, Denver, Colorado.

51. *Rocky Mountain News,* December 8, 1903; *Denver Republican,* December 9, 1903.

52. King, *History of Denver,* 233–36; Perkin, *First Hundred Years,* 410; DeLorme, "Turn of the Century Denver," 1.

53. Snyder, "The Election of 1904," 19; *Denver Post,* September 16, 1904.

54. Keating, *Gentleman From Colorado,* 328.

55. *Rocky Mountain News,* May 5, 1904.

56. *Rocky Mountain News,* January 18, 1894; *Denver Times,* June 21, 1905.

57. *Rocky Mountain News,* May 5, 1904.

58. Ibid.

59. Ibid.

60. *Rocky Mountain News,* May 19, 1904; Lindsey, *The Beast,* 162, 163; Lincoln Steffens, *Upbuilders* (New York: Doubleday Page, 1909), 236–43.

15: Constructive Contempt

1. *Denver Post,* September 21, 1904.

2. *Rocky Mountain News,* November 9 and 10, 1904; *Denver Republican,* November 10 and 11, 1904.

3. *George's Weekly,* November 13, 1904; *Rocky Mountain News,* November 10–13, 1904.

4. *Rocky Mountain News,* January 9 and 20, 1905; J. Richard Snyder, "The Election of 1904: An Attempt at Reform," *Colorado Magazine* 45 (winter 1968): 24, 25.

5. 35 Colo., 326-329; Charles A. Johnson, *Denver's Mayor Speer* (Denver, Colo.: Green Mountain, 1969), 78–81.

6. *Denver Times,* March 15–17, 1905; Colin Goodykoontz, ed., *Papers of Edward Costigan Relating to the Progressive Movement in Colorado, 1902–1917* (Boulder, Colo.: University Press of Colorado, 1941), 40–48; Carl Ubbelohde, Maxine Benson, and Duane A. Smith, *A Colorado History,* 6th ed. (Boulder, Colo.: Pruett, 1988), 279; Snyder, "Election of 1904," 25; Benjamin B. Lindsey and Harvey J. O'Higgins, *The Beast* (New York: Doubleday Page, 1910), 203–06.

7. *Rocky Mountain News,* January 1 and June 24–30, 1905; Benjamin B. Lindsey, "The Rule of Plutocracy in Colorado: A Retrospect and a Warning." Pamphlet. (Denver, Colo., 1908), 38; Edward Keating, *The Gentleman From Colorado* (Denver, Colo.: Sage, 1964), 101, 102. The *Rocky Mountain News* also claimed that President Theodore Roosevelt had denounced the Republican plans. January 4, 1902.

8. *Rocky Mountain News,* June 28, 1905.

9. *Rocky Mountain News,* June 30, 1905.

10. *Rocky Mountain News,* November 28–30, 1905; *Denver Times,* November 28–30, 1905. Complete coverage can be found in the reply that Patterson and his lawyers filed in answer to the attorney general's suit. *Colo. Reports,* 36: 281–355.

11. The fine was described by one historian as a "cowardly slap on the wrist" to a person of Patterson's wealth and position. Robert L. Perkin, *The First Hundred Years* (Garden City, N.Y.: Doubleday, 1959), 412. See also Arthur C. Johnson, diary entry, April 15, 1906. Arthur C. Johnson papers, Western Historical Collection, University of Colorado at Boulder.

12. *Denver Republican,* February 6, 1906; Keating, *Gentleman From Colorado,* 102; *Colorado vs. Patterson,* 205 U.S. 454, 1906.

13. *Denver Republican,* November 21 and 30, 1905.

14. Benjamin Lindsey and Harvey J. O'Higgins, *The Beast* (New York: Doubleday Page, 1910), 212.

15. In recounting support for Tom Patterson across the state, Keating also mentions a drive by a mining-camp editor to pay Tom's fine by collecting a penny from each sympathizer. The drive was halted by Patterson, who feared that such a move might incur ridicule from his enemies. Keating's *Gentleman From Colorado,* 103. It should be noted Patterson had purchased the *Denver Times* in October 1902.

16. *Denver Express,* October 24, 1913.

17. *Pueblo Chieftain,* December 1, 1905; B. O. Fowler, "Liberty Imperiled Through the Encroachments of the Judiciary," *Arena* 35 (January 1906): 189–94; William E. Doyle, "Patterson Vindicated," *Dicta* 18 (July 1941): 169–72.

18. Elmer Ellis, *Henry Moore Teller: Defender of the West* (Caldwell, Idaho: Caxton, 1941), 365.

19. *Denver Post,* June 14 and 21, 1905.

20. *Rocky Mountain News,* November 11 and 12, 1905.

21. *George's Weekly,* June 17, 1905; *Denver Republican,* March 16, 1906; *Rocky Mountain News,* April 8 and May 19, 1906; Johnson, *Mayor Speer,* 83.

22. *Rocky Mountain News,* May 19, 1906; Lindsey, *The Beast,* 251; *George's Weekly,* May 24, 1906; Johnson, *Mayor Speer,* 111.

23. *Rocky Mountain News,* June 14, 1906; Goodykoontz, *Papers of Edward P. Costigan,* 25.

24. *Rocky Mountain News,* August 17 and September 29, 1906.

25. *Denver Times,* August 16, 1906; *Rocky Mountain News,* July 12, 1906.

26. *Washington Post,* February 8, 1906; T. M. Patterson, Washington, D.C., to William Howard Taft, Washington, D.C., June 25, 1906. William H. Taft papers, Library of Congress.

27. Keating, *Gentleman From Colorado,* 328; *George's Weekly,* June 21, 1906. The newspaper outside Denver most consistently supporting the Patterson newspapers appears to have been the *El Paso County Democrat.*

28. Johnson, *Mayor Speer,* 84–87.

29. *Denver Republican,* September 9, 1906; *Rocky Mountain News,* September 12 and 13, 1906.

30. *Rocky Mountain News,* September 13, 1906.

31. Arthur C. Johnson, diary entry, September 17, 1906. Johnson papers.

32. DeLorme flatly declared that the greatest problem of the Denver reformers was lack of unity. "The Shaping of a Progressive: Edward Costigan and Urban Reform in Denver, 1910–1911" (Ph.D. dissertation, University of Colorado, 1965), 184.

33. Benjamin B. Lindsey, Denver, Colorado, to T. M. Patterson, Denver, Colorado, August 23, 1906. B. B. Lindsey papers, Library of Congress.

34. Lindsey, *The Beast,* 103, 104, 122–26, 128, 167, and 251.

35. B. B. Lindsey, Denver, Colorado, to T. M. Patterson, Denver, Colorado, October 11, 1904. Lindsey papers.

36. B. B. Lindsay, Denver, Colorado, to T. M. Patterson, Denver, Colorado, Lindsay papers. January 11, 1905.

37. T. M. Patterson, Denver, Colorado, to B. B. Lindsey, Denver, Colorado, December 19, 1904. Lindsey papers.

38. B. B. Lindsey, Denver, Colorado, to T. M. Patterson, Denver, Colorado, December 27, 1904, and December 20, 1905. Lindsey papers; Lindsey, "Rule of Plutocracy," 64.

39. Lindsey, *The Beast,* 268–70.

40. *Rocky Mountain News,* September 1, 1906.

41. Charles Larsen, *The Good Fight* (Chicago: Quadrangle, 1972), 254, 255.

42. *Rocky Mountain News,* September 27, 1906; Thomas R. Garth, *The Life of Henry Augustus Buchtel* (Denver, Colo.: Peerless Printing, 1937).

43. Johnson, *Mayor Speer,* 117; George Creel, *Rebel at Large* (New York: G. Putnam, 1947), 121, 122.

44. *Denver Times,* May 15 and 16, 1908; *Rocky Mountain News,* May 15–17, 1908.

45. *Rocky Mountain News,* April 14, 19, 23, and 24, and May 20, 1908; *Denver Times,* May 19 and 20, 1908. Tom Patterson's impact has been recognized in Johnson, *Mayor Speer,* 117, and Creel, *Rebel at Large,* 121, 122.

46. *Rocky Mountain News,* November 1, 2, and 5, 1908; *Denver Post,* November 5, 1908; Ellis, *Henry Moore Teller,* 383.

47. DeLorme, "Shaping of a Progressive," 136.

48. *Denver Post,* May 16, 1910.

49. *Denver Times,* April 16, 1910; Fred Greenbaum, *Fighting Progressive: A Biography of Edward Costigan* (Washington, D.C.: Public Affairs Press, 1971), 27.

50. *Rocky Mountain News,* April 15 and 28, and May 17, 1910; *Denver Times,* April 16 and May 10 and 17, 1910; J. Paul Mitchell, "Municipal Reform in Denver: the Defeat of Mayor Speer," *Colorado Magazine,* 45 (winter 1968): 43; Keating, *Gentleman From Colorado,* 276.

51. *Rocky Mountain News,* October 24–28, 1910; George Creel, *Rebel at Large* (New York: G. Putnam, 1947), 91, 92; B. B. Lindsey, Denver, Colorado, to Edward Costigan, Denver, Colorado, July 11, 1910. E. Costigan papers, Western Historical Collection, University of Colorado; J. S. Temple, Denver, Colorado, to E. Costigan, Denver, Colorado, October 6, 1910. Costigan papers.

52. *Rocky Mountain News,* November 10, 1910.

53. *Rocky Mountain News,* October 19 and November 6–8, 1910.

54. T. D. Palmer, Canon City, Colorado, to T. J. O'Donnell, Denver, Colorado, January 31, 1911. O'Donnell papers, Western Historical Collection, University of Colorado at Boulder. Greenbaum, *Fighting Progressive,* 31.

55. *Denver Post,* May 7, 1911.

56. Edgar C. MacMechen, ed., *Robert W. Speer: A City Builder* (Denver: City of Denver, Colo., 1919).

57. *Rocky Mountain News,* May 1–5, 1911.

58. *Rocky Mountain News,* December 1, 1911.

59. *Rocky Mountain News,* December 10–11, 1911.

60. Mitchell, "Municipal Reform in Denver," 43–45.

61. *Rocky Mountain News,* December 5 and 14, 1911; *Denver Express,* December 15, 1911; *Denver Republican,* December 15–17, 1911; *Denver Post,* December 15, 1911.

62. *Denver Republican,* December 16 and 17, 1911; *Rocky Mountain News,* December 16, 1911.

63. Creel, *Rebel at Large,* 101; Mitchell, "Municipal Reform in Denver," 51, 52; *Rocky Mountain News,* December 18, 1911.

64. *Rocky Mountain News,* April 19–23, 1912; Perkin, *First Hundred Years,* 412. Quarrels among members of the reform steering committee portended serious disunity should they ever gain power. Mitchell, "Municipal Reform in Denver," 54; Keating, *Gentleman From Colorado,* 109, 110.

65. *Denver Post,* May 23, 1912; *Rocky Mountain News,* May 22–24, 1912.

66. Keating, *Gentleman From Colorado,* 109, 110.

67. *Rocky Mountain News,* April 30, 1913; Greenbaum, *Fighting Progressive,* 36.

68. Creel, *Rebel at Large,* 109, 115, 116.

69. *Rocky Mountain News,* June 1, 1913.

70. Ubbelohde, *A Colorado History,* 281.

71. *Rocky Mountain News,* November 3, 1912.

72. Patterson recognized the weakness of the Progressives in Colorado when he observed that they were divided internally and had not been able to fill out a complete legislative ticket, being forced into a fusion with Old Guard Republicans. *Rocky Mountain News,* November 3, 1912. For a discussion of the Progressives in Colorado and the struggle between the Edward Costigan and Philip Stewart factions, see Greenbaum, *Fighting Progressive,* 41–48.

73. *Rocky Mountain News,* November 3 and 4, 1912; Creel, *Rebel at Large,* 101.

74. William Jennings Bryan, *The Commoner,* quoted in *Rocky Mountain News,* May 21, 1913.

75. Bray Hammond, "Andrew Jackson's Battle With the Money Power," in *Times of Trial,* ed. Allan Nevin (New York: Knopf, 1958), 79–94; Bray Hammond, *Banks and Politics in America* (Princeton: Princeton University Press, 1957), 329.

76. *Rocky Mountain News,* December 12, 1911.

77. *Rocky Mountain News,* July 23, 1916.

78. Russel B. Nye, *Midwestern Progressive Politics* (East Lansing: Michigan State University Press, 1959), 189.

79. *Rocky Mountain News,* December 12, 1911.

80. *Rocky Mountain News,* November 11, 1910, and May 22, 1912.

81. Johnson, *Denver's Mayor Speer,* 204, 205.

82. *Rocky Mountain News,* July 24, 1916. This was the opinion of J. K. Mullen, president of the Colorado Milling and Elevator Company.

83. Samuel Yellen, *American Labor Struggles* (New York: Harcourt Brace, 1936), 225, 226.

84. *Denver Times,* June 18, 1914; *Rocky Mountain News,* June 18 and 19, 1914.

85. Patterson and the *News* had supported Ammons against Costigan in 1912. *Rocky Mountain News,* November 2, 1912.

86. Edwin A. Miller, Fort Collins, Colorado, to E. Costigan, Denver, Colorado, August 1, 1914. Costigan papers.

87. T. M. Patterson, Denver, Colorado, to Richard Campbell, Exeter, New Hampshire, April 14, 1916. Patterson papers, Western Historical Collection, University of Colorado [hereafter referred to as Patterson papers].

88. *Denver Times,* July 24, 1916.

89. Charles S. Thomas, "Thomas Patterson" (Unpublished article in the C. S. Thomas papers), 14. Colorado State Historical Society, Denver.

90. Keating, *Gentleman From Colorado,* 113.

91. Statement to author Robert Smith by Thomas Campbell, Denver, Colorado, August 28, 1969.

92. Thomas, "Thomas Patterson," 14. Thomas papers.

93. Keating, *Gentleman From Colorado,* 113.

94. *Denver Post,* July 24, 1916.

95. Margaret Patterson Campbell, S.S. *Cartago,* to T. M. Patterson, Denver, Colorado, February 28, 1916. Patterson papers.

16: The Editor and the Man

1. For an excellent history of the *Rocky Mountain News* see Robert Perkin, *The First Hundred Years* (Garden City, N.Y.: Doubleday, 1959). For numerous personal references and anecdotes about Patterson and the *News-Times* operation, see Edward Keating, *The Gentleman From Colorado* (Denver, Colo.: Sage, 1964) and George Creel, *Rebel at Large* (New York: G. Putnam, 1947). Credit to the *News* for its impact on Denver and Colorado also appears in Benjamin B. Lindsey and Harvey J. O'Higgins, *The Beast* (New York: Doubleday, Page, 1910) and Charles A. Johnson, *Denver's Mayor Speer* (Denver, Colo.: Green Mountain, 1969).

2. *Denver Times,* February 21, 1902.

3. *Washington Post,* February 1, 1906.

4. Thomas F. Dawson, *The Life and Character of Edward O. Wolcott,* 2 vols. (New York: Knickerbocker, 1911), 1:219, 220.

5. T. M. Patterson, Washington, D.C., to Margaret Patterson Campbell, Denver, Colorado, December 14, 1903. Patterson papers, Western Historical Collection, University of Colorado at Boulder [hereafter referred to as Patterson papers].

6. Horace Hawkins, "Tribute to the Memory of Honorable Thomas M. Patterson," a speech delivered on the occasion of a memorial service held by the Denver Bar Association, March 26, 1917. Arthur C. Johnson papers, Western Historical Collection, University of Colorado.

7. *Rocky Mountain News,* April 2 and May 21, 1893.

8. *Rocky Mountain News,* October 3, 1893.

9. *Rocky Mountain News,* October 5, 1893.

10. *Rocky Mountain News,* January 5, 1894.

11. *Rocky Mountain News,* October 4, 1894.

12. Ellis Meredith, "Three Distinguished Figures of the *Early Rocky Mountain News,*" *Colorado Magazine* 27 (January 1950): 48.

13. Meredith, "Three Distinguished Figures."

14. Stephen J. Leonard and Thomas J. Noel, *Denver: Mining Camp to Metropolis* (Niwot: University Press of Colorado, 1991) 100.

15. *Rocky Mountain News,* April 7 and 11 and March 14, 1897.

16. *Rocky Mountain News,* February 21, 1897.

17. T. M. Patterson, New York City, to K. M. Patterson, Denver, Colorado, February 8, 1898. Patterson papers; Richard C. Campbell, Denver, Colorado, to T. M. Patterson, Butte, Montana, September 22, 1899. Patterson papers; Perkin, *First Hundred Years,* 398; *Rocky Mountain News,* May 7, 1897; *Cripple Creek Morning Journal,* August 17 and October 21, 1894.

18. *Rocky Mountain News,* January 2, 1911.

19. Jerome C. Smiley, *The History of Denver* (Denver: Times-Sun, 1901), 672.

20. Keating, *Gentleman From Colorado,* 119, 120.

21. *Denver Post,* September 30, 1897.

22. Creel, *Rebel at Large,* 110.

23. *Rocky Mountain News,* March 9, 1900.

24. Mary Fonda Adams, "Thomas M. Patterson: Some Aspects of His Political Career" (Master's thesis, University of Colorado, 1933), 108.

25. Thomas, "Thomas M. Patterson," 8.

26. T. M. Patterson, Denver, to Margaret Patterson, Block Island, Rhode Island, August 16, 1897. Patterson papers.

27. Richard C. Campbell, Denver, Colorado, to T. M. Patterson, Butte, Montana, September 22, 1899. Patterson papers.

28. T. M. Patterson, Denver, Colorado, to A. C. Johnson, Manilla, Philippine Islands, April 24, 1899. Arthur C. Johnson papers, Western Historical Collection, University of Colorado at Boulder.

29. Gene Fowler, *Timberline: A Story of Bonfils and Tammen* (Garden City, New York: Garden City Books, 1951), 99.

30. *Denver Times,* November 2, 1904; Perkin, *First Hundred Years,* 406.

31. Fowler, *Timberline,* 95.

32. Ibid., 229, 230.

33. *Rocky Mountain News,* October 23, 1913.

34. S. B. Strang, Denver, Colorado, to Edward Costigan, Trinidad, Colorado, February 26, 1914. Costigan papers.

35. Perkin, *First Hundred Years,* 429.

36. *Rocky Mountain News,* October 23, 1913.

37. *Denver Express,* July 24, 1916.

38. F. Edward Little, "Thomas M. Patterson: Gamecock of the Colorado Courts," *Rocky Mountain Law Review* 11 (April 1939): 3:158.

39. *Denver Times,* July 11, 1902.

Sources

Articles

Abbott, Ernest H. "Religious Life in America-Colorado." *Outlook* 72 (October 11, 1902): 366–71.

Ammons, E. M. "Colorado Strike." *North American Review* 200 (July 1914): 35–44.

Baker, Ray Stannard. "The Reign of Lawlessness in Colorado." *McClures* 23 (May 1904): 43–57.

Bayard, Charles J., "The Colorado Progressive Republican Split of 1912." *Colorado Magazine* 45 (winter 1968): 61–78.

Bechtol, Paul T. "The 1880 Labor Dispute in Leadville." *Colorado Magazine* 47 (fall 1970): 312–25.

Brenneman, Bill, "Block 175—A New Era in Old Denver." *Lawyers Title News* (June 1970): 11–16.

Coletta, Paolo E. "Greenbackers, Goldbugs, and Silverites: Currency Reform and Policy, 1860–1897." In *The Gilded Age*, edited by H. Wayne Morgan, 111–39. Syracuse, N.Y.: Syracuse University Press, 1963.

Collins, George W. "Colorado's Territorial Secretaries." *Colorado Magazine* 43 (fall 1966): 204–7.

Cornish, Dudley Taylor. "The First Five Years of Colorado's Statehood." *Colorado Magazine* 25 (July 1948): 179–88.

Creel, George. "The High Cost of Hate." *Everybody's* 30 (June 1914): 755–70.

Dawson, Thomas F. "Major Thompson, Chief Ouray and the Utes." *Colorado Magazine* 7 (May 1930): 113–22.

DeLorme, Roland, "Turn-of-the-Century Denver: An Invitation to Reform." *Colorado Magazine* 45 (winter 1968): 1–15.

Doyle, William E. "Patterson Vindicated." *Dicta* 18 (July 1941): 169–72.

Fitch, John A. "Law and Order." *Survey* 33 (December 5, 1914): 241–58.

Fowler, B. O. "Liberty Imperiled Through the Encroachments of the Judiciary." *Arena* 35 (February 1906): 189–94.

Fuller, Leon W. "Governor Waite and His Silver Panacea." *Colorado Magazine* 10 (March 1933): 41–47.

————. "A Populist Newspaper of the Nineties." *Colorado Magazine* 9 (May 1932): 81–87.

Goldstein, Marcia T., and Rebecca A. Hunt. "From Suffrage to Centennial." *Colorado Heritage* (spring 1993): 40–48.

Griswold, Don and Jean. "Leadville: A City of Contrast." *Leadville Herald Democrat*, July 2, 1965.

Hammond, Bray. "Andrew Jackson's Battle with the Money Power." In *Times of Trial*, edited by Allan Nevins, 79–94. New York: Knopf, 1958.

Horner, John W. "Boyhood Recollections." *Colorado Magazine* 20 (September 1943): 168–75.

Hough, Merrill. "Leadville and the Western Federation of Miners." *Colorado Magazine* 49 (winter 1972): 19–34.

Johnson, Jerome W. "Murder on the Uncompahgre." *Colorado Magazine* 43 (summer 1966): 209–24.

Lindsey, Benjamin B. "The Rule of Plutocracy in Colorado: A Retrospect and Warning." Pamphlet (1908): 38.

Little, F. Edward. "Thomas M. Patterson: Gamecock of the Colorado Courts." *Rocky Mountain Law Review* 11 (April 1939): 149–58.

Lonsdale, David L. "The Fight for an Eight Hour Day." *Colorado Magazine* 43 (fall 1966): 339–53.

Meredith, Ellis. "Three Distinguished Figures of the Early Rocky Mountain News." *Colorado Magazine* 27 (January 1950): 34–49.

Miners Magazine, July 1902; January, August, April, and October 1903; June 1904.

Mitchell, J. Paul. "Municipal Reform in Denver: The Defeat of Mayor Speer." *Colorado Magazine* 45 (winter 1968): 42–60.

Pinckney, James F. "Moses Hallett." *Rocky Mountain Law Review* 2 (April 1930): 173–83.

"Real Home Rule in Denver." *Outlook* 75 (September 12, 1903): 97.

Robinson, William H. "Charles S. Thomas: The Tall Sycamore of Cherry Creek." *Rocky Mountain Law Review* 3 (April 1931): 157–67.

————. "James B. Belford—The Red Rooster of the Rockies." *Rocky Mountain Law Review* 4 (February 1932): 77–86.

Rush, John. Article on taxation. *Rocky Mountain News* (May 17, 1908).

Smith, R. E. "Colorado's Progressive Senators and Representatives." *Colorado Magazine* 45 (winter 1968): 27–41.

Snyder, J. Richard. "The Election of 1904: An Attempt at Reform." *Colorado Magazine* 45 (winter 1968): 16–26.

Steffens, Lincoln. "Ben B. Lindsey: The Just Judge." *McClures Magazine* 27 (October 1906): 563–82.

Strangeland, Charles E. "Preliminaries to the Labor War in Colorado." *Political Science Quarterly* 23 (March 1908): 1–17.

Thomas, Charles S. "The Pioneer Bar of Colorado." *Colorado Magazine* 1 (July 1924): 193–205.

Vaile, Joel F. "Colorado's Experiment with Populism." *Forum* 18 (February 1895): 714–23.

Valesh, E. M. "The Strength and Weakness of the People's Movement." *Arena* 5 (May 1892): 726–31.

Van Wagener, Theodore F. "Views on the Admission of Colorado in 1876." *Colorado Magazine* 3 (August 1926): 86–88.

Werner, Jane. "The Press and the Populists." *Colorado Magazine* 47 (winter 1970): 44–61.

West, Elliot. "Jerome B. Chaffee and the McCook-Elbert Fight." *Colorado Magazine* 46 (spring 1969): 145–65.

Wortman, Roy T. "Denver's Anti-Chinese Riot, 1880." *Colorado Magazine* XLII (fall 1965): 275–291.

Books

Bagehot, Walter. *Lombard Street: A Description of the Money Market.* New York: Scribner, Armstrong, 1874.

Baker, James H., and Leroy R. Hafen. *History of Colorado.* 5 vols. Denver, Colo.: Linderman, 1927.

Bardwell, George E., and Harry Seligson. *Labor-Management Relations in Colorado.* Denver, Colo.: Alan Swallow, 1961.

———. *Organized Labor and Political Action in Colorado: 1900–1960.* Denver: Denver University, 1959.

Beale, Howard K. *Theodore Roosevelt and the Rise of America to World Power.* Baltimore: Johns Hopkins Press, 1956.

Beisner, Robert L. *Twelve Against Empire.* New York: McGraw-Hill, 1968.

Berman, Edward. *Labor Disputes and the President of the United States.* New York: Columbia University, 1924.

Beshoar, Barron. *Out of the Depths.* Denver: Colorado Labor Historical Committee of the Denver Trade and Labor Assembly, 1942.

Billington, Ray Allen. *America's Frontier Heritage.* New York: Holt, Rinehart, and Winston, 1966.

Binkley, Wilford Ellsworth. *American Political Parties: Their Natural History.* New York: Knopf, 1945.

Blum, John Morton. *The Republican Roosevelt.* Cambridge: Harvard University Press, 1954.

Bowers, Claude G. *Beveridge and the Progressive Era.* Boston: Houghton Mifflin, 1932.

Braeman, John. *Albert Beveridge: American Nationalist.* Chicago: University of Chicago, 1971.

Breck, Allen du Pont. *William Gray Evans, 1855–1924: Portrait of a Western Executive*. Denver: Alan Swallow, 1964.

Brissendon, Paul F. *The I.W.W.: A Study of American Syndicalism*. New York: Columbia University, 1920.

Brown, Joseph G. *The History of Equal Suffrage in Colorado, 1868–1898*. Denver: Denver News Job Printing, 1898.

Bryan, William Jennings. *The First Battle*. Chicago: W. B. Conkey, 1896.

Bryan, William Jennings, and Mary Baird Bryan. *The Memoirs of William Jennings Bryan*. Philadelphia: John C. Winston, 1925.

Chessman, G. Wallace. *Theodore Roosevelt and the Politics of Power*. Boston: Little Brown, 1969.

Coletta, Paolo E. *William Jennings Bryan*. 2 vols. Lincoln: University of Nebraska, 1964.

Creel, George. *Rebel at Large: Recollections of Fifty Crowded Years*. New York: G. P. Putnam, 1947.

Croly, Herbert. *The Promise of American Life*. New York: Macmillan, 1912.

Davis, Sally, and Betty Baldwin. *Denver's Dwellings and Descendants*. Denver, Colo.: Sage, 1963.

Dawson, Thomas Fulton. *The Life and Character of Edward O. Wolcott*. 2 vols. New York: Knickerbocker, 1911.

Dewitt, Benjamin Parke. *The Progressive Movement*. New York: Macmillan, 1915.

Dill, R. C. *The Political Campaigns of Colorado*. Denver, Colo.: Arapahoe, 1895.

Donnelly, Thomas C., ed. *Rocky Mountain Politics*. Albuquerque: University of New Mexico Press, 1940.

Dorset, Phyllis Flanders. *The New Eldorado*. New York: Macmillan, 1970.

Durden, Robert F. *The Climax of Populism: The Election of 1896*. Lexington: University of Kentucky Press, 1965.

Dyer, Frederick, ed. *A Compendium of the War of the Rebellion*. National Historical Society. Dayton, Ohio: Morningside, 1979.

Ellis, Elmer. *Henry Moore Teller: Defender of the West*. Caldwell, Idaho: Caxton, 1941.

Ely, Richard T. *Monopolies and Trusts*. New York: Macmillan, 1900.

Faulkner, Harold Underwood. *The Decline of Laissez Faire, 1897–1917*. New York: Rinehart, 1951.

———. *Politics, Reform, and Expansion, 1890–1900*. New York: Harper, 1959.

Filler, Louis. *Crusaders for American Liberalism*. Yellowsprings, Ohio: Antioch Press, 1950.

Foot, Michael R.D., and J.L. Hammond. *Gladstone and Liberalism*. London: English University Press, 1952.

Fowler, Gene. *A Solo in Tom Toms*. New York: Viking, 1946.

———. *Timberline: A Story of Bonfils and Tammen*. Garden City, N.Y.: Garden City Books, 1951.

Friedman, Milton. *Capitalism and Freedom*. Chicago: University of Chicago Press, 1962.

Fritz, Percy Stanley. *Colorado: The Centennial State*. New York: Prentice-Hall, 1941.

Garth, Thomas R. *The Life of Henry Augustus Buchtel*. Denver, Colo.: Peerless Printing, 1937.

Glad, Paul. *The Trumpet Soundeth*. Lincoln: University of Nebraska, 1960.

Goodykoontz, Colin P., ed. *Papers of Edward P. Costigan Relating to the Progressive Movement in Colorado, 1902–1917*. Boulder: University Press of Colorado, 1941.

Greenbaum, Fred. *Fighting Progressive: A Biography of Edward P. Costigan*. Washington, D.C.: Public Affairs Press, 1971.

Griswold, Don L., and Jean H. Griswold. *The Carbonate Camp Called Leadville*. Denver: Denver University, 1951.

Hafen, Leroy R., ed. *Colorado and Its People*. 4 vols. New York: Davis Historical Publishing, 1948.

———. *Colorado: The Story of a Western Commonwealth*. Denver, Colo.: Peerless, 1933.

Hall, Frank. *History of the State of Colorado*. 4 vols. Chicago: Blakeley, 1895.

Hammond, Bray. *Banks and Politics in America*. Princeton: Princeton University Press, 1957.

Hammond, John Lawrence LeBreton. *Gladstone and Liberalism*. London: English Universities Press, 1952.

Hicks, John D. *The Populist Revolt*. Minneapolis: University of Minnesota Press, 1931.

Hofstadter, Richard. *The Progressive Movement, 1900–1915*. Englewood Cliffs, N.J.: Prentice-Hall, 1963.

Holbrook, Stewart H. *The Rocky Mountain Revolution*. New York: Holt, 1956.

Hollingsworth, J. Rogers. *The Whirligig of Politics: The Democracy of Cleveland and Bryan*. Chicago: University of Chicago Press, 1963.

Hoover, Dwight W. *A Pictorial History of Indiana*. Bloomington: Indiana University Press, 1980.

Jensen, Vernon. *Heritage of Conflict: Labor Relations in the Nonferrous Metals Industry up to 1930*. Ithaca, N.Y.: Cornell University Press, 1950.

Jessup, Philip C. *Elihu Root*. 2 vols. New York: Dodd, Mead, 1938.

Johnson, Charles A. *Denver's Mayor Speer*. Denver, Colo.: Green Mountain, 1969.

Keating, Edward. *The Gentleman From Colorado*. Denver, Colo.: Sage, 1964.

King, Clyde L. *The History of the Government of Denver With Special Reference to Its Relations With Public Service Corporations*. Denver, Colo.: Fisher Book, 1911.

Koenig, Louis W. *Bryan: A Political Biography of William Jennings Bryan*. New York: Putnam, 1971.

Lamar, Howard. *The Far Southwest, 1846–1912, Territorial History*. New Haven, Conn.: Yale University Press, 1966.

Larsen, Charles. *The Good Fight*. Chicago, Ill.: Quadrangle, 1972.

Leonard, Stephen J., and Thomas J. Noel. *Denver: Mining Camp to Metropolis*. Niwot, Colo.: University Press of Colorado, 1991.

Lindsey, Benjamin B., and Harvey J. O'Higgins. *The Beast*. New York: Doubleday, Page, 1910.

Lindsey, Benjamin B., and Rube Borough. *The Dangerous Life*. New York: Horace Liveright, 1931.

Link, Arthur S., and William M. Leary. *The Progressive Era and the Great War, 1896–1920*. New York: Appleton-Century-Crofts, 1969.

McCarthy, Fitzjames. *In Political Portraits*. Colorado Springs, Colo.: Gazette, 1888.

McCarthy, G. Michael. *Hour of Trial: The Conservation Conflict in Colorado and the West, 1891–1907*. Norman: University of Oklahoma Press, 1977.

MacMechen, Edgar C., ed. *Robert W. Speer: A City Builder*. Denver, Colo.: City of Denver, 1919.

Magnus, Philip M. *Gladstone, a Biography*. New York: Dutton, 1954.

Martin, Curtis Wilson. *Colorado Politics*. Denver, Colo.: Big Mountain, 1963.

Mowry, George E. *The Era of Theodore Roosevelt, 1900–1912*. New York: Harper, 1958.

———. *The Progressive Era, 1900–1920: The Reform Persuasion*. Washington, D.C.: American Historical Association, 1972.

Nevin, Allan, ed. *Times of Trial*. New York: Knopf, 1958.

Nugent, Walter T.K. *The Tolerant Populists*. Chicago: University of Chicago Press, 1963.

Nye, Russel Blaine. *Midwestern Progressive Politics: A Historical Study of its Origins and Development*. East Lansing: Michigan State University Press, 1959.

Pease, Otis. *The Progressive Years*. New York: G. Braziller, 1962.

Penick, James L. *Progressive Politics and Conservation: The Ballinger-Pinchot Affair*. Chicago: University of Chicago Press, 1969.

Perkin, Robert L. *The First Hundred Years*. Garden City, N.Y.: Doubleday, 1959.

Pollack, Norman. *The Populist Response to Industrial America*. Cambridge: Harvard University Press, 1962.

Portrait and Biographical Record of Denver and Vicinity. Chicago: Chapman, 1898.

Pringle, Henry F. *The Life and Times of William Howard Taft*. New York: Farrar and Rinehart, 1939.

———. *Theodore Roosevelt*. New York: Harcourt, Brace, 1931.

Rastall, Benjamin M. *The Labor History of the Cripple Creek District: A Study in Industrial Revolution*. Madison: University of Wisconsin, 1908.

Rhodes, James Ford. *The McKinley and Roosevelt Administrations, 1897–1909*. New York: Macmillan, 1922.

Rickard, Thomas. *A History of American Mining*. New York: McGraw-Hill, 1932.

Rodman, Paul. *Mining Frontiers of the Far West, 1848–1880*. New York: Holt, Rinehart & Winston, 1963.

Roosevelt, Theodore. *An Autobiography*. New York: Macmillan, 1913.

Smiley, Jerome C. *The History of Denver*. Denver, Colo.: Times-Sun, 1901.

Spencer, Frank C. *Colorado's Story*. Denver, Colo.: World, 1930.

Sprague, Marshall. *Money Mountain: the Story of Cripple Creek Gold*. Boston: Little, Brown, 1953.

Steffens, Lincoln. *Upbuilders*. New York: Doubleday, Page, 1909.

Stone, Wilbur Fisk, ed. *History of Colorado*. Chicago: S.J. Clarke, 1918.

Suggs, George G., Jr. *Colorado's War on Militant Unionism*. Detroit: Wayne University Press, 1972.

Swisher, Carl Bent. *American Constitutional Development*. New York: Houghton Mifflin, 1943.

Thomas, Sewell. *Silhouettes of Charles S. Thomas*. Caldwell, Idaho: Caxton, 1959.

Thornbrough, Emma Lou. *Indiana in the Civil War Era*. Bloomington: Indiana Historical Bureau and Historical Society, 1965.

Tolman, William H. *Municipal Reform Movements in the United States*. New York: F. L. Revell, 1895.

Ubbelohde, Carl, Maxine Benson, and Duane A. Smith. *A Colorado History*. 6th ed. Boulder, Colo.: Pruett, 1988.

Western Federation of Miners Official Proceedings, 1904. Denver, Colo.: Western Newspaper Union, 1904.

Wilcox, Delos F. *Great Cities in America: Their Problems and Their Government*. New York: Macmillan, 1910.

———. *Municipal Franchises*. Rochester, N.Y.: Gervaise, 1910.

Yellen, Samuel. *American Labor Struggles*. New York: Harcourt, Brace, 1936.

Manuscripts

Beveridge, Albert J. Papers. Library of Congress.

Campbell, Thomas Patterson, III, "Thomas McDonald Patterson, Wabash 1868: One of Our Wayward Sons Comes Home" (Unpublished speech presented to the Ouiatenon Club, November 10, 1992).

Carmack, Edward W. Papers. Southern History Collection, University of North Carolina.

Costigan, Edward P. Papers. Western Historical Collection, University of Colorado.

Dawson, Thomas. Papers. Colorado State Historical Society.

Hawkins, Horace, "Tribute to the Memory of Thomas M. Patterson" (speech on the occasion of a memorial service held by the Denver Bar Association, March 26, 1917).

Johnson, Arthur C. Papers. Western Historical Collection, University of Colorado.

LaFollette, Robert M. Papers. Library of Congress.

Lindsey, Benjamin B. Papers, Colorado State Historical Society.

O'Donnell, Thomas J. Papers. Western Historical Collection, University of Colorado.

Patterson, Thomas M. Papers. Western Historical Collection, University of Colorado.

Roosevelt, Theodore. Papers. Library of Congress.

Speer, Robert W. Papers. Western Historical Collection, University of Colorado.

Spooner, John C. Papers. Library of Congress.

Taft, William Howard. Papers. Library of Congress.

Teller, Henry Moore. Papers. Colorado State Historical Society.

Thomas, Charles S. Papers. Colorado State Historical Society.

Newspapers

Aspen Union Era. July 7 and August 4, 1892.

Boulder Banner. July 1, 1883.

Boulder Camera. January 8, 1908.

Central City Post. September 23–October 21, 1882.

Colorado Springs Gazette. October 31, 1884; Sept. 1–Nov. 5, 1888: May 31, 1894–April 26, 1895.

Cripple Creek Morning Journal. Aug. 17–Oct. 31, 1894.

Denver Express. Oct. 24, 1913; July 24, 1916.

Denver Post. August 10, 1892; 1895–1914; July 24, 1916.

Denver Republican. 1880–1914.

Denver Times. 1880–1914; July 24–26, 1916; Jan. 8, 1917.

Denver Tribune. 1875–1880.

Ft. Collins Argus. Sept. 30, 1902.

George's Weekly (Denver). Jan. 12, 1901–April 22, 1905.

Grand Junction News. Sept. 22–Oct. 6, 1888.

Leadville Herald-Democrat. 1965–1970.

Loveland Leader. Oct. 21, 1892.

New York Times. July 12, 1893; Jan. 1901–June 1907; Nov. 10, 1908.

Pueblo Chieftain. Aug. 3, 1874; Oct. 23, 1884; Oct. 14–Nov. 7, 1886; Sept. 13–Oct. 20, 1888; Sept. 12–14, 1892; June 18, 1905.

Rocky Mountain News (Denver). June 25–Sept. 2, 1874; Nov. 1, 1880– Dec. 1, 1914; July 24–26, 1916; Feb. 10 and June 2, 1929; Nov. 29, 1954; June 14, 1959.

Rocky Mountain Sentinel (Denver). June 6, 1914.

Silver Cliff Rustler. Oct. 25, 1888.

Silver Cliff Weekly Herald. Oct. 19, 1882.

Washington Post. Jan. 1, 1901–June 1, 1907.

Washington Star. Jan. 1, 1901–June 1, 1907.

Official Documents

Colorado. *House Journal.* 9th Sess. Denver, 1893.

   Colorado Reports.

Congressional Record. 44th Cong., 1st Sess., vol. 44–45th Cong., 2nd Sess., vol. 7 (December 6, 1875–June 20, 1878).

Congressional Record. 56th Cong., 2nd Sess., 34–59th Cong., 2nd Sess., vol. 41 (December 3, 1900–March 4, 1907).

Congressional Record. 63d Cong., 2nd Sess., vol. 49 (December 2, 1912–March 4, 1913).

Pacific Reporter.

U.S. Congress. *Congressional Directory,* 58th Cong., 3d Sess., Washington, 1904.

U.S. Congress. House. *Biographical Directory of the American Congress.* 85th Cong., 2nd Sess., H. Doc. 442. Washington, 1961.

U.S. Congress. House. *Patterson vs. Belford,* 45th Cong., 2nd Sess., H. Doc. 14. Washington, 1877.

U.S. Congress. Senate. *Hearings on Affairs in the Philippine Islands,* 3 vols., 57th Cong., 1st Sess., S. Doc. 331.

U.S. Supreme Court Records.

U.S. Statutes at Large.

Theses and Dissertations

Adams, Mary Fonda. "Thomas M. Patterson: Some Aspects of His Political Career." Master's thesis, University of Colorado, 1933.

Campbell, D'Ann M. "The Last Drive for a Dry Utopia: The Prohibition Movement in Denver, 1907–1914." Honor's thesis, The Colorado College, 1972.

DeLorme, Roland L. "The Shaping of a Progressive: Edward P. Costigan and Urban Reform in Denver, 1910–1911." Ph.D. diss., University of Colorado, 1965.

Fritz, Percy S. "The Mining Districts of Boulder County, Colorado." Ph.D. diss., University of Colorado, 1933.

Huber, Frances A. "The Progressive Career of Ben B. Lindsey, 1900–1920." Ph.D. diss., University of Michigan, 1963.

Kountze, Harold. "Davis Waite and the People's Party in Colorado." Master's thesis, Yale University, 1944.

Linnevold, B.L.J. "A Study of the Attitudes on Public Questions of Colorado's Territorial Delegates, 1861–1876." Master's thesis, University of Colorado, 1944.

MacColl, E. Kimbark. "Progressive Legislation in Colorado, 1907–1917." Master's thesis, University of Colorado, 1965.

Morris, John R. "Davis Hanson Waite: The Ideology of a Western Populist." Ph.D. diss., University of Colorado, 1965.

Musselman, Lloyd K. "Governor John F. Shafroth and the Colorado Progressives: Their Fight for Direct Legislation, 1909–1910." Master's thesis, Denver University, 1961.

Smith, Robert E. "Colorado Congressmen and National Reform Legislation During the Progressive Era, 1901–1916." Master's thesis, The Colorado College, 1963.

Smith, Robert. "Thomas M. Patterson: Colorado Crusader." Ph.D. diss., University of Missouri, 1973.

Index

Ute Indians, 20, 34
Utilities, 160, 168, 169, 179, 202
  municipal ownership of, 149, 186
  Patterson and, 149-50, 158-59, 165–66, 177
  problems with, 157-58
  taxation of, 149

Vanatta, J. K.: on Patterson, 102
Vindicator Mines, explosion at, 107

Waite, Davis Hanson, ix, 72, 73, 77, 79, 82–83,
    90, 100, 201, 222n28
  city hall war and, 84
  governorship for, 78
  greenbacks and, 82
  Patterson and, 74-75, 83-84, 86-87, 102
  photo of, 76
  Populists and, 83, 84, 85
  pressure on, 84–85, 101–2, 220n51
  silver industry and, 82
  support for, 74, 81, 120, 221n65
Washington Evening Star, on Patterson, 144
Washington Post
  on Patterson, 129, 132, 133-34, 137, 142,
    143-44, 145, 149, 235n28
  on *Rocky Mountain News,* 187
Water companies. *See* Utilities
Watson, Thomas, 90

Weaver, James B., ix, 72, 75, 78, 79
  Populist party and, 71
  support for, 73, 77
West
  exploitation of, 67
  welfare of, 156
Western Federation of Miners (WFM), 100,
    104, 109, 110
  Cripple Creek strike and, 99, 107
  decline of, 108
  at Leadville, 103
White, Michael D., 4
Wilbur, Harry, 174
Wilson, Woodrow, 118, 155, 181, 190
  New Freedom and, 201
Winters, George, 241n10
Witter, Mrs. John A., 49
Wolcott, Edward O., 69, 119, 124
  Stratton Home and, 48
Women's Home Club, Kate Patterson and, 125
Woman Suffrage Association, Kate Patterson
    and, 83, 189
Women's suffrage, 125
  Patterson and, 83, 188-89

Young Women's League auxiliary, Patterson
    daughters and, 83, 189
YWCA, Kate Patterson and, 125